Barbara
1972

150.

DESTINY TIMES SIX

DESTINY TIMES SIX

AN ASTROLOGER'S CASEBOOK

by Katherine de Jersey
with Isabella Taves

Published by M. Evans and Company, Inc.
and Distributed in Association with
J. B. Lippincott Company,
Philadelphia and New York

NOTE

Names, places and certain circumstances have been changed in these case histories to protect the identity of my clients and those involved in their lives. The personal conflicts and problems, however, are real life situations, involving real people, as is the counseling approach I undertook in handling these cases.

KATHERINE DE JERSEY

Contents

Contents

DESTINY TIMES SIX

1

Pisces
Mystery

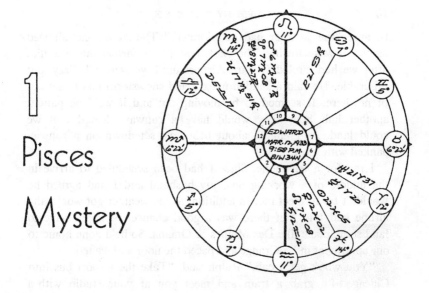

THE storm hadn't been predicted. When our plane took off from
Los Angeles International Airport, the pilot said cheerfully, "It
looks like a fine day for flying. Clear and cold in Chicago. We have
a tail wind so we should get in before our scheduled arrival time
of 4 P.M."

Which sounded great, except I didn't believe it. I had a wicked
inclination to tell the stewardess I was willing to bet the pilot any
reasonable sum that by the time we reached Chicago it would be
snowing. Last night, just before I'd fallen asleep, I had checked
Chicago weather conditions astrologically. Neptune, which is liquid
and causes rain, fog, and snow, was adversely aspected to the
planet Saturn, which indicates cold. There would be a full moon
and weather changes invariably occur either on the full or new
moon. In my opinion, it was going to snow—hard.

However, I decided to fly anyway. I was tired. I hadn't seen my
husband for two weeks. I wanted to get home and get a good
night's sleep in my own bed. I'd been on a lecture tour around the
Middle and Far West, talking about astrology, and there had been
too many late night receptions and early morning flights.

But I couldn't resist a secret feeling of triumph when, about a
half hour out of Chicago, the pilot asked us to fasten our seat belts

because "the weather had deteriorated." The stewardess allowed as how it was snowing. The pilot went a little further than she did, after we had circled O'Hare Airport until we were all dizzy and miserable. He said a sudden unexpected snowstorm had come out of nowhere. It seemed to be moving out and if we'd be patient another half hour they would have a runway cleared and we could land. And finally, about 6:30, we set down on a runway banked with snow.

I ran for a telephone. Since I had been scheduled to arrive in the middle of a working day, my husband and I had agreed he wouldn't try to meet me. In addition, as the weather got worse, the airline had told him there was a good chance we might have to land some place like Des Moines or Omaha. So he'd gone home to our apartment in La Grange and paced the floor and waited.

"You won't get a cab," Ralph said. "Take the airport bus into Chicago. I'll grab a train and meet you at your studio with a picnic."

My studio was in the old Italian Court Building at Michigan Avenue and Ontario. I stood down in the courtyard with my bags and yodeled for help. In summer, the Petit Gourmet restaurant put out tables where Ralph and I used to have long lunches when we were courting. Today, the winds off Lake Michigan had piled snow in waist-high drifts. My husband hurried down and together we skidded up the stairs with my luggage.

But upstairs there was warmth and wine and thick hero sandwiches. After a while, he said, "Was it a lousy trip?"

"Just great. The pilot said if we were patient, we might land in another half hour. My seatmate asked what was the alternative."

"What sex seatmate?"

"Male, naturally."

"Handsome?"

"Divine. Bald as a billiard ball. You know how I go for baldies. A doctor. I don't know what kind. His name was Fuller."

"Henry Fuller?"

"We didn't get on a first-name basis. But I have his card in my coat pocket, if you have the energy to move. I haven't."

I'm married to a Gemini, the most curious man in the world. He got to his feet and found the card. "Katie, my God. Henry Fuller. Probably the greatest brain surgeon in the country. What did you talk about?"

"Why, astrology. What else? He was fascinated." I ducked the pillow he threw at me.

We were late getting to bed on the folding bed in my studio and up early, as Ralph had to take the train out to his electronics company. We had breakfast in a small hotel around the corner and I snowplowed back to the Italian Court Building. It was bitter cold and the concrete steps up to my third-floor studio were slick with ice. I stepped carefully, mainly concerned with saving my own skin.

I didn't notice the tall blonde who was coming toward me until we collided. "If you're Katherine de Jersey, I've been waiting half an hour. Your studio is locked and nobody answers the telephone."

I said I wasn't surprised. The telephone service didn't start working until 9 A.M. and Maggie, my part-time secretary and full-time friend, was probably detained by the storm. "I wouldn't be here myself, if I hadn't been snowbound at the airport last night, coming in from California, and not able to get home to La Grange."

"I know," she said. "That's why I'm here."

It didn't make sense. But then, I wasn't quite awake. Usually I don't get up so early. My first appointment isn't until ten o'clock, unless there is an emergency, and it is only a half-hour's drive from home, so I sleep while Ralph makes the morning coffee. I said, "Do you have an appointment with me?"

"Appointment? Of course not. I never heard of you until last night. I am staying with an old school friend of mine. Her husband came home and said he'd had a fascinating experience on the plane, he'd met an astrologer named Katherine de Jersey. And Louise—that's his wife—said to me, 'Grace, I think you should go to see her.' So here I am."

I felt stunned. She was an overwhelming woman. Straight and tall, hatless despite the cold, her pale blond hair long and pulled back in a knot to reveal what some people call a widow's peak, but I, as an astrologer, always recognize as a Leo peak. Of all the signs of the zodiac, the Leos are to me the easiest to spot. They so often have the snub lion nose, the regal bearing. And, of course, the distinctive catlike walk, on the balls of their feet. My visitor had the Leo nose and I was interested in watching her walk. So I said, "Come on up and get warm, anyway. My secretary will be in soon and can give you an appointment."

"I don't have time to make an appointment. I have to see you now."

I let her go up the stairs ahead of me. She moved quickly, and gracefully, as I had suspected. I knew my schedule would be tight, murderously tight, after two weeks away. It always was. And I had no intention of letting myself be overpowered by this early morning visitor, even if her friend was the wife of Dr. Fuller. I would leave her to my secretary, Maggie, who fought off fiercer dragons than this one every day for me. Luckily, she had just arrived and was busy stamping the snow off her boots.

I said, "This is—"

"Grace G.," said my visitor. "I must see Miss de Jersey immediately. She says I have to have an appointment. That's ridiculous. She's here and I'm here so why—"

I escaped to my own office and shut the door. A widow with three children, Maggie is my age but she sometimes treats me as though I didn't have good sense. Which I guess I don't—at least money sense. She studied astrology in one of my classes after her husband died. Then I had to give up teaching because of the number of private clients who began to count on me, and my increasing schedule of lecture tours. Maggie came and suggested she act as my secretary in the mornings when her children were in school. The whole arrangement had been a blessing and a delight. My only fear was that one of these days some man would realize how great she was and take her away from me.

Maggie had left the day's schedule, and it was a full one, on my desk, together with the folders containing the charts of people who were regulars. I picked up the mail she had considered important enough for me to see right away and was hurrying through it when Maggie slipped in and closed the door behind her.

"She's won. I hate to admit it. But we had a cancellation for your ten o'clock."

"I give up," I said.

Whatever she had done to herself while she was waiting, Grace G. looked trim and immaculate, hazel catlike eyes glistening, every hair in place. She sat down opposite me. For a moment neither of us said anything. Then she finally smiled, putting me at my ease as deliberately as though we were in her home, she the hostess, I the guest who had arrived at a particularly difficult time.

"I'm afraid you think I'm a bully, Miss de Jersey. But as a matter of fact, it is rather urgent. That is, I'm leaving town this afternoon. And I always believe that if you want something, the way to operate is to go out and get it. Don't you agree?"

"When were you born, Mrs. G.?" I asked. She had a wedding ring on her left hand, a thin circle of diamonds, and an engagement ring with a huge diamond, the kind my dentist had once described to me as "the size of a fourth molar."

"April 9. I'm not mentioning the year."

"I'm afraid I can't help you unless you do. Everything that is said in this office is confidential. I'd like to know not only the year, but the hour and the place."

"What if I lie to you? Even my husband doesn't know the correct date."

"Then you will be wasting my time as well as yours."

"Can you tell when people are lying to you?"

"Usually, yes. Only it's so senseless. I have to place the planets in the exact positions in the heavens that they occupied at the time of your birth in order to do what we call a natal chart. Ideally, I would like to have the moment which was listed on your birth certificate. But not all doctors do that. When clients aren't certain, or I'm not sure their parents remember correctly, I do what is called rectifying the chart. It means working in reverse. I take important events in a person's life, such as marriages and deaths and illnesses and work backward. It can be done but it's time consuming."

"I'm an Aries. I've always known that."

"Yes, but you have Leo rising."

"I don't have any idea what that means." Her voice quickened, the annoyance of a hostess who has been rebuked by an impudent stranger. I should have been annoyed in turn. But I enjoyed looking at her. And I also had, tucked back in my mind, the fact that anyone who was a friend of Dr. Fuller or of his wife, must be worth patience on my part.

So I explained carefully. "Aries is your sun sign, the zodiac sign the sun was in at the time of your birth. That is simple enough to find out. But it's just the beginning. In every chart, there are approximately one thousand seven hundred and fifty factors, variables, and three very strong basic elementary influences. The sun sign is usually considered first, because the sun represents the life force. But frequently people don't feel at ease with the characteristics of their sun sign. Then we say they aren't true Virgos or Geminis or whatever. These people often are more influenced by

the sign rising over the eastern horizon at the time of birth, what
we call the rising sign, or ascendant. It always influences the appearance. That's why I know you had Leo rising. I can see it in the
way you walk, your hairline, your nose, everything, even your
eyes."

She pulled a package of cigarettes out of her bag and spent more
time than necessary lighting one, putting it in a position in my little ashtray which pleased her. "All my life, it has amused me to
collect lions. I have them as wall plaques and ornaments and
jewelry. I never knew why. Whenever my husband or one of my
children doesn't know what to give me, he finds some kind of a
lion. Maybe there is something in astrology."

"Where were you born?"

Her tidy eyebrows rose. "Barrington, Illinois. Louise Fuller and
I were children together up there. We've been best friends a long
time. She knows everything about me."

"Except your birthdate."

She smiled. "She even knows that. But she has forgotten it
conveniently. I'm being silly, I suppose. I came to Chicago from
South Carolina last week because I had decided to leave my husband. My children are grown, one is married and it seemed ridiculous for me to live a farce. I was trained as a nurse and I'd hoped
Louise, through her husband, might be able to get me on the staff
of some hospital here. I have no money of my own and I wouldn't
take his if I left him. She persuaded me it was a mistake. I should
return to him."

"Then you don't want to ask me about that."

"No. I've already called and told him I'm coming home. He
didn't exactly get hysterical with delight, but he said he was glad
I'd come to my senses."

"Then why do you want your horoscope done?"

"It's Louise's idea." Impatiently. "She's had some problems of
her own and she's been reading all sorts of odd books. She's seen
you on television. When Henry—that's Dr. Fuller—talked about
meeting you last night she decided it was meant to be, it was a
message for me. She came into my bedroom and woke me up to
say I must try to see you, you would help me."

"I'll try, if you will help me. I need the time of your birth as
well as the year."

She put out her cigarette and stood up. She was at the door
when she turned around. "It does seem a little silly for me to be

guarding the secret of my birthdate when I've been so frank about other things. I was born in 1903. I'm fifty-five, or will be too soon. Frank just turned fifty-three and he's a very attractive man; at least that is what most women think and you would, too, probably. So I lied about my age to him. And when you lie to your husband, you have to lie to everyone else. Do you understand?"

"Of course I do. I'm a woman." Our eyes met and she came and sat down again. I said, "Have you any idea of the time of day or night?"

"I think so. It was between noon and 2 P.M. I remember my father, who always went to bed early and got up to see the sunrise, said he knew I was going to be exceptional because I chose to be born at noon, not at midnight, like most contrary little girls. I loved him very much, Miss de Jersey, and it pleased me I'd been born at the right time. I was an only child. I never minded. Nobody stole my toys or mussed my dolls. Does that make me selfish?"

I said, "You were born closer to 2 P.M. Your moon is in Virgo. Your eyes are very round, yet deep-set, slightly oblique—that's the Leo—with Aries eyebrows which arch up from the outside corner, like the Ram. You have the Ram pointed chin, the square Leo jaw. It's amazing, sometimes amusing, to study people's looks, because the characteristics of the signs are so clearly reflected in our looks, the way we walk, move our heads and bodies. For example, although the way you walk is Leo, the Aries is also evident. You walk directly across the room, fast. You must get there now, waste no time."

Later, she checked the family Bible. She had been born at 1:30, which put her moon definitely in Virgo. Actually, I had other indications which made me sure of that. Virgo people usually have high-pitched, thin voices but occasionally when they are lovely, they are exceptional—like Ingrid Bergman's and Grace G.'s. Her meticulous appearance was Virgo, even the fact she'd chosen nursing as a profession. Although an aware astrologer can see the influence of the moon in a client's appearance, the moon is really the key to his inner nature, the side he does not care to show to the world, which is why it is the third strong basic influence in a chart.

Ordinarily we think of Cancer and Pisces people, gentle and sympathetic, as choosing nursing as a life work—and meticulous Virgos as going into the more technical fields of surgery or research, if they are inclined toward medicine. But this just isn't true. Virgo women frequently go into nursing or marry men who are invalids or otherwise incapacitated. They want to serve, not because they are soft and sentimental, but because they feel strong and capable, and it is good for their egos to care for other people. Actually Virgo women are often better nurses than some of the gentler signs and they certainly make more efficient supervisors.

A natal chart, a horoscope for the moment of birth, is divided into twelve segments, called houses. Each house represents a different phase of a person's character or life—one is marriage, another is love and romance, another is the mind, and so on. Each house is also ruled by a different sign of the zodiac, which in its turn has a ruling planet. The way we do a chart is to translate the time of birth into sidereal time, consult tables giving the position of the planets at that moment, and place them on the chart. A great deal depends not only on the houses and signs the particular planets fall into, but also on their relation to each other.

I had expected Grace G.'s dubiously aspected planets would be related to her house of marriage, for obviously she was having difficulties with her husband. Instead, all the trouble aspects pointed to her fifth house, which relates to children.

"I don't think you came to me to talk about yourself. You must have a child in trouble."

She looked around my desk, hunting for something. I said, "You slipped your cigarettes in your bag a few minutes ago." She nodded, found them and put one in her mouth without lighting it. After a few minutes, I did it for her. Finally she said, "I smoke too much. But you are right. I didn't come here to talk about myself. I have a son Edward, my youngest. He is in trouble. You may even have read about Edward in the Chicago newspapers. He—"

I said, "Please don't tell me what happened. Tell me when he was born and give me his birthdate. Let me find out what is wrong, from the chart. That's the way I want to work. It is less confusing to me and I think it is more convincing for you. Especially as you have come to me a bit reluctantly, only on the advice of a friend."

Her eyes closed and her long dark lashes stood out against her pale cheeks. "Edward was born in March 1933. March 12, around two o'clock in the morning. I'd had trouble with the other two boys. But this was like a miracle. I hardly suffered at all, and afterward I felt wonderful. Maybe I was a little drunk from whatever they had given me but I kept telling everyone he was the most beautiful baby in the world. He looked like my father. You know, newborn babies sometimes look like little old men. It vanishes in a few hours. But it filled me with joy."

Edward had his sun in Pisces, a water sign, which has produced people of extraordinary talents, like dancers Nijinsky and Nureyev. But a man with his sun in Pisces is often a mystery to other people. He is too gentle, too sensitive to cope with brutal reality, unless he has great supporting strength in his moon, his rising sign—or his wife. Many men of genius have been born in the sign of Pisces, but on the whole, in my limited experience, I have known few men of genius who were happy. And occasionally, a tortured Pisces withdraws from the world through drugs or alcohol or even psychosis.

"Have you a picture?" I asked. For some reason I could not define, I was having a problem with my calculations. The instant I saw the picture, I saw why. It was a snapshot taken on some festive occasion, a party or wedding. The three young men, her sons, were all in dark suits and white shirts, strikingly handsome. But the youngest, Edward, was different from his brothers. They were big-boned, tall, grinning openly and cheerfully into the camera. Edward was shorter, with the soft Scorpio-Pisces mouth touched by the gentle Venus, ruler of Libra, and a dark, beautiful sensuous face. His eyes avoided the camera.

"All the boys were darling babies and I was terribly proud," she said. "But Edward was special. An artist friend came to town and begged to paint him. For nothing. Afterward Frank bought the picture. We had it over our fireplace in the living room for a long time until—"

"Where was Edward born?"

"In Columbia, South Carolina. All my boys were born in the hospital there. We have our farm about 30 miles outside the city, near my husband's steel mill."

The calculations I was making based on the 2 A.M. hour of birth just weren't making sense. I had thought perhaps he had been born abroad, or in some faraway place. The longitude and latitude must be taken into consideration when we translate the time of birth into Greenwich mean time, and then into star time. That is why we have always to know the place of birth.

I said, stubbornly, "The time you've given me can't be right,

2 A.M. He would have his ascendant in Capricorn, a strong earth sign. I don't think he has."

She seemed to come out of a trance. "Did I say 2 A.M.? How ridiculous. Edward was born in the evening, around ten. I remember well. My father wasn't well and Frank was glad the baby arrived at a reasonable hour so he wouldn't disturb his sleep with the long-distance call. I'm sure I didn't say 2 A.M. You must have heard me wrong."

I didn't try to argue. Her appointment hour was nearly over. And with the correct birth time, everything made more sense, painfully more sense. It didn't take me long to do Edward's chart. Hardly more than twelve minutes, I think. Then I said, "I can tell you three things. Your son is confined, either in a hospital or some kind of institution. He is there against his will, at any rate. Something of a violent nature has occurred. And the base of all his trouble is sibling rivalry—jealousy of his brothers."

"You have read about it in the papers."

I shook my head. "If I did, I don't remember. No, it is there in his chart. The various planets in certain houses, and in relation to each other, tell the story."

"I don't believe it."

"This is what astrology is about, why you do a chart. Some day, when we have more time, I'll explain exactly why I saw these three things, tell you the astrological explanation. Right now, I think you must have questions to ask me which are more important."

"I have, but I don't know where to begin. There are so many things I don't understand. When I left my husband and asked Louise Fuller to help me, I was beside myself. My life, everything I had worked for, had all fallen apart. I wanted to escape. It was she who told me I couldn't. Edward had tried to escape—and look how that had hurt so many people."

"Mrs. Fuller sounds like a fine person."

"Too good." Grace G. shook her head. "Too good for me. Please let me have that picture. It's the only one I have. His father hid all the others the night of the—accident. I was locked in my room, under morphine. He went all over the house, taking every picture of Edward we had. I don't know where he put them. He says he will tell me some day. I've hunted but I can't find them. I think he burned them. He's a violent, cruel man. He says this is all my fault. I spoiled Edward, and he needed discipline because he had inherited bad blood from my side, from my father. Could that be true?"

"The planets emanate electromagnetic energy which constantly changes with their movements in the heavens. At the instant of birth, as the first breath enters our bodies, we take on the pattern of that particular field. When Edward was born, the sun hit almost 23 degrees in Pisces, held by the fixed star Markab. We learned long ago that this is called a degree of sorrow. It meant he would have more than his share of trials and suffering."

"But why did this happen? It isn't fair."

"Why do some people die of cancer? I wanted the answer to that question when I began to study astrology. My father was dying of cancer, I kept asking, why did it happen to him?"

"And did you get the answer?"

I nodded. "There is always growth through suffering. We are put on this earth not by accident but for a purpose. Sometimes people who suffer greatly go on to reach the heights and become great artists or geniuses of another sort, who contribute much to mankind."

"Does that give you comfort?"

I nodded again. "I happen to believe that my father did benefit from what he learned during his illness."

"What comfort is that to me, when my son is in a jail for the criminally insane? My God, Miss de Jersey, have you ever seen one of those horrible places? And there he is like an animal. My beautiful Edward." Grace G. tried to stand up. She fell back in her chair. Maggie, in her coat and boots, hurried in, alarmed. Between us, we helped her to the couch in the reception room, the couch which in emergencies served also as a bed. She slumped with her head down for a long time, refusing the water or tea we offered her. Finally she sat up. Her color was better but she was still having trouble breathing. She pushed her handbag at me. "There's a pillbox somewhere. A yellow pill. I'd better take it."

Maggie produced water again, and I found the pill. She swallowed it and closed her eyes. "Asthma. The doctor says it's psychosomatic. It started after the accident. I'll rest here a minute and go back to Louise's. I hate the pill because it makes me groggy. Perhaps you could find me a taxi?"

Maggie said, "I'll drive you. I was going home anyway, early because the roads are bad."

Grace G. nodded. "It isn't far. Louise lives up on Astor Place, near Division. May I wait here a moment? I don't want to frighten her."

Over her head, Maggie and I looked at each other, questioningly. I could see she was as worried as I, so I said, "Are you sure we hadn't better call Mrs. Fuller? Perhaps you need a doctor."

"Of course not. Do as I say." I glanced at Maggie again, and she shrugged. After a minute, Grace G. opened her eyes. "I am perfectly all right. Except that when I take a pill I want to go to sleep for a while. It was a shock, your telling me what you did about Edward. I still can't quite believe it."

"But I was right?"

"Yes. Yes, you're right." She sounded defeated.

"Do you want to tell me about the accident?"

"Edward killed someone. At least, that is what everyone believes. His psychiatrist. It was in all the newspapers, even back here in Chicago, because my family was from Barrington. Edward shot his psychiatrist. That is what all the newspapers said. Of course, he was insane; insane, they said. He should have been put away in an institution years ago, because he was dangerous. They tried to keep the newspapers away from me. But there was a big editorial in some Nashville paper about letting known psychotics run loose, endangering lives."

"What do you think happened?"

"I don't know. But it had to be an accident. Edward wasn't dangerous. He wouldn't kill a fly. But they all turned against me. Even his father blamed me for spoiling Edward. They say I ruined the lives of my other sons because Edward was my favorite. That is why I left home. I never wanted to see any of them again."

"Including Edward?"

"Dear God." She turned her head so we wouldn't see her tears. Maggie brought her the box of tissues from her desk. I went into my office and motioned to Maggie. "Close the door and call Mrs. Fuller. Tell her you and I are bringing Grace G. home."

"Not you. Your next client is due." Maggie picked up the telephone. "I'll manage. I'll go downstairs and get my car and bring it around on Michigan and you can help her down. Give me about ten minutes."

I picked up Edward's and Grace G.'s charts and left the room, closing the door behind me.

Grace G. was still crying, but softly. I sat down quietly at Maggie's desk, studying Edward's chart in more detail. This might have been the first time Grace G. had broken down and, in my opinion, it would help her.

An astrologer first casts a natal chart for a client, which represents the basic pattern of the life ahead, a blueprint showing all the potentials and liabilities. Then we do what we call "progression"—casting ahead, following the planets and their positions in relation to the natal chart. We can see periods of good aspects ahead, when we urge our clients to embark on new projects, to take reasonable risks. But we also can recognize times when aspects are bad, when it is wise to lie low, withdraw. Certain planets are beneficent: Jupiter, Venus, the sun, which represents the life force. Others are more questionable: Mars, which can mean both sex and violence; Saturn, which can indicate both good and bad fate; Pluto, which is tricky, subtle. In certain relationships to each other, these planets can trigger explosive events.

Edward's natal chart had the three trouble aspects I had described to Grace G. In addition, his moon was opposed to Uranus in the sectors which govern the subconscious. The first star Formen was involved—a dangerous and malevolent influence. But he had managed to escape disaster for nearly twenty-three years. Then, in the past two months, there had been an arrangement of formidable bad aspects in the heavens, working against him, triggering his fate. His moon was in the twelfth house of incarceration. Uranus, the planet which always means change, was at a 90-degree angle to Pluto, the planet of trickery; this is an aspect we refer to as "Uranus squaring Pluto" and it usually means that there will be a sudden accident, and that elements of mystery, trickery, will be associated with it. In fact, at the time of Senator Edward Kennedy's accident on the bridge at Martha's Vineyard, the aspects in his chart were very similar to those in Edward G.'s chart at the time of the shooting.

I often am asked the question: Could you have warned Grace G. if she had come to you before the accident? Of course, I could have. Unfortunately people usually come to astrologers only after they are in trouble, not when things are going well.

Grace G. sat up. "I shouldn't smoke, my doctor says. But it helps. Could I have an ashtray?" I found one on the table and put it beside her. She stared at it as though she didn't know what it was for. "Where is that girl—your secretary?"

"She went to get her car. I'll take you downstairs in a few minutes. I've been studying Edward's chart. Early in April 1939, something happened which colored his whole life. He must have been six years old."

Her head jerked toward me. "What on earth are you talking about?"

"In his progressed chart, the chart which shows where the planets were in 1939, there is a trouble aspect which can occur only once in a person's lifetime. Edward's ascendant squares the planet Saturn, indicating disappointment through a parent, rejection. Saturn in this position always triggers something of far-reaching significance. In addition, the moon was in the third house, the mind, in the same trouble aspect to Uranus. A blow which he kept hidden from the world, a disappointment which he kept secret, until it became exaggerated."

She dropped the cigarette she was holding. I picked it up and put it in the ashtray, unlighted. "No one alive knows about that but Edward and me. How could you—"

"The potential sibling rivalry which is in his birth chart was stirred up, set aflame by what happened. I'm not wrong, am I?"

"No." Her voice was almost a whisper. "No, but I can't believe this is happening. Louise was right. There are things around us which we have grown too blind to recognize. When Edward was six years old, I hurt him badly. God knows, I didn't want to. And I never knew it until years later when he was being analyzed and it came out under hypnosis. His doctor, a sweet old man, told me about it and then tried to explain to Edward. I don't know whether he ever really got over it. And it was such a little thing."

"Do you want to tell me about it?"

"I love him. I love him dearly. It was just—I wanted to be an actress. So I did live in the triumphs of the two older boys. I wanted to fulfill myself in them. But Edward—"

The room was silent. The snow muffled the traffic outside. I waited. She cleared her throat. "It was his sixth Christmas. I loved Christmas. I used to start getting ready months in advance, baking cookies, fixing special little stockings for each child, full of toys. We had lots of help then, servants all over the place and they seemed to enjoy everything as much as I did. But it was tiring. And that year Christmas disappointed us. We had hoped for cold weather, if not snow. It was muggy and warm and—I guess we all overdid.

"Right afterward, Edward came down with a cold. I wouldn't let him go to school and it made Frank mad. He didn't dare take it out on me so he began to tease Edward; was he made of sugar, if a drop of rain fell on him, would he dissolve? That sort of thing. The boys took it up, as boys will. One day Edward insisted he wanted to go back to school. He didn't. We found him miles from home, in an old tenant shack, playing with a bunch of colored kids. He had lost his coat and had only his little play suit and sneakers. He was terrible that night. The doctor said he was afraid of pneumonia."

I glanced at my watch. Maggie's ten minutes were nearly up but I hated to stop her. And maybe I couldn't have anyway. "My husband wanted to take the boy into Columbia to a hospital. I said yes, if I could stay and nurse him, but they refused. So I kept him at home. I slept in a cot in his room. I nursed him night and day. One night I must have been dreaming because when he called me, I stumbled to my feet saying, 'Billy, what do you want?' I called him by his oldest brother's name. What was so terrible about that? But the doctor said he never forgot. He talked to him about it during the treatment and Edward agreed he still thought I preferred Billy."

"Edward is a Pisces. They are easily hurt. I don't know about the other two boys but I suspect they are stronger, less vulnerable."

"Billy was born January 20 and Neil on September 6."

"A Virgo and a Capricorn. Curiously, there's a problem here in Edward's chart, an antipathy toward Capricorns. And Billy was born first. Mothers sometimes prefer their first-born sons. What time was he born?"

"Billy? Let me think. Around 2 A.M."

"You gave me Edward's birth time as 2 A.M. when I first asked you."

"I didn't. That's impossible."

"It was a slip." I got her coat and mine. "Maggie must be out in front, and my next client is due. I'll leave the door open and take you down."

"It isn't necessary."

"I know. But I would like to be sure you're all right. And to say good-bye."

On the way downstairs, she turned to me. "Miss de Jersey, is Edward guilty?"

"I don't know. I can't tell."

"Is there any way you could?"

"I could do a chart of the time of the shooting. That might indicate something to me."

"It was just a month ago. January 18, 1958, at 7:07 P.M. What does that tell you?"

"Nothing—until I do a chart for that specific moment and compare it with Edward's."

"Do it. Please." She stopped on the steps.

"You're going home today. I'll mail it to you."

"No, I'm not. I can't go home until you tell me whether or not Edward is guilty. I have to know."

Maggie honked. I put my hand under Grace G.'s elbow to hurry her. "I can't put my regular clients aside. Many of them have desperate problems."

"As desperate as mine?"

"They think so. One woman is coming tomorrow to ask me to fix a date for surgery, major surgery. A young man wants to know if his wife is cheating on him. And here comes one of our local millionaires to tell me about his latest romance. You may not think it's important but he does." I introduced my Taurus client to Mrs. G. and saw his eyes brighten. Even with traces of tears on her face, she was a remarkably handsome woman. I said to him, "Go upstairs. I'll be there in a minute. I'm taking Mrs. G. to her car."

"May I help?" I said no, and pushed her along. She had enough problems without my amorous Taurus. I put Grace G. in Maggie's car and was about to close the door when she said, "I have an idea. Dr. Fuller and Louise are going to the country tonight, for a long weekend. Why don't you have dinner with me?"

"I must get home. I just came back from California. My husband took my bag with him on the train this morning. I haven't a thing to wear."

"You could go home after dinner."

"No, it would be too late."

"Please. I can't go back without knowing."

In the old days, before I was married, I had worked at night frequently. While my mother was alive, I spent five nights a week at the studio, and went home over weekends. I didn't want to start that again. I wouldn't have a husband if I did. But once you have done a client's chart and seen something dramatic, it is almost essential to do a chart for the moment of the incident.

"Are you sure the gun went off at 7:07?" I asked.

"Positive. I was looking at the clock, wondering whether Frank would be home shortly when I heard it. Then you'll come?"

"I'll have to explain to my husband that it's an emergency."

"It is, really. Here is the address. I've written the time of the accident down, in case you forget. Come at 6:30."

"I can't get there until nearer seven. I should rough out the chart before I come."

She nodded and closed the door. I looked at the folded slip of paper in my hand. And wondered what Ralph would say.

One of the amazements of my new life is that I'm married to a man who understands about my business. He doesn't always go along with me when I'm seeking out auspicious dates as against what he considers practical arrangements, but he understands. "I don't want you to get too tired," he said. "You keep your date but I'll drive in and pick you up at ten o'clock. That will give you a chance to break away."

"But you can't—it's too much to ask."

"I can and I don't like sleeping alone. Be downstairs at ten."

Anyone can learn to set up a chart accurately, given a fair sense of mathematics and some lessons from an astrologer who knows his business. But learning to interpret what you see is an art, not a science. There is one basic thing any astrologer has to guard against. If you are a person who thinks negatively, you are in the wrong business. You cannot help people and, indeed, you are capable of inflicting great harm.

I have a client who hopes one day to be an astrology teacher. She is a negative Capricorn, who sees the dark side of everything, including her husband. She recently complained to me that he was against everything about astrology. When I agreed to see him, I found him open-minded and interested, a typical Aquarian, and all I could do on the positive side was get him to try to persuade her to give up her professional ambitions in this area and go into something for which she is more suited. "Like being a witch in *Macbeth*?" he had asked unhappily. One day she came to me in a state because Uranus squared her sun. Of course, the square, the 90-degree aspect, does mean things get stirred up. There can be trouble. But this position also can be terrific, because it lifts us up from our little rut, and gives new perspective. When she said, "It never seems that way to me," I broke my rule about trying to be upbeat and begged her to take up some field where she wouldn't be transferring her own gloom to other people.

On the other hand, you cannot be so insecure yourself that, in order to please your client, you see things which aren't there. Not long ago, I was asked to judge an "election" chart; that is a chart cast for the best time to select a corporation name. Another astrologer who had been asked to set up the chart had done a perfectly adequate natal chart of the firm, using the moment it was incorporated as its birthdate. Then she had chosen a time when the ascendant would be in good aspects to Saturn (standing, in this case, for good fortune, lasting success) and a day shortly after the new moon, for growth of the project. But she had completely overlooked the fact that there was a planetary aspect operating at that time which encourages trickery, loss, frustration, and subtle deception, and this fell into the sectors of the chart which represent the public and the partners. In addition, Saturn was in the second house, money, in a trouble aspect to good fortune, Jupiter. This meant money would come very slowly, if at all.

"Didn't she point out these adverse aspects?" I said. And the president of the concern replied, "Yes, but she thought that the new moon would take care of everything." Actually, that is like saying a child will live, but not whether he will live in good health . . . and I only discovered later why she was so falsely optimistic. The president's own birthday was on that date and she wanted to please him!

I've had the good fortune in my life to know two astrologers who perfected the interpretation of charts to a fine art. These were people—one a man, the other a woman—who deeply researched the ancient lore and read all the books written about the meaning of the various degrees and aspects—but who also continued to learn every day, from their own observations. I think the advice I cherish most came from the man, my dear old teacher, who told me, "Be humble. Always listen to others; you may learn something even from fools. Read endlessly. Try to encourage action, not blind resignation to fate. And never copy what others have said unless you believe it yourself. Every astrologer must learn to trust his own instincts. Better to sit silent than talk before you are ready, before your interpretation comes through clear and decisive, filtered through the mass of knowledge you have accumulated and are adding to every day."

My last client left at six. I put the day's charts on Maggie's desk, except for Edward's, and started to work. Nothing came through clearly. The chart showed sudden tragedy in the home, a blow dealt by fate (Uranus next to Saturn) and a tricky situation (Pluto) in which something underhanded had gone on. Mars (which stands for both violence and sex) was six degrees in Virgo, the same position where it was in Edward's natal chart. I was inclined to think that in this case, it stood for sex; if you know the astrological symbol for Mars, you will recognize its phallic origin. And Uranus was badly aspected to Mars, making it unexpected sex—not the routine man-woman relationship.

It was nearly seven. I hadn't even put on lipstick. I stopped to dial my husband. "Ralph, answer a question off the top of your head. If someone made a pass at you, a homosexual pass, and there was a gun handy, would you shoot him?"

"Hell, no. I would just tell him to get lost. What sort of a client are you having dinner with, anyway?"

"A lady," I said. "A mixed-up lady."

I managed to find a taxi so I wasn't as late as I'd feared I would be. But Grace G. was waiting—impatiently, I could tell—and so was Mrs. Fuller. Louise Fuller was one of those marvelous simple aristocrats which only Chicago seems to produce. She was thin, almost too thin, but she wore the classic country skirt and sweater with easy chic and her manner was so open and friendly I felt as though I had known her for years. She sent Grace G. into the kitchen to discuss what the cook was leaving us for our dinner— "We're driving up to the country tonight and I'm afraid I'm going to have to take the cook with us because I'm having a dinner on Saturday night for our anniversary"—and took me around the apartment. Like its mistress, at first glance it seemed simple and understated. But in every corner there were precious bits which she and her husband had collected: a Picasso sculpture, a jade Buddha, African masks, an enchanting painting of Caracus done on wrapping paper by a famous Indian artist.

Finally she took me over to the fireplace. "Henry and I are both grateful for what you are doing for Grace. She's a complicated woman. Her parents were old Chicago society, lovely people but improvident, especially her father. Grace adored him and he adored her. Yet, in a curious way, he was hard on her. She wanted to be an actress, first. That horrified him because he didn't think ladies went on the stage. Then she wanted to study voice. By that time, there was too little money, or so he said. Grace became a nurse and as soon as she graduated, she left Chicago. In a way, it was her rebellion against her father."

"Do you know her husband?"

"Frank? He's a dear and everything Grace's father wasn't. Frank makes no bones about being a self-made man and he enjoys making money and spending it. Grace likes having enough money, for a change; goodness knows, there were periods in her girlhood when we wondered if she was really on a diet, as she claimed, or just couldn't afford lunch. Yet in a way she has always resented Frank's way of marching through restaurants passing out tips. And the cash he always insists on carrying with him, three or four hundred dollars, just in case."

"Yet she didn't marry him for money."

"Oh, no. Not Grace." Louise Fuller glanced toward the kitchen. "She was always so beautiful. She could have married money seven times over, if that had been what she wanted. I think Frank attracted her because he was so unlike her father, in the first place. But later, she resented the very qualities she admired when she was young. And then this business about Edward. She was stubborn and that made Frank angry and when the accident occurred last month, it ripped them apart. They both said and did many foolish things."

"Do you believe it was an accident?"

"I believe it because Grace does. Or wants to. That is why she needs you."

"I have to tell her the truth, as I see it. And to be honest, I can't see what happened. I didn't want to disappoint her tonight by not coming, but I don't think I will be of much use. I could suggest her going to her lawyers but—"

"Billy, her oldest son, is a lawyer. Of course he isn't attempting to handle Edward's defense. But one of the partners in his firm is. I'm afraid the popular conclusion is that poor Edward just cracked and shot the psychiatrist. It does happen, you know."

"What does your husband think?"

"Henry never cared for Edward, I'm afraid. He was a difficult boy to like. The other two were always so outgoing and delightful. You felt they were glad to have you in their home. Edward was always chasing down to the basement and locking himself in. If you tried to talk to him, he answered in grunts."

"Yet he was good-looking. I saw his picture."

"Beautiful, I would say. In the same way Grace's father was beautiful. It's not my taste in males. I like my Henry, plump and bald and masculine. However, if you would like a tiny bit of advice, Miss de Jersey, about Grace—"

She hesitated. I said, and meant it, "There is nothing I would appreciate more."

"She's a strange, proud woman. She will talk to me about Frank because I really believe she wanted me to advise her to go back to him. Deep in her heart, now that Edward is lost to her she needs to take care of someone. Her two older sons don't need her. Billy is married and Neil is living away from home, doing his medical residency in Baltimore. Frank is as lonely as Grace is. And Grace needs to be needed."

"I saw that in her chart."

Louise Fuller's slender hand dropped swiftly on my arm. "Let her talk about the—accident, as we call it. I think she is ready now because she trusts you. I didn't ask her what you said today and she didn't volunteer. But she's been on a high pitch all afternoon, waiting for you."

Soon after that, Louise Fuller and the cook were off. Grace G. and I were left alone, in front of the fireplace. I was grateful for the glass of sherry she poured for me. "I want to study Edward's chart in more depth. It would be unfair, and unwise, for me to try to make guesses about the accident while I am still in the dark myself. It would help if you could find out the birthdate of the psychiatrist. And perhaps send me a photograph."

"It was all in the newspapers. I threw them out."

"You can go to the newspaper offices and buy back copies."

"I suppose I could." She didn't sound happy.

"I need to see the whole picture. And I really don't know what actually happened."

"It's a long story."

"I have until ten o'clock."

She leaned forward. "Louise put you up to this, didn't she? I knew she sent me out of the room for some reason." I didn't answer. Grace G. suddenly smiled. "I don't mind. I love Louise and I know exactly what she is doing, or trying to do. She doesn't have much time left and she is trying to see to it that the lives of people she loves are in good order before she goes."

"Before she goes?"

"She has cancer. Lymph glands. When they first found out, Henry raced her around the world, seeing specialists. He was frantic. Then one day, she told him to stop. She wanted to spend what time was left in peace. And strangely enough, I think she is at peace. Trying to help the rest of us is part of it."

"That is what I mean about accepting the pattern."

Grace G. studied me. "All right. If I have to accept Edward's guilt, I will. That is what you are trying to get me to say. And you think he killed the doctor."

"I don't know yet. I need more information and more study."

"Well, let's have dinner and then I'll talk."

It was all delicious and I couldn't have told you afterward what we had been eating. Because Grace G. began to talk, rambling at first, then more concisely. I had to know the background, she said. First, about her husband.

"He swept me off my feet," she said. "I was in the Veterans Hospital in Columbia. Another nurse and I were working our way around the country, having fun. Staying as long as we wanted in one place and then moving on. But then Frank came along."

I got out the notebook and pencil I always carry with me. "When was he born?"

"January 8, 1905—I told you he was younger than I. But from the first, he took charge. He was working his way through college, nights at the hospital. Actually, he'd fixed it so he was put in charge of the orderlies on our floor, so mostly he studied or read books. I remember the first night I really noticed him. I came in with a copy of the *Reader's Digest* and he borrowed it from me."

Capricorn is the sign of the ambitious, self-made man, and it was obvious Frank G. was as typical of his sign as is President Nixon. The Capricorn is difficult really to know, even for those closest to him. Yet he often can establish surface rapport with everyone, especially his employees.

Each zodiac sign has one planet which acts as its "ruler," its guiding influence, and in the case of Capricorn this is strong, indomitable Saturn. So Capricorn men tend to be father figures in their businesses or professions, paternalistic with employees. Yet when it comes to the more intimate contacts in their family, they draw back. Quick to discipline, often harsh in judgment of those they love best, they can be stern fathers, demanding too much.

I've often said on the lecture platform that it's happier for a Capricorn male to have daughters instead of sons. Pretty daughters who can adore from afar are more acceptable than sons who challenge, or disappoint. I think this is obvious so far as Richard Nixon is concerned, and his delightful daughters have learned to make their conquest of him with charm and flattery—just as his Piscean wife is happier to stay in the background, not attempt a "style" of her own. I was certain one of the deep problems of Grace G.'s marriage was that she wasn't a background type—and, of course, she had produced sons instead of daughters.

"Do you remember I told you Edward showed resentment of Capricorns in his chart?" I asked.

She nodded. "And he and his father were so different. In fact, Frank is different from anyone I have ever known. He comes from simple laboring people. His mother is barely literate. His father ran away when Frank and his sister were babies and his mother supported the children working on the cotton platform, weighing bales. Frank worked, too, from the time he fought in the streets for the quarters the plantation owners would toss out to the youngsters, until he was old enough to go into the cotton mills himself. But he was smart, and he learned fast. He knew how to please the bosses. And if he had to drop out of school for a semester to work full time, he always studied at home and went back."

"Have you a picture of him?"

"Oh, he's a fine-looking man, even now. He photographs well and knows it. In fact, there are more pictures of him in our house than anyone else, even the children when they were babies. But when I left him this time, I threw away every picture of him I ever had."

"In revenge for what he did to Edward?"

"I don't know. There was a silver frame with a picture of him on my dressing table. When he came up and found I was really going, I don't know which made him more furious—the fact I was leaving him or that I'd thrown away his wonderful picture, which he'd given me for a valentine."

"Yet you fell in love with him."

"He fell in love with me. I couldn't say no. He has charm, if he cares to use it. He can get anybody to do anything he wants, from the watchman at the mill to those fine old Southern ladies whose daddies used to toss the quarters Frank fought for. I didn't tell my parents we were married until six months later, when I found out Billy was on the way. Daddy was wild, my marrying what he called white trash. But he got along with Frank, too. I hate to say it, but maybe it was because Frank used to send them money."

I said, "I did your chart today. You have Venus squared by

Saturn. We interpret such an aspect to mean that, much as you loved your father, you were afraid of him, adored him from a distance. Your husband's sign is Capricorn, ruled by Saturn. In a way, I am sure you chose your husband because he represented a kind of father figure. And did you feel rejected by him in turn?"

"I didn't *feel* rejected. He did reject me. Frank is always telling people what a man's man he is, how he is never happier than when he is out with his gun and his hunting dogs, or on one of those silly coon hunts when all they do is get drunk. But there have been more women than men in his life. Women in the mill, sometimes. And nice women, too. They can't resist him. He used to flaunt them in front of me and the boys."

"Yet you never thought of leaving him?"

"I threatened, when I was younger. Billy and Neil loved me, but I knew they would survive without me. I offered the boys to him, in exchange for my freedom. But he wouldn't let me go. Once he insisted he'd kill himself if I deserted him. I thought it was love. Actually, I suspect he needed me because marrying someone like me, from a different background, was part of his whole program of success. He told me once he had planned to be President of the United States when he was a little boy. I honestly think he would have made it, if he had really wanted it hard enough."

"Why didn't you leave him before?"

"I don't know." She got up from the table abruptly and lighted a cigarette. I followed her into the living room. "I guess I was afraid of being poor. And then Edward was born. And everything was different. I can't explain it. He was my baby, my very own. Billy and Neil had always been—they never needed me the way Edward did."

"Was your husband fond of Edward, too?"

"I don't know. I suppose so. He could be very sweet, at times. But I told you about his teasing him when he was just a baby, six years old, and I had to keep him out of school. He always made fun of Edward because he would rather be out studying butterflies or watching birds than hunting or fishing. I used to beg him to stop; I needed one son who would be a companion to me. He said I was making a pansy out of the boy."

She stopped and stared at me. "Is that what you're driving at?"

"I'm not driving at anything."

"Yes, you are. Well, let me tell you this. Edward was gentle and he was sensitive and dear. But he was not a homosexual. The first analyst made that very plain. He told us to get such notions out of our heads."

She disappeared, abruptly, into the kitchen. I heard dishes clattering. A plate smashed. I didn't know what to expect. But when she returned, she was carrying a tray with coffee. I accepted mine and asked, "And why did you send him to an analyst?"

"Lots of reasons." She sat down. "Frank went into the Army during World War II. He came back a full colonel, trailing clouds of glory. I thought everything was going to be all right. Then he got the idea it was time to teach Edward to be a man. He taught him to use a gun and made him go out hunting. Edward went. But he wouldn't shoot and he refused to eat anything his father killed. He went without meat for about six months. I begged his father not to notice, to pay no attention. Frank, though, couldn't do things that way. One night he threatened to beat him if he didn't eat a big slice of roast beef. Edward did—and then he went out and vomited in the kitchen sink. Edward was just fourteen. I told him if he ever threatened the boy again, I would leave and take Edward with me. And I would have."

Life tends to divide itself into seven-year cycles. At six, almost seven, Edward had his first shock; he was called by his oldest brother's name by his mother. At fourteen, he was rejected by his father. And at twenty-one, he entered analysis.

Painfully, stopping to refill her cup, Grace G. told me the story. Edward graduated from high school with failures in many subjects and brilliant grades in a few. His average was not good enough to get him into Harvard, the college his brothers had attended. And he refused to settle for any of the smaller schools which would have taken him. So, before dropouts became fashionable, he irritated Frank G. by becoming a dropout. Billy planned to be a lawyer, Neil had set his heart on medicine, so Frank G. put Edward into the steel mill, on the assembly line. The second day, he was hit on the head and hurt, because, against several mill rules, he had taken off his hard hat. That finished the career at the mill.

The boy showed some interest in labor relations. But Frank G. refused to let him "start at the top." So Edward stopped doing anything, so far as they could see. Quarrels became a regular feature of the dinner table. Eventually Grace G. encouraged Edward to eat his meals—snacks, they really were—in his room, or in the basement where he had set up his record player and had a cot and bookshelves.

Once he ran away, bumming a ride to California. He sent a postcard to his mother saying he was going into the movies. But things went sour again. He hired out as a stunt man and, repeating the pattern at the mill, was so badly injured after being thrown from a bucking horse his mother had to go to California and bring him back in a private plane. He was hospitalized for a month. After that, nobody mentioned working. He spent his days sleeping, and his nights reading. He never had meals with the family. When Grace got up in the morning, she usually found evidence he had been eating during the night.

She was afraid to bring in professional help. Frank G. was dead-set against such things. Like another Capricorn, President Nixon, he mistrusted psychiatrists. But eventually, Edward made it clear he needed help. (Later I was to see on his chart that this cry for help was one of the best things that ever happened to him.) One evening when he was alone in the house he got out of the bed where he had been lying naked, walked several blocks through the soft summer night to the country club—the white neighbors were all at the end-of-summer dance and the blacks, attempting to stay out of trouble, pretended not to see him—climbed over the fence which had been built to keep non-members out of the pool, and jumped in. At first, no one paid any attention. There had been considerable drinking and, although the pool was supposed to be closed at seven o'clock, those who heard the splash figured it might have been some member who was jumping in on a dare.

Then Edward, naked, appeared on the diving board. He posed there until everyone recognized who it was. Billy had the presence of mind to tell his father to go to the locker room and find clothes. He waited at the end of the pool, after Edward executed a perfect swan dive, and persuaded his brother to come out. Wrapping his own white coat around his brother's exposed midriff, Billy rushed him off to the locker room, and then home. Frank G. and Neil went with them.

Grace G. sat stunned, suffering agonies of apprehension and embarrassment. She and her husband had been at a table alone. She endured the glances of sympathy and curiosity directed at her. Finally the family doctor sent his wife over to suggest they drive Grace home. On the way, he told her Edward was a sick young man who needed treatment which might not be available locally. By the time they reached the house, Neil had convinced his father that it might be a good idea to send Edward away for help and suggested a retired analyst in Charleston who accepted patients in his own house and let them feel they were part of the family.

"Frank was glad to get him out of the house," Grace G. said. "He is that way. If he doesn't see it, it isn't there. And I guess he was afraid Edward might do something worse."

"And you?"

"I was numb. I drove him down to Charleston. Neil insisted on going along. I guess maybe he thought we would both escape if he didn't. But Edward wasn't in any state of mind to try anything and I was too heartsick. He just sat in the back, without talking. When we would stop for gas, or something to eat, Neil would lead him off to the rest room like a child. He even seemed to enjoy the ride, as though it were a kind of holiday."

"Did he get better?"

"Yes. Not right away. Eventually, though, his doctor let him come home for a weekend. I'd been to Charleston to visit him but it was the first time he saw his father. He seemed to want to talk to him about what was going to become of him. Of course, without a college education so many areas were closed to him. But he told Frank he realized he must find some way of helping others if he were to find himself."

For over three years, Edward was under the doctor's care. He finally was able to share an apartment with three other young men in Charleston and work in a settlement house. He also enrolled in night school, studying philosophy and psychology and, because he was interested, leading the class in grades. But in the autumn of 1957, his analyst died suddenly. Edward stopped night school. Then he began skipping work at the settlement house. One of his roommates called Grace G. to complain about Edward's drinking.

"I wanted to go up to Charleston and bring him home right then," Grace G. said. "Frank said no, he'd have to find himself, grow up. So, against my better judgment, I waited. One morning when I was out, Edward came walking up our road. He had hitch-hiked home and was so dirty and unkempt our old cook didn't recognize him until he called her by name."

This time, Frank G. took charge. He selected an analyst, a new man in Columbia who agreed to treat Edward at home, rather

than hospitalize him. "He's not suicidal or dangerous," he assured
the G.'s after an interview. "What he needs is stabilization, not
analysis in depth. That was the mistake made by the Charleston
analyst. I can give him tranquilizers and have him at work in six
months."

"I want him to go back in the steel mill," Frank G. had said.
And the thirty-eight-year-old analyst had agreed, adding, "Sometimes a certain amount of routine and discipline does the trick in
these cases. Permissiveness, overpermissiveness, makes an unstable person feel no one cares about him. Obviously the boy
doesn't have the maturity to stand on his own feet. When his doctor died, he regressed."

Grace G. tried hard to understand the new treatment. Dr. James
drove out to their farm from Columbia, a 30-mile trip, three times
a week. The sessions lasted from six to seven o'clock and, at her
husband's suggestion, they invited the analyst to have dinner with
them afterward. But in her opinion, Edward was not responding.
He refused to come to the dinner table with Dr. James, reverting
to his old habit of snatching the makings of a sandwich and escaping to the basement. He seldom left the house and showed
no interest in the books Grace G. selected carefully and brought
him from the library.

"Don't worry," Dr. James assured them one evening after dinner when they were having coffee in the living room, and Edward
had locked himself downstairs. "This is absolutely natural. He had
come to depend upon his analyst, too much in my opinion but
many of the old Freudians feel this is necessary, and the death
was a kind of rejection. My problem is not to be a father figure,
but a kind of older brother, even a competitor, if you like. Hos-
tility is natural in this relation in the beginning but when I have
managed to make him want to show me I am wrong, then, you
will see results fast. And lasting results."

By the time she reached this part of the story, Grace G. had
emptied the pot of coffee, virtually without help from me, and
smoked half a pack of cigarettes. She looked at the ashtray
ruefully.

"I didn't know much about psychiatry, except the short course
we took when I was studying nursing. But he made me feel hope-
lessly out of date and guilty, too. I have no idea whether he was
trying to diminish me in Frank's eyes deliberately, but he was
succeeding. I was the one who had hurt Edward in the beginning

by my permissiveness. I think Dr. James and Frank would have laughed at me if I had told them the story of calling Edward by his brother's name when he was six. And I had no intention of telling either of them, anyway. I wasn't talking much those days."

"It wouldn't have shown in his chart if it hadn't been important."

She got up and went over to the window and stood there for a long time. When she began to talk, she did not turn around.

"The night of the—accident—was Dr. James's seventh or eighth visit. I forget. It was all in the newspapers. When I read them, they seemed to know more than I did about what happened. But it's all so mixed up now. I see everything as though it all happened under water. So bear with me. If you have to know."

"It will help," I said.

"All right. I'll think back and try to remember. Edward and Dr. James used the big front room upstairs for their sessions. When the boys were little, it was the nursery, and later Frank made it over into kind of a television and gun room. He had pictures of his dogs all over the wall and hanging over the fireplace some old gun he'd brought back from the war as a souvenir. It wasn't my kind of room and it certainly wasn't Edward's, but Dr. James liked it because he said it was 'neutral territory'."

She whirled around. "You may think I don't like him now because of what happened. I never liked him. He was—too sure of himself. Whenever he talked about anything, he knew more than anyone else. Frank didn't mind. Or, if he did, he wouldn't admit so. For he was Frank's discovery and Frank had persuaded him to make house calls, something most analysts don't like to do.

"Anyway, I went along, or tried to. We were having a rib roast that night, which is why I was watching the time. Florence, our old cook, knew Frank liked it rare and she was afraid it would be overdone if he came home late. I had set the table earlier—poor old Florence is so big and fat now I've seen her crawl on her hands and knees when she had to go upstairs to get something—and was fixing some flowers I had bought at the greenhouse, for ours were all gone. Then—it happened."

She caught the back of a chair. I stood up. She motioned me away. "I'm all right. It's just—remembering. I heard a shot. It didn't really startle me that much. Down our way, everybody hunts and I'm always telling Frank he has to keep our place posted because they come too close to the house, especially when it's little kids who get excited chasing a rabbit or a game bird. And then I heard a scream. I knew it was Edward."

She circled the chair awkwardly and sat down. "I ran upstairs. Edward was just coming out of the gun room. He said, 'Mama, the doctor is dangerous. Don't ever let him in the house again.' Then he fell to the floor. Old Florence was right behind me—I don't know how she ever got up those stairs so fast—and she ran into the bathroom to get water. We were trying to bring Edward out of his fainting spell when Frank came home. He went in the gun room and found Dr. James dead. He'd been shot through the heart. That's what they said, anyway. I fainted, too. When I came to, someone had carried me into my own room and locked the door. I guess Frank didn't want me to see the body. Or see them taking Edward away, either. The doctor gave me a shot of morphine and I really didn't know anything until late that night. I went downstairs where Frank was sitting at the kitchen table drinking—drunk—and he told me so far as he was concerned, Edward was dead, too."

She stood up and looked around her. I said, "Can I get you anything?"

"No. No, of course not. It's just that—I think Billy and Neil went with Edward in the police ambulance. They put him in a security hospital. He didn't talk, even move. He just lay there in bed like a dead person with his eyes closed. Frank said a lot of things that night I'll never forgive him for. He said I was to blame."

"He was drunk. And upset."

"That's what he said afterward. Just the same, you don't forgive someone for deliberately trying to hurt like that."

"He thinks Edward was guilty?"

"Of course. It was all so simple. Edward had shown he didn't like Dr. James. So he shot him. Oh, there was a struggle. They found his and the doctor's fingerprints on the gun, although it was so rusty there was nothing conclusive. Frank said the doctor must have tried to snatch it out of Edward's hands."

She walked over to me. "But they are wrong, all of them. I'll tell you why. It would never have occurred to Edward to touch that gun over the fireplace. It was old, it had been there forever. I didn't know it was loaded—I hate guns and I wouldn't touch one, even to dust it. Maybe one of the boys tried to use it years ago and left a bullet in it. But we all regarded it as just an ornament.

A nasty kind of ornament but it was Frank's room. He wouldn't put his guns in the basement because it was too damp. So he built racks for them and there they were—all kinds of shotguns and powerful rifles lined up against the wall. If Edward wanted to use a gun—and he had been taught to handle guns like Billy and Neil— he would have taken one from the rack. There was all kinds of ammunition in the drawers. If he had intended to kill the doctor, he would have loaded a gun and had it ready."

"Nothing was locked up?"

"Never. Not then. Frank ordered glass cases and locks after the accident. But guns are so much a way of life where we live that it never occurred to any of us to lock them up."

"What if Edward shot him in self-defense?"

"Edward wouldn't have killed an animal, even to save his life. Besides, what kind of a threat could Dr. James have made?"

I hesitated. Edward's sun and the planet Venus were in Pisces in the birth chart. This made him beautiful rather than handsome, gentle, impressionable to all that is sensuous, hurt by anything ugly or sordid. His moon in Libra (whose ruling planet is Venus) also contributed to his general softness of character and looks. There was nothing to indicate he had any ambivalence in his sexual attitude; if anything I would have instinctively cast him as one of those Scorpios (he had that sign rising) who was as yet unawakened, fearful of sex, who pushed his feelings deep inside where they festered and caused trouble. Yet he was drawn to people who admired him, men and women, and needed flattery desperately.

"I wish I knew when Dr. James was born. Even his sun sign would help. Would you say he might have made a homosexual advance toward Edward?"

"No, never. Frank wouldn't have chosen him if there had been anything of that sort in Dr. James. I know he wouldn't. Frank loathes what he calls sissies."

"Sissies aren't necessarily homosexuals and vice versa. In fact—" I stopped. I could see any mention of homosexuality upset her. Yet Edward's chart at the moment of birth indicated that trouble would come through his beauty. His sun and Venus in Pisces were directly opposite the planets Mars (violence), Neptune (frustration) and Jupiter (luck, happiness). Opposites indicate face-to-face encounters, struggle. I finished lamely, "What do you think happened?"

"It was a complete accident. Dr. James took the gun up from over the mantel because he was curious. Edward must have told him it was no good, it was just something his father brought back from Korea as a souvenir. And it went off."

"Then how do you account for what Edward said to you, that the doctor was dangerous?"

"Maybe that he didn't know how to handle firearms. Boys who are around guns must know how to use them. Much as I dislike guns, I agreed with Frank about that."

"Would that be a reason for not allowing the doctor in the house again? Wasn't that what Edward said?"

"Stop torturing me. I think that is what he said. Florence can't remember. The rest think I'm hallucinating. Do you think I'll ever have him back?"

She broke away and lighted another cigarette. "They can put him away for life. Right now they say he is dangerous and have him in solitary confinement. Dangerous? He sits on the floor and cries like a baby. He can't talk, or he won't. Sometimes I take him in my arms and he looks at me as though he knows me. I can't be sure. They say not, it only upsets him for me to visit. I know it upsets me."

"You mustn't expect miracles."

"What do you mean?"

"It's going to be a long time. His chart doesn't show any dramatic changes for a number of years. Then something crucial is due to happen. The planet Uranus will cross his ascendant, Scorpio, and there will be an eclipse of the moon in Scorpio. I can't tell you exactly what it means right now. I have to know more about his brothers, the doctor, his father. I need to do their charts. Then perhaps—when do you plan to go home?"

"Tomorrow. I can give you the information about Billy and Neil now. I don't know the time Frank was born and I doubt if he does. About the psychiatrist. Is that necessary?"

"Yes. If you want me to try to find out whether Edward is guilty or not."

"I do. More than anything. I think I could live with Frank in peace if I knew Edward was not dangerous, that I didn't give birth to a monster."

"He isn't a monster and I don't think he killed the doctor. I agree with you it was an accident. In spite of the evidence."

"I wish I could convince my husband of that."

"Perhaps you can. Be patient. Send me everything you can, as soon as you can."

"I wish—am I doing right in returning to my husband?"

"I think so. These next few years aren't going to be easy. But periods of trial and dissatisfaction are periods of growth. I hadn't planned to discuss your horoscope with you, yet. I can only tell you, briefly, that you have an exceptionally quick mind but you have never learned balance. You make decisions too fast, without regard for their effect on others. In your natal chart, both Mars and Venus are in Libra where they are not well placed. I think these coming years are going to change you a great deal, for the better."

"That is very small comfort, Miss de Jersey."

"Think about it from time to time. And there is light at the end of the tunnel. By the time any changes occur in Edward's life, you will be wise enough to make balanced judgments."

"I'll be an old woman. I must say you've disappointed me. I'm sorry I wasted my time."

"I'm sorry, too." I looked at my watch. "My husband will be downstairs in a few minutes. I don't want to make him wait."

I went for my coat and boots. She followed me to the door and handed me a slip of paper. "Billy's and Neil's birthdates, although I don't know why you bother. And my address. You can have your secretary send me a bill."

"For this morning, yes, because it was a regular session. Let's forget tonight since you feel it was so unsatisfactory. Thank Mrs. Fuller for me."

"You don't need to be so disagreeable. After all, I did most of the talking."

I said good night and left. Ralph was early, for which I was thankful. On the way home, we didn't talk much. Finally, he said, "Forget her. She sounds like a horrible woman."

"She isn't, really. It's just one of those cases of a beautiful, potentially bright woman who has a great deal to learn. I told her that, which was my mistake."

He repeated, "Forget it, Katie. Those are orders. For you have lots of people who need and appreciate you."

Maggie was even more vehement the next morning when I gave her the slip of paper from Grace G. "You are seven times an idiot to have told her you wouldn't charge her for last night. And what are these birthdates?"

"Her two older sons."

"Honestly, Katie." Maggie opened Grace G.'s folder and slammed the slip of paper inside. "I should bill her for the ride home I gave her. However, since you are going to be poor but proud, I guess I'll have to go along. Then we'll have a celebration and burn the whole folder."

I said it was up to her. However, left to her own devices, Maggie isn't without her own bump of curiosity. In the week that followed I noticed she had been working on two charts. One noon hour, when we were having sandwiches and soup sent in to save time, I asked her what she'd been doing. She pulled them out from her top drawer.

"Two lost souls," she said. "Just as I suspected. That horrible woman. Here's Billy, January 20, 1930, 2 A.M. Sun in Capricorn, Scorpio rising, moon in Sagittarius. He has musical talent, he loves athletics, but he's in some field he doesn't like because he needs to please his mother and father."

"Law," I said.

"Anyway, he's frustrated. Women are crazy about him and he's very sexy, he has this strong Mars. But he'll never stay married. Though he will achieve typical Capricorn success."

"Did he like his brothers?"

"No. The chart shows sibling rivalry. But he is always off in the clouds some place. He thinks of his brothers only when they interfere."

"What about Neil?"

"Virgo. September 6, 1931, 7:30 P.M. He's in the degree of Virgo you call 'the dictator.' He has to be running things and he wants to be a success, Aries rising. His moon is in Cancer, which gives him tenderness but he is absolutely terrified of his father. What does he do?"

"Medicine. She didn't say what field."

"Four planets in Virgo. Very bright. He'll do well in any field involving children."

I looked at the chart: "Either obstetrics or gynecology."

"He'll always be a square. A bore. If you ask me, with all his faults, Edward was the big brain of the family. Well, that closes the book. I got a check from Mrs. G. this morning. No comment. Just a check."

But we didn't burn the file. Or throw it out. For it was unfinished business. And unfinished business affects me like a nagging toothache. Sometimes I can forget it entirely for weeks, months. Then in the middle of the night, when I am in a strange hotel bed, I wonder what is bugging me and I discover it is the case I wasn't able to solve. For two years, on and off, I forgot about Mrs. G. Then one day I was in Lincoln, Nebraska, speaking before a function sponsored by a bank. As usual, there was a group of women who came up afterward to ask questions or, delightfully, thank me. One of them looked familiar; suddenly, with a chill, I remembered the face. But Mrs. G. had changed. She was still beautiful, but ravaged. She hadn't looked her age before. Now she seemed much older than she actually was. Yet she was still a woman who stood out in a crowd. I couldn't dredge up any resentment. When her turn came, I called her by name.

She looked surprised. "I didn't think you'd know me. I've changed so. Frank says it is for the better but I don't look in my mirror much these days. I promised to write you and give you some information and I never did. I guess I was ashamed of the way I acted."

"You were under a lot of pressure."

"In a way, I still am. One of these days I'll write you a long letter. Are you at the same address?"

I said no and gave her my card. I'd moved into the Marina Towers. We chatted, not really saying anything. I didn't like to ask about Edward, and she, apparently, had no desire to mention him. The line stretched out behind her and I had a TV show to tape, in a few minutes. So I had to ask urgently, "How are you, really?"

"And what am I doing here? Louise died, a year ago. She left me quite a lot of money. I'm spending most of it trying to do something about conditions in mental hospitals. I go around the country lecturing. I don't get audiences like yours. Sometimes I'm sure nobody listens to me if they do come. But if I save just one boy from hell, it's okay by me."

"And your own boy?"

She smiled, and her face was beautiful again. "No better. Oh, he goes through stages when he can talk almost rationally. Then he reverts. He has no memory of the accident. I go and see him about once a month, oftener when he is rational. Once in a while his father goes along, or one of his brothers. The boys are both married and living away from home. Billy has been divorced and is married again, a widow with grown children. It hasn't helped him in his law firm. And Neil married his office nurse, a nice enough girl but terribly conservative. It's queer how life turns out, isn't it? You must come and see us when you are in South Carolina."

I said I would like that, being polite, not meaning it, and she smiled again and moved on. After my television show, I was driven to the airport by a charming retired dentist, a Leo widower who drove a Cadillac and had women of all ages swooning over him. He insisted on waiting with me until the plane was announced. While we were chatting, I heard myself being paged; I was wanted, they said, on the telephone. It was Grace G.

"I didn't mean to tell you. But I decided I owed it to you. My son Neil was able to check out Dr. James. He was born December 28, 1919."

"That makes him a Capricorn. It explains why your husband selected him and why Edward didn't respond. I doubt if he ever would have liked him."

"There's another thing. I don't exactly know where this puts us and we've not told anybody outside the family. Dr. James had to leave New York because one of his patients accused him of making homosexual advances. The family threatened to take him to court if he didn't get out of the state. He came down South very eager to blot out his past. I don't know whether or not he was a homosexual—he certainly didn't look or act like one—but it's apparent now why he was so eager to accommodate Frank and make house visits to treat Edward."

"What is apparent?"

"I think he was attracted to boys. He did have many young boys among his patients in New York, Neil was told. Miss de Jersey, do you think it is possible that Dr. James killed himself because he couldn't resist approaching Edward?"

I said I didn't know. In fact, the possibility hadn't occurred to me. "I wish I had more information about where Dr. James was born and his birth hour. I can only guess, and that doesn't help you much. But I'll look at the chart for the moment of the accident again, and Edward's chart, and see if I can come up with any suggestions."

To my surprise, she said, "No, please. Let it go. Frank and I have reached a kind of plateau where we have accepted what has happened. They won't release Edward, I am afraid, unless he improves enough so he remembers what happened and is able to stand trial. I'm not sure I could go through that and I hate what the publicity has already done to Frank and my other sons. Let it go."

I gave Maggie the scribbled notes I had made about Dr. James to file with the rest of the chart. This time she did put the folder away in the inactive files. It stayed there until the summer of 1969 when we were moving over to the John Hancock Building and ruthlessly weeding out what had to be kept from what could be thrown away. One hot day, she tossed Grace G.'s chart on my desk.

"It's over ten years and we only billed her for that one session. Don't you think we can throw the folder out?"

I opened it. "I suppose so. It just irritates me that I never could figure out what happened. The doctor might have been a homosexual and it could well be he was attracted to Edward. But I don't think he would pick up a gun and shoot himself if Edward rejected him. Nor would Edward grab a gun he didn't think was loaded to shoot the doctor for making a homosexual advance."

"Dr. James might have been afraid of exposure again. Or decided he just couldn't control himself. It wasn't any use."

"Then he would have killed himself at home, quietly. And not with a gun, when doctors have such easy access to pills. It doesn't make sense." I studied Edward's yellowing chart again, shaking my head.

"Let's forget the whole thing." Maggie reached for the folder. I caught her wrist.

"Wait. Maggie, something is going on right now. There was an eclipse last March which coincided with some of the aspects I had seen in the accident chart. I wonder—sometimes this means the old problem is eclipsed out. And both the moon and Saturn are in the twelfth house, the house of confinement. Maggie, it means he has served his karma, at least some part of it. I have to know what is going on. I have her address here somewhere. Try to get her on the telephone, please."

"She told you to let it go. Besides, you know how she acted that night you were kind enough to go up and have dinner with her. She practically ordered you out of the house."

"She was under pressure. She's changed."

"Now, Katie." Maggie faced me across the desk, defiantly. Her hands were black with dust from the files and there was a streak of dirt across her forehead. "Let's think of it this way. What if you are wrong? I've never put it this way before but I am going to say exactly what I think now. That woman is a bitch. If you call her and put yourself out on a limb saying what just happened and if nothing did, she's going to make you a laughingstock. She's going to call her friend Louise Fuller and Louise is going to tell the doctor and the doctor will tell somebody else and it's going to be all over Chicago."

"Louise Fuller is dead."

"Okay, then Grace will call the doctor. I wouldn't put anything past her. She is a selfish woman. And you've taken everything you should from her."

"You're afraid I'm wrong, that is what is bothering you. Don't you have faith in astrology?"

"I don't want you to make a fool of yourself." I stared at her amazed. She was my dear friend. She worked with me because she believed in what I did. She liked some of my clients better than others. She felt some of them made unfair and unreasonable demands on my time. But never before had she opposed me with this determination.

I went back to Edward's chart again. I remembered how I had felt the night I had done the accident chart; nothing had come through clearly. I had gone to the dinner with Grace G. in a disturbed mood, uncertain. But on a hot Saturday in July more than ten years later, I knew I was right. "Call her, Maggie. Take my word for it. Something has happened."

And something had happened. On the telephone, Grace G.'s first words were, "Miss de Jersey, we've been thinking of you all day. I wanted to call you but Frank felt we had treated you too badly. Edward is home. He's talking rationally. It's like a miracle."

Of course, it wasn't quite a miracle—yet. Several strange things had happened. Edward had improved in the last year, so much he was allowed to help other patients in the therapy hours. He taught painting and had done several portraits which had been exhibited in the building. The guards had grown used to him, trusted him. He also worked out in the gardens and spelled them when it came time to mow the bedraggled lawn. One afternoon, he tossed down the trowel he was using in the annual bed and walked out of the grounds. The guards didn't report him missing until dinnertime.

A doctor called Frank G., to tell him they were looking for Edward. They either hadn't looked very hard, or Edward had been extremely clever. Two days after the G.'s heard he was missing, he turned up at the house, tired and terribly sunburned. He had walked and hitched rides. He hadn't eaten. Grace G. had put him to bed and begged the doctors to let her keep Edward for a little while, until he recovered from the trip. She said sadly, "But of course he has to go back. Eventually. Do you see that?"

"Yes. But I also see regeneration. He is under excellent astrological aspects for the next ten months. The moon is moving through his chart in a way which means he is going to have another chance, a different path is there for him if he can only take advantage of it. That is where you come in."

"What can I do?"

"Get him the right kind of help. If it isn't available wherever he is, go to court and have him moved. I think he can be saved. But you must fight."

"Neil thinks this is just a remission. He wanted to take him back the day he came home. He says Edward is dangerous."

"What do his doctors think?"

"I suppose they'd have to agree with Neil. But there is one, an older man, who used to be a general practitioner and who has been back to school again, studying now to be an analyst. He called me after he heard about Edward and told me he felt there were new drugs which might help him if I would give my consent. Not the old sedatives, but something experimental. What do you think?"

I could see Maggie watching me warily. She had heard enough of the conversation to realize what was going to happen. I was going to get myself involved again. That meant broken appointments, schedules switched around. In the middle, I would be spreading myself too thin, missing sleep, inviting the germs which are always ready to attack when you exhaust yourself. But on the other hand, there would be excitement. Not the pseudo-excitement you get from books and movies, but real-life drama. And she would be sharing it with me, as always.

"Go ahead," I said. "And look. I'm going to be in Baltimore in a month or so, I have a speaking date. I'm not quite sure just when, I'll have my secretary call you. Would you like me to fly down and spend the night with you?"

Grace G. said they would send a private plane for me; Frank G. would come up with the pilot "any time, any place."

I looked at Maggie, dirty hands, dirty face—with a wide grin across it, suddenly. Once you've been exposed to the practice of astrology, you are trapped. There is nothing in the world quite so fascinating. I said to Grace G., "And may I bring my secretary? You remember—that nice girl who drove you home that day when you weren't feeling well."

We didn't arrive in South Carolina until a warm Saturday in late October. But meanwhile, even my Gemini husband, who had taken as dim a view of Grace G. as Maggie had in the beginning, had become involved. He studied medical articles about the use of chemicals to correct imbalance in mental illness; during the course of his reading, he telephoned Dr. Fuller, who was also involved. Meanwhile, every Sunday night Grace G. and I had an appointment call, all through the summer and early autumn. The progress in Edward's condition was not dramatic. But it was progress. The danger, of course, is that if he is pushed too fast, he might regress. And of course, I, as the astrologer, am well aware of other hazards.

For 1975 is going to be his crucial year. An eclipse 10 degrees in Scorpio at that time will square the position of Saturn in his natal chart. Uranus in Scorpio will cross his ascendant, and cause upheaval. I am not sure what will be the result. But whatever it is —a recovery or a relapse—is sure to be conclusive. And, meeting Frank G. for the first time, I was also well aware that the key to the solution might lie, simply, in his attitude.

Of course, he charmed Maggie and me immediately. He was a Southerner, born and bred. Yet he was not the old-style Southerner who was still fighting the War Between the States. The new South had offered him opportunity and made him rich; he said cheerfully, he now had more money than he ever thought there was in the world, when he was a boy. He and Grace G. lived in what had once been the manor house of a plantation, in a soft, sleepy little country town near his new steel mill.

The approach to the house was lined with beautiful old trees hung with dark Spanish moss. Frank G. told me in the old days the plantation owners used to have slaves holding flaming torches to light the drive when they expected guests. Today, he views this kind of thing in proper perspective. He took the tenant farmers and sharecroppers in the neighborhood, the descendants of freed slaves, and trained them to work in his steel mill at good wages. He loaned them money to build proper houses, with bathrooms and electricity. Yet he enjoys being "Mr. Frank" to everyone. With true Capricorn paternalism, he delivers orations at black funerals and sits behind the picture window in his office at each change of shift, watching "his" men. The old slave quarters behind the house, where some of the mothers and fathers of his present employees were born, have been remodeled into air-conditioned kennels for his prize hunting dogs. Yet when he hunts, side by side with him are his black neighbors—not that he can bring himself to call them "black"; "colored" is his term when he is being polite.

In the house, the only full-time servant left was old Florence, now so heavy and arthritic her small grandchildren are paid baby-sitting fees to come in and help her. Frank talks constantly about the local girls who aren't available to do housework because they are standing side by side in the mill with men, earning equal wages. But he hires them because they are as good as men, sometimes better. And when he spots a particularly bright young girl—or man—he sends him off to college, to get an education and "better" himself.

Frank G. and I had plenty of communication on the man-woman level. As his wife had promised, I found him attractive and it was easy to respond to his gallantry. Yet he was a Capricorn, a father figure who was completely charming so long as he had his own way. And I knew, despite the easy warmth with which he was making Maggie and me welcome, that he was ready to be tough. He was waiting, cautiously, for my first approach. And he had the big guns in reserve in case they were needed.

We arrived in time for dinner, and Maggie and I were shown our suite, a charming big bedroom with canopied beds and a dressing room attached to a magnificently modern bath. We were on the first floor and all of our windows overlooked the huge S-shaped pool, heated so we could swim in the morning. By the time we had slipped on cocktail dresses, the guests had arrived, Billy and Neil and their respective wives. Billy's wife was tall and angular, the kind of woman who enjoys being referred to as a good sport. She talked all the time (I cast her immediately as a Sagittarius and I was proven right) while Neil's wife, mouselike, hardly opened her mouth and, on the few occasions she answered a direct question, had such a thick Southern accent I couldn't make out what she had said.

But it was, mostly because of Frank G., a pleasant dinner. The cook's niece, a college-educated woman who taught school and worked in the local hardware store owned by her husband, had been brought in to help serve. Although Frank G. didn't mention it, I suspected he'd been the one who sent her to college because they were on intimate terms, laughing and exchanging sometimes private jokes throughout the meal. He directed the conversation and a great deal of it was about himself. But the stories he told were amusing. His sons laughed at them, although they must have heard them many times before. So did their wives. Grace G. didn't; I had the feeling she was worried about what might happen when Frank G. stopped being the gracious host and began to discuss his son Edward. Frankly, so was I.

I was glad when dinner, and the air of false conviviality, was over. The cook's niece left coffee and cups in the living room and vanished. I guess that had been the instructions. Outside there was a new moon, winking through the trees. Mr. Neil's wife passed the cups and cream and sugar. Mr. Billy's Sagittarian wife talked—until she was silenced by a look from Frank G.

Then he turned to me. "Edward is far from well."

"But he is responding." That was Grace G. "They say the trip home set him back, and of course this new treatment is a—a challenge."

"Mother expects too much." A new voice of authority, high and rather too shrill, very Virgo Brother Neil. I studied him and wondered whether he was saying what he really believed or was trying to please his father. "The work is strictly experimental. Personally, I was against offering my brother as a guinea pig. He had made a reasonable adjustment. But now anything can happen."

"If he gets well—" Grace G. again tentative. Frank G. turned to me.

"And what do you think, Miss de Jersey?"

I put down my coffee cup. "I've already told you. This is a period of good aspects for Edward. I think it was wise of you to decide to let him have this new treatment. The benefit of knowing astrological aspects is being able to select times which are propitious for going ahead, trying new things."

Silence. Even Billy's Sagittarius didn't care to add to that. Then Frank G. again. "I wish I could believe in your astrology, Miss de Jersey. You have really persuaded my wife that you have a special pipeline to the stars. I've tried to understand what you're driving at. But it doesn't make sense. How can a science which was based on the assumption that the world was flat have any relevancy today?"

Maggie moved uncomfortably. Otherwise, silence. The floor was mine. I spoke up. "It makes sense to me. And I know more about it than you do. Do the tides make sense to you? Do you know why they respond to the pull of the moon? I've studied astrology for more than twenty years and I am sure of one thing. The fact we don't understand why certain things happen is no reason we should try to turn our backs and deny their power."

He smiled. Charm, charm, charm. "Don't get upset, my dear. This is just a little friendly discussion, in the bosom of the family. I grant you there are mysteries in this life and perhaps beyond it which we aren't supposed to understand. I'm just concerned about my son. On your advice, or the advice of your stars, we are making Edward undergo a new kind of treatment. Neil was against it, and he's a doctor. I was against it, and I'm the boy's father. Billy was on the fence; poor Billy believes being on the fence proves he has a legal mind. You were for it. So you won."

I took a deep breath. "I saw in his chart that something had happened to him. When I called your wife, she said Edward was home, he had run away from the hospital. She told me one doctor wanted to try a new kind of treatment. I said the prospects for good results in the next ten months were there in his chart. That was all. I don't tell people what to do, Mr. G., I tell them what the aspects are."

"Calm down, my dear. I'm not attacking you. All I want is to do the best thing possible for my family, my sons and their wives as well as my wife. If the boy gets well enough so he can stand trial, if he remembers what happened that afternoon with the psychiatrist and can stand up and prove his innocence, fine. I'm all for it. But if he can't face reality, which is what happened to him before, and retreats into—being a vegetable again, I don't like the idea of being responsible. And I'm sure you don't, either."

"Does he have to go to court and prove his innocence? Isn't it enough if he is well and able to come home?"

"Well, now. Billy, you're the legal expert. If Edward gets well, won't he have to stand trial?"

"Dad, that's a technical point. I wish I could say exactly—"

"I wish you could, too, son." Frank G.'s voice was hard. "In any case, when we get the truth, when we find out what really happened and if Edward is innocent, which I hope to God he is, I want him cleared legally. We all have suffered enough. He should be cleared in the eyes of the world."

Period, paragraph, I thought. I glanced at Maggie. Her eyes were closed but she was far from asleep. At the end of the table,

I heard a match strike. Grace G. hadn't smoked at all during dinner, or since. But now she had lighted a cigarette. Her husband frowned at her, then turned back to me. I was obviously the pigeon for tonight.

"My wife told me there was something in Edward's horoscope which showed that his whole problem started at the age of six. Now, Miss de Jersey, if you had seen my son's chart before that time, or done it shortly after birth, how could you have helped? Would Edward now be sitting here with the rest of us, a nice, normal human being instead of being behind bars?"

Abruptly, my rising anger was gone. "You're more interested in astrology than you admit, Mr. G., I think you have even studied it a bit. For you are asking a basic question on which even some astrologers disagree."

"Give me your opinion. To hell with the rest."

"Let me put it this way. I do not believe that any astrologer could have changed the basic pattern of Edward's life. It is too strongly indicated. But I could have warned you of dangers ahead. I could have told you that this child would suffer more acutely from the simple, common problems of sibling rivalry and fear of rejection by his parents, than most children. That he was more sensitive, more highly strung, than his older brothers. I would have begged you to treat him differently from them. Not necessarily try to keep him a baby, but to understand his vulnerable Pisces nature and to have compassion for his depressions and withdrawals instead of trying to make him conform."

"Would he have killed somebody anyway? No matter what?"

"I don't believe he killed his doctor. I think it was an accident. I don't know precisely what happened, but I am also sure there was something to do with the fact that the doctor was homosexually inclined."

"Do you think this could have been avoided—the thing you say was an accident?"

"Yes, I do."

"How?"

"Perhaps some kind of therapy earlier. And a difference in your attitude toward him. He must have clung to his mother because he was terrified of you."

Silence. I looked around. Maggie's eyes were open wide, staring at Frank G. His wife had put out her cigarette and was watching him, too. I wondered if I had gone too far. If I had, I didn't care. As a guest in the house, I hadn't asked to be interrogated.

"I think she has a point, Dad." Neil's voice was low. "I used to lie because I was afraid of you. When you were gone during the day, I used to sneak home and get one of your guns and pretend you were coming home and somebody would attack you and I'd shoot him and you would like me because I saved your life."

"Neil, my God. How ridiculous. You weren't scared of me, were you, Bill?"

Bill straightened. Like most athletes, he had gained weight and looked soft. His face was slack and his smile uncertain. "Why am I practicing law today? To please you, Dad. I wanted to stay in athletics, maybe become a high school coach. I would have been good at it. Or I might have studied music. You remember I had a piano teacher who said I showed aptitude. I can remember what you said to her: 'If my son isn't going to show more than aptitude, let's quit right now. Either he is going to be the best goddamned musician in the world or he isn't going near a piano.' "

"I never said anything like that." Bill looked away. Frank G. turned to me again. "Miss de Jersey, do you take pride in upsetting all your clients this way?"

"You're not my client. Your wife came to me about Edward."

"I certainly didn't expect you to come down here for free."

"If I'd known you wanted to consult me professionally, I would have asked you to come to Chicago. Or Washington. I wouldn't be here in your home as a guest. I came, quite honestly, because I wanted to try to help Edward. Or at least help you understand to a small extent why he has had to suffer so much. Under these circumstances, I think Maggie and I had better leave right now."

Grace G. stood up. "She is right. I want you to apologize to Miss de Jersey. You have been—insufferable."

Frank G. got up and walked over to her. "I'm sorry. I apologize to Miss de Jersey and to my sons, all three of them, and their wives, and my wife. I apologize to Miss Maggie, here. It turns out in this little truth session that I've been the one to blame all the time, that nothing would have happened if I hadn't been such a bastard."

The man was incredible. Even now, I couldn't help admiring him, responding to his magnetism. "I am only saying to you that astrology might have helped if you had understood your pattern, and that of your wife and sons. You would have recognized why you are all different and been perhaps a little more tolerant."

"You do think I'm a bastard, don't you?"

"You were born in the sign of Capricorn, I know that. It's a good strong sign. If I knew your exact time of birth, I could tell you more about yourself. I do think if you had realized what you were doing, your attitude toward your sons would have changed. The other two were strong enough to survive. But Edward, terrified of displeasing you, retreated into mental illness."

"But why was Edward born weaker than the other two? Was it in his genes?"

"Some people think so. I think it is in his stars. I believe he was meant to suffer more than most people. He was born in a degree of sorrow."

"What in hell is a degree of sorrow?"

"At the moment a child takes his first breath, the position of the planets in the heavens affect the pattern of his life. When I make a natal chart, I am simply putting down this pattern in terms which are clear to me, if not to the average person. Each chart is divided into houses, each containing 30 degrees. The sun, when Edward took his first breath, was in Pisces at 23 degrees. Over the centuries we have discovered that anyone born when the sun is 23 degrees in Pisces will suffer more keenly than his fellows. That is why we call it a degree of sorrow."

"But why do certain people have to suffer more than others?"

"That's a question which theologians try to answer. I don't know the whole answer. But, as I told your wife, I went into astrology in the first place because I wanted to find out why my father, whom I adored, had been chosen to die a painful death of cancer. I'm sure Mrs. G.'s friend, Louise Fuller, was trying in her own way to find out why she had been inflicted, when others weren't. My answer is merely that we are put on earth for a purpose, perhaps to be ennobled by suffering, perhaps to learn so that in this life, or the next, we can contribute more."

"Are you talking about reincarnation?"

"Perhaps. Or regeneration on this earth. It can happen. I've seen it. Through suffering, people have changed."

Frank G. walked over to me and put out his hand. "I'm really sorry, Miss de Jersey. I have given you more than you deserve tonight. My other apology was made in anger. This one is from the heart. I hope you and Miss Maggie sleep well under my roof. And if you care to, tomorrow, I'll take you when I exercise the dogs."

He disappeared and Grace G. told me he had gone to give the

dogs their nightly run. She said sadly, "Sometimes I think if he had loved his sons as much as his dogs everything might have been easier. But he isn't a happy man, Miss de Jersey. I think his suffering has been worse than mine because he cares so terribly what people think of him."

I nodded. "That's a Capricorn trait, too. I would like to do his chart. You don't know his birth hour, I remember."

She shook her head. "I think I told you he was born on January 8, 1905. But at what time—his mother might know. He calls her every day. He could ask."

Shortly after that, Neil and Bill left with their wives. With Frank G. out of hearing, the Sagittarius wife babbled over our good-byes. I could hear her talking in the car as they drove off. Grace G. turned to me. "I can't believe it, still. It seems incredible that I as a human being, an insignificant human being, should be influenced by planets so far away. Yet—I used to wonder why God, with so many important things to worry about, would care whether I forgot my prayers or not. Perhaps we aren't meant to understand."

We said good night and still she hesitated. "Miss de Jersey, you were very understanding about Frank tonight. He didn't mean to be rude. It is just his way. He always thinks he's right. He used to be much more difficult. But Edward's trouble has softened him. I used to think I didn't love him any more. This past year, he has needed me. That's made a lot of difference in our relationship. Sleep as late as you like, tomorrow. Breakfast is when you get up. Frank always gets up early and is out with the dogs."

Maggie and I were too tired for conversation, and too full of our own thoughts. We turned out the light quickly. Even as I dropped off to sleep, I could hear the dogs barking in the distance.

Some time later, I wakened with a start. There was scratching at my door. When I was awake enough to realize where I was— sometimes on a fast lecture tour I forget where I am when the telephone rings to get me up—there was more scratching and an imperious bark. In order not to waken Maggie, I got up without turning on the light. An animal moved past me toward Maggie's bed. Enough moonlight was coming through the dressing room windows so that I could see that the dog—a silver-gray Weimaraner—was wearing a collar. I took him by it and led him through the hall into the dining room; I was sure he had been left in the house by mistake and I could at least find the kitchen and close him in there. The dog came willingly enough. He seemed friendly, but distressed. When I pushed open the swinging door to the butler's pantry, I saw there was a light in the kitchen. Frank G. was sitting at the big old-fashioned drop-leaf table with a pint bottle of bourbon and a glass in front of him.

He looked up. I had slipped on my robe but I was barefooted so he hadn't heard me. He called the dog, who broke away and ran to him. "Come here, baby. He's gone away again but he'll be back, one of these days. I promise you. Poor old boy, why did you have to pick him to love? I was the one who brought you home, who's fed you and trained you all these years. And you still miss him."

My first instinct was to vanish. But I have my pride, too. I didn't want Frank G. to think I was running away from him, if he ever discovered I'd been there. I said, "He was trying to get in our room. I didn't know anyone was awake. I brought him out here, thinking I'd close him in the kitchen for the rest of the night."

Frank G. jumped to his feet, nearly spilling the glass in front of him, buttoning his hunting shirt with one hand as he reached for the glass with the other. "I'm sorry. This time when Edward was home, he slept in the guest room. We thought it was better than if he went upstairs or went back to his old cot in the basement. So Hans—I had him out here with me and I guess he thought Edward was in the house. I hope he didn't disturb you."

"It's all right. I love dogs."

Frank G. looked at the whisky bottle and then at me. "I suppose I seem like an old drunk to you. That's not true. It's just that sometimes I can't sleep and I come downstairs and pour myself a drink and go out to the kennel and bring in a dog with me for company. I don't know why I picked Hans tonight; maybe because he's Edward's dog. Would you like a drink?"

I shook my head and said I'd better go back to bed.

"Why do we have to suffer? Even a dog. I'm the one who loves him and exercises and feeds him. Why does Hans want him and not me? Why do I put my head on the pillow every night thinking, God, why did this have to happen to me?"

"Because every Capricorn, sometime in his life, has to suffer severe disappointment or defeat in order to soften him, make him a better person. I don't know how you feel about President Nixon but I happen to think his defeat a few years ago has made him far more sensitive and responsible."

"How do you know I'm a better person? I behaved like an ass tonight."

"Because your wife thinks you are. I suspect you married her for the reason many men marry—particularly ambitious Capricorns. She was beautiful, she came from an old Chicago family, she had the kind of background you lacked. But you never really loved her until there was trouble and you needed her. And she is a gentler and lovelier person than when I first met her."

"You really believe this astrology, don't you?"

"Of course I do. And because I know your sign, I can understand you a little. That's why I wasn't really too upset tonight, even though I threatened to leave. The very characteristics which made you such a successful man also inhibited you from being the kind of father your sons needed, the husband your wife wanted. Until now, you thought everything you did was for your family, didn't you?"

"Who else would it be for?"

"Yourself. Your own ego. But now you realize there is something besides money and success."

He pulled the dog to him and stroked behind his ears. The dog sighed and dropped his head on Frank G.'s knee. "Maybe you're right. But it's the kind of thing you only admit late at night, with a little whisky for courage."

"I think you were born at night."

He looked up at me teasingly. "And what has that to do with anything?"

"I told you I'd like to do your chart. Ask your mother when you were born."

He turned toward the back door. "Come on, Hans, I'll put you to bed. And I'll get upstairs myself. Miss de Jersey, I don't know why, but I trust you. I'll call my mother tomorrow morning and ask her when I was born and she will really think I've gone off the deep end. Then will you come out and walk the dogs with me?"

I said I would. I went back to bed and to sleep instantly. And, which is very unlike me, I also wakened instantly when Frank G. tapped on the door and reminded me of the middle-of-the-night promise.

We ate breakfast in silence, Frank G. and I, a huge breakfast of all the fattening delectables I never touch at home, including leftover pie. Frank G. prepared it. As he was stacking dishes for the cook, he told me, "I called my mother. She's in a kind of nursing home down near where I was born and I have a phone by her bed so we can talk, first thing in the morning. She is near ninety but her mind is clear as a bell."

"What time were you born?"

He smiled. "She didn't look at the clock. Or maybe they were so poor they didn't have a clock. But she does know she sent my daddy across the fields to get the midwife and he had to wake her up. After I was born, she left and went home and my daddy had to get to the cotton platform so my ma wrapped me in a blanket and got up and fixed breakfast."

I said, "I'll put a notebook and pencil in my pocket and we'll talk while we walk. While I was eating breakfast, I made some calculations on my own. I think you must have been born between 12 and 2 P.M. That period is associated with the second house, which controls money. I think your rising sign is Aries, your wife's sun sign. That explains your attraction, despite many difficulties. It's a strong sign, the one we connect with the ram, always going forward, butting his way if necessary. But that is why your marriage has endured, will endure, and why you and your wife make a strong team."

"You figure out all that because my mother thinks I was born late at night?"

"I suspected that before. Now I am sure your moon is in Aquarius. You have a public conscience, a need to help, which is why you have done what you have for the poor people in your area. But you have, all your life, tended to pull away from deep involvement with people. Isn't that true?"

"I'm boss. I care about my people. Hell, I love them. But I have to be boss, so they will respect me."

"Exactly. And you raised your sons the same way."

"Miss de Jersey, go and put on a pair of walking shoes and some rough clothes. I'll meet you outside by the kennels in twenty minutes. And bring that pad and pencil along."

"By that time I'll have done your chart."

I slipped in and out of the bedroom without waking Maggie. In the deep pocket of my jacket, I had my notebook, where I had sketched out Frank G.'s natal chart. Under ordinary circumstances I would have been sleepy at this hour in the morning, after an interrupted night. I had never felt more wide awake. Like the dogs —there were fourteen setters ("red" dogs, Frank G. called them) and two Weimars besides Hans—I knew I was on the trail of something, but what remained to be seen. The dogs circled and sniffed, wild to get out in the woods. I fell in behind Frank G. We didn't talk until we had reached the old lumber trail. Then he said, "And what is your prognosis, Miss de Jersey? Am I going to be a believer?"

"Yes. You already are interested because you, with an Aquarius moon, have an open mind. You have read about astrology, haven't you?"

"Since Grace saw you in Chicago. I was intrigued, I admit."

"Let me go on a little. Each zodiac sign is strongly influenced by a certain planet, called its ruler. In your case, Capricorn is ruled by Saturn. Saturn stands for many things—destiny, the father figure, the inevitable. The inevitable is often something tragic, either a loss of prestige or the loss of someone close to you. In your case, you have had both. As I understand it, you lost your father at an early age. Oddly enough, the loss of a parent in early childhood is often part of the Capricorn pattern."

"He ran away and left us."

"In a way, that was worse than his dying. And your mother had to work so hard to support you that, in a way, you lost her, too. Most people think of Capricorn as a solid sign, earthbound. So it is, astrologically. But, because of the peculiar fate which seems to affect this sign, Capricorn people need affection desperately but are too proud to ask. If anything, they demand love and loyalty and are furious when this is withheld. When your wife left you, what did you do to get her back?"

His face was grim. The shotgun swung easily in his hand. He didn't answer.

"You have Jupiter, the planet of happiness, right on her Aries sun; I just compared your natal charts. You are suited and your sex drives are similar. But I'm sure, when I do your progressed chart, I will discover that only recently has she felt you needed the affection she wanted to give you. Before that, she must have had the impression it was her duty to love you."

He said, "You don't get days like this up north in October. Or do you?" He strode ahead again.

"Take Onassis, for example," I said. "He is a Capricorn, an attractive, ambitious, self-made man, highly sexed. But he has always played it cool. It could be, late in life, he sought the kind of affection and warmth he has always needed from his beautiful new wife. Perhaps he married her only for that. But I do suspect that she fascinated him because, as the widow of an assassinated President, she was one of the most desirable and talked-about women in the world."

"You don't make us Capricorns sound like very nice people." But he turned and waited for me.

"One thing I discovered which is, to my mind, astonishingly revealing. Venus, which stands for love, is in the sign of Pisces in your chart. There is a deep sweetness and sensitivity in your nature which you have tried to keep hidden. You loved your son Edward very much, so much that when you recognized evidence of a sensitivity similar to yours in him, you tried to stamp it out. So he turned toward his mother. And you were jealous."

"God damn you." He whirled toward me. For an instant, a passing instant, I was afraid. The man was angry and had a gun in his hand. We were in deep woods. No one would hear a shot; even if they did, what was more natural than the firing of a gun in this fine hunting country? He couldn't get away with it, of course. Maggie would know I hadn't just walked away. But what good would that do me, if I were dead?

Then he smiled. The sun moved through the trees and shone on us. A red dog flashed by, after some personal quarry. "No, I'm not a murderer. Don't be afraid. But I will tell you something, Miss de Jersey. For a long time, I thought I was to blame. I thought I had killed Dr. James and my son. I went through the worst kind of hell, for I couldn't tell anyone."

I waited. It was very still. "You just said I was jealous of my wife because my son preferred her. I never thought of it that way. But I was jealous of her, I suppose. Partly it was because I never understood her. She was my wife but she wasn't mine. And men always admired her. Always. I was jealous of that, too. I liked them to admire my wife but I didn't want her to enjoy it.

"All right. Dr. James, whom I hired to come and treat Edward —I didn't believe in psychiatry and I didn't like him. But I had an idea Grace went for him. I decided to bring him in the house, let them see a lot of each other, push them together. Then if anything happened, I would throw them both out. You see what I mean?"

"But he was—"

"I know. But I never guessed it. And I'm pretty smart about spotting homosexuals as a rule. Anyway, after a couple of weeks, Edward came to me and said he didn't like Dr. James and didn't want to continue treatment with him. And I said he damned well had to because his mother was in love with the guy."

"You didn't believe that."

"I don't know. Afterward, I decided Edward had killed the doctor because of what I had said. I felt as though I had pulled the trigger myself. Yet I couldn't tell anyone. In a way, I was glad— glad, do you hear—that Edward couldn't talk, couldn't remember what had happened, because he would have told people what I had said. Yet night after night, I would go down to the kitchen and sit there with Hans and sweat it out, wondering if it would do any good if I would confess. The only person I could have helped was Edward, and he was already lost."

He dropped the gun and let it lie there. Far away, a bird—an unidentified bird, to a city woman like me—sang its heart out. "You despise me. All right. Go and tell Grace what a coward I am. And a fool. She'll leave me again. And I deserve it."

"No, I don't despise you." My voice sounded rusty. "But I still don't think Edward intended to kill the doctor. He knew guns. Why, with all the guns he had been trained to shoot handy, would he pick an old war souvenir which, so far as he was concerned, was a decoration over the fireplace?"

"I don't know. Maybe he had it sitting there, loaded. Maybe he had planned the whole thing."

"Wait a minute. You didn't know Dr. James was homosexual. Neither, presumably, did Edward. I don't think Edward would have shot the doctor for making a sexual advance toward him. My husband said a man just wouldn't, and it makes sense to me. But what if Edward accused the doctor of having an affair with his mother and the doctor, as such a man might do, simply laughed and said that wasn't the way he was, and made some slighting remark about your wife, as a homosexual might? Wouldn't it have been natural for Edward to grab anything, not a gun, but a club, to hit him? And what if that available club turned out to be the old decoration hanging all these years over the mantel? The doctor didn't think it was harmless. He tried to get it away from Edward. They struggled—and it went off."

I was breathing hard, as though I'd been running. So, I discovered, was Frank G. After a long time he said, "We can't prove it."

"No, but if the time comes when Edward does remember, and I am right, your testimony will be important. Even if he never comes to trial, your wife and your sons will appreciate knowing what you have just told me."

"I can't. I can't face them."

"They'll respect and love you more if you do. In your chart, Saturn and the moon are side by side. That usually means some deep disappointment, overcome. In this case, I think you did something which disappointed your opinion of yourself, and caused you great shame. But your acknowledgment of guilt is going to bring you great happiness."

"Is Edward going to be well—ever?"

"I don't know. The year 1975 is crucial, as I've told your wife."

"You mean he may go back to where he was?"

"That. Or the whole ordeal might be too much for him. His health might suffer. All we can do is be prepared."

"Don't frighten my wife."

"Of course not. If you will tell her what you just told me. And my theory about the accident."

"If you don't mind, Katherine, I would like to call you by your first name." He put out his hand. I shook it. "Grace will continue to consult you as a client. She will want your advice about Edward. I hope you can encourage her. Within reason."

"And with honesty," I said. "But don't worry, I will be careful."

"And if you are sure the worst may happen, will you get in touch with me at the mill? Or leave word for me to telephone you?"

I promised. He picked up his gun and we headed back to the house. Back there, we returned to our formal basis. Nor does he use my first name when we talk on the telephone, which happens frequently on Sunday evenings. For, although Frank G. insists on regarding each call as a client consultation, and paying for it, we are almost on a family basis. Frank has invited Ralph down to hunt and Grace G. has promised me long beautiful drives through the country, with the promise of homemade collector-piece quilts and other beautiful things at bargain prices. I don't know whether we will ever go or not.

Edward is home now, in the guest suite Maggie and I shared. Hans, although he is showing his years and doesn't care for hunting any more, is always with him. Edward, after the chemotherapy, had some psychiatric treatment. He is quiet, not as depressed and withdrawn as he was before, but also without the spurts of sudden energy and enthusiasm. He does not talk about his future. He never mentions the accident. Nor does he like to leave the house and if he does, only after dark so he can avoid the neighbors. Often he stays up all night reading the books his mother brings him from the library. Then he sleeps during the day.

Perhaps someday I will open Edward's chart and see his improvement clearly marked. Or I will only see that his sufferings will be soon over. Then I will have to get on the telephone and call Frank G. . . . by his first name.

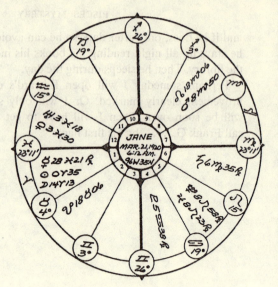

2

Sagittarius Rising

FEBRUARY can bring out the worst in Chicago. The last snow-storm had turned to gray muck, then frozen into a permanent ice cap. Lake Michigan was dull and sullen, burdened with chunks of ice. My friends and clients were either bedded down with colds or up and barking like vicious dogs. To top it all, my car had developed what the garage could only diagnose as a bad case of stomach flu; "Wait until spring," they told me, "and maybe she'll feel better."

And my mainstay, my secretary, had deserted me and taken off for a month in Mexico with the beautiful people. There was a card from her in my morning mail: *Weather heaven, swimming like mad, staying in the shadow of Mt. Popocatepetl and meeting loads of glorious men, all millionaires. Love,* Maggie."

I tossed it in my wastebasket; or, rather, Maggie's, because I had to start each day at the desk she usually occupied, making a list of the day's appointments so I could get out the charts of regulars. Meanwhile, the telephone was bleating, and the answering service was slow because usually Maggie took all the calls until noon. And I was faced with the prospect of coping with Maggie's filing system.

I had just broken a fingernail hunting for the chart of my four o'clock, Harriet L., who had been having an affair with a married man for going on ten years. She made appointments about once a year, hoping I would change my mind and see something in her chart which meant he would marry her. And once a year, with monotonous regularity, I'd been telling her, "No, he won't. He's a Sagittarius and you know what that means. The chase is his thing. The minute he's sure of you, off he goes after another girl. Of course he is sincere at the moment—but only at the moment—when he says he wants to marry you, but that's because he can't. Sagittarius is known as the idealist of the zodiac—he is constantly seeking the ideal woman, who doesn't exist, so she can't be found. You can have a lot of fun with a Sagittarian, so long as you don't try to fence him in and keep yourself a bit elusive, too. But don't count on marriage if he already has a wife because he'll invariably run back home when he is sure he has you in his pocket—nothing like a nice cosy little safe haven to go back to for a Sag!"

Or I'd say simply, "It is no use. Forget him."

Only she couldn't. Once Maggie, in a fit of exasperation, had told Harriet to stop wasting her money on having her horoscope brought up to date and go out and get herself another man. But it did no good. Harriet was a true Taurus, sweetly set in her ways, difficult to move as a bull and terrified of any kind of change. In her professional life, she was alert and bright; she made excellent money as a fashion photographer. She dressed in advance of fashion, which sometimes fooled people into thinking she was a swinger in other ways.

Far from it. In addition to having her sun in Taurus, a solid earth sign, she had the moon in Cancer. Cancer in its positive aspects means devotion and affection for family and children. But she had the negative Cancer moon, making her too clinging, super-sensitive. And unless she happened to be working, sat by her fake fireplace in a charming (I must admit) apartment on the near North Side, baking cookies or making draperies, waiting for her lover to call. Which he did, if he felt like it.

Yet, like a Taurus, she was loyal to the point of being a doormat, and kind and generous to the point of foolishness. She was always putting off a job, to baby-sit for a stranger or do an errand for a sick friend, usually a needless effort which wasn't appreciated because she was too available. Instead of thanking her, you fell into the trap of using her because she "enjoyed it." And I'm afraid even I was no exception. Once when Maggie had chicken pox (funny but serious in an adult), Harriet had offered to fill in for her. And I'd been graceless enough to snap at her when she was slow. Poor Harriet.

But her chart eluded me and I was silently cursing Maggie and blaming her also for my fingernail when the telephone on my private line rang. The answering service doesn't pick that up, and only my husband and Maggie and a few special friends know the number.

So I ran. First there was a torrent of Spanish. Then something was mentioned about long distance. And then silence. Prolonged. I was about to give up and go back to the files when Maggie's voice came in, loud and clear. "Katie, how are you?"

"Furious. Where in hell is Harriet's chart?"

"Let me think. Anyway, I didn't call you about that. I wanted to fill you in on the five o'clock appointment. It's a dame who gave me a phony name. I forget what."

I checked the book. "Jane Austen, March 21, 1920. She isn't the Jane Austen I know."

"Do you suppose I made a mistake in the date? She's coming from New York just for the interview. Going back the same night. I thought it was somebody very jet-setty, like Jacqueline Onassis, she sounded so mysterious and upperclass. But if Jane Austen is a friend of yours—"

"Not a friend, an author. And she's been dead quite a while."

"Oh, that one." Maggie sounded relieved. "This girl sounded terribly refined and glamorous. The kind of accent which makes any girl born in Chicago think her stockings have runs. Anyway, I wanted to alert you. I was in such a hurry getting off I forgot to mention her. In fact, I'd forgotten about her until I woke up this morning and heard my hostess—she's Laura Bergquist, the writer— mention Jackie Kennedy. Do you suppose she's pregnant or something?"

"Maggie, come back to earth." Yet, in spite of myself, I was interested. Jane Austen had been scheduled for an hour and a half, which meant she probably wanted to discuss someone else. All astrologers have a weakness for doing the horoscopes of celebrities in their spare time; it's a form of doodling. But since you nearly always have to guess at the moment of birth, and can't be sure you are accurate, it is interesting to get a chance at a celebrity in person, when you can sit him or her down opposite you, study the physical characteristics which give you clues, and ask pertinent questions.

"Katie, I have a hunch. Call it my ESP. This client is going to be very interesting. I wish I were there to see her. Is it snowing?"

"Not at the moment. It's just cold and sunless. And where is Harriet's chart?"

"Let me see. Isn't it under L.?"

"I don't think so, I broke a fingernail looking for it. I'll try again if you're sure."

"I'm not sure. In fact, I think I did something with it. She called and said it was really important, that she was sure David was getting a divorce. I wanted to put her off if I could, I know how you feel about her hanging on when there is no hope, so I studied his chart and said, 'Honey, save your money,' for he wasn't marrying her but she insisted and—I know. Look for it under Sagittarius. I was thinking so hard about David that I might have made a mistake."

"Thanks. And come home. I really miss you. I even miss the way you rationalize your filing system. I'm keeping all the charts for you to put away when you get home. And that will be—"

"Next week, maybe. It depends."

"On what?"

"On whom. I am going to a party at a house where they have the bathroom carpeted in real growing grass. Do you suppose they bring in a lawn mower to cut it?"

"What has that to do with your staying on?"

"Well, they're terribly rich. Or must be. If I meet my dream man and he has yachts and stuff—"

I said good-bye reluctantly. One of these days Maggie was sure to marry again. I live in dread of that day—not only because I'd have to learn to find my way around her filing system. In her own special way, she is a tower of strength. She may complain—but nothing is too much trouble so long as it's for me.

My first client, at 10:30, had a very bad cold. He said he should have stayed in bed but he had a pressing problem with a female who wasn't his wife. I fed us both orange juice and vitamin tablets and told him to get rid of the other woman, as fast as possible. She was a Gemini and both he and his wife were Virgos.

For lunch, I had two eggs beaten up in milk, more vitamins, and I walked around the block for a brief gulp of sooty air. All in the interests of maintaining my health because an astrologer can't afford to be sick, not with clients and appearances booked solidly ahead. Just the same, when four o'clock came, I was feeling wan. It may have been the prospect of breaking bad news to Harriet, for I kept hoping she had forgotten as the hands of the clock moved on to 4:15, 4:20, then 4:25.

However, at 4:29 she arrived, looking blooming and apologetic in a black cape and boots, with a leopard mini skirt. "I'm sorry. I meant to be on time. But I was meeting David and he didn't show."

"Harriet, you—"

"He said he'd come. He promised. Three o'clock at the Museum of Contemporary Art. Do you suppose he made a mistake and went to the regular museum? Maybe he's waiting there. Do you think—"

"Sit down. You know he didn't intend to come. He just hasn't the courage to hurt your feelings and refuse to see you. So he ducks out."

She let her cape fall to the floor. And walked away from it, like one of her own fashion models. She had a marvelous little figure, a pretty face (she had Libra ascending) and she was a darling. A darling idiot when it came to David.

"He's marrying a stewardess. He met her on a plane. His divorce isn't even final and he's shacking up with her. She is just twenty-one and he's forty-five. You know it can't last."

I glanced at his chart. Maggie had been right. David was getting a divorce, but he was marrying an off-beat character I had seen in his chart. "What if it doesn't last? He'll never marry you, my dear. Leave him alone."

"She has the Chicago–Los Angeles run. She's gone a lot of the time. I'm sure he isn't eating right. If I only could cook dinner for him occasionally—"

"Harriet, skip it."

"She's Swedish. Sex-mad. She'll ruin him."

"Did you tell him that?"

"I really care about him. I'm thinking of his own good. I'd rather have him go back to his wife than marry the stewardess. You know I really love David."

I knew. I also knew Harriet could be possessive, clinging as Scotch tape. Twelve years ago, when David was one of the up-coming newspapermen in Chicago, his wandering Sagittarian eye had spotted Harriet at some kind of a press club party and he had taken her home. After they made love, she noticed he had a hole in one of his socks and that, so far as Harriet was concerned, did it. A married man with a hole in his sock. It had been useless for me to point out everything she would not see: that he was meant for a double life, that he would always be chasing the elusive woman who didn't exist, that if I were his wife, I wouldn't mend his socks, either. She fell completely in love with him.

Nothing could put her off. He would leave for months, take out other girls including models she photographed. He would try in every way he could think of to show Harriet he was no longer interested. Then she would call him, catch him in a weak moment, and the affair would be on again. For a while.

David was not a mean man, or heartless. He was simply a man who should never have married and who should have had the wisdom to have many girls, and keep it light. For men who have their sun signs in Sagittarius, or who have Sagittarius importantly in their horoscopes as the rising sign, are bachelors at heart. Like Frank Sinatra, they are always seeking a dream woman, an ideal. Sometimes they think they have found her. But, because their freedom is more important than anything else, they are always disillusioned. A Sagittarian may marry many times; if he does come back to one woman, it usually is his first wife, who often represents his lost dreams. But as he grows older, he is more apt to look for younger and younger women, the playgirls of the youth which is slipping away from him.

It had not helped that recently, belatedly, Jupiter had brought David the success which had been withheld for so long. He had been noticed on a local television show and now was network. Magazines were asking him for articles. A book had been accepted. He had quit his job, his wife and family, and his mistress, in one full sweep. It was quite in character for him to have moved in with a young girl, a stewardess whose very schedule made her as unlike a wife, and a Taurus mistress, as possible. Yet he never could be honest with Harriet, in the way he was with his wife, because it is impossible to be brutally frank with a sweet, loving Taurus. For a man, it's like kicking a puppy.

Yet someone had to level with her. So, much as I loathed it, I said, "Harriet, give him up. Everything is finished. It is here in your chart, as I've told you for years. You are still young and attractive. Your life isn't over. But face the fact he is gone. Just the fact he didn't meet you today—"

"He might be sick. The stewardess is away. Something might have happened. He didn't answer the telephone. Perhaps he's had a heart attack. Maybe I—"

"Harriet, you are not to go there on your way home."

She faced me, sweetly stubborn. "He may need me."

"Harriet, this is outrageous. He doesn't want you. Why do you insist on pushing yourself at him?"

"You're being mean. You know I love him."

"I know you are thirty-five years old. It's time you grew up. David may never marry the Swedish girl. But he is through with you. Forget him. Find someone else. You are still young and you never looked prettier. In another five years, it may not be so easy for you to—"

I stopped, horrified at her face. Okay, I had kicked the puppy.

"You mean that in another five years, I'll be too old to attract anyone, including David."

It was hopeless. It always had been hopeless. Somewhere along the line, Harriet had become a misfit. Her mother, a dress buyer for one of the more expensive Michigan Avenue shops, and a three-time divorcée with a talent for handling men, had pushed Harriet into a career, more to get rid of her than to give her an outlet. Harriet should have married and devoted her life to photographing her husband and a large brood of demanding children. It wasn't too late for that, yet. If she could extract David from her mind.

"Harriet, listen to me. You don't need to pay an astrologer to hear this. Your own intelligence should tell you David is tired of you. And you'll never meet a man, or even people who can introduce you to a man, sitting home by that fake fireplace of yours. You are a very pretty girl. Go out and let people see you. Show them you aren't eating your heart out over David."

"But I am."

It was no use. I put my hand on her shoulder while I picked up her cape. "Honey, it isn't the end of the world. He's an attractive man but he'll never stay with one woman. Forget him."

She threw her cape over her shoulders. "Sometimes I think I don't want to know the future when you say things like that."

"I'm trying to help you. I don't like hurting people."

"I know. Just the same—" She left without saying goodbye. I made a note on her chart for Maggie: "Harriet mustn't have another appointment if all she wants to talk about is David."

Back in the days when Fannie Hurst was writing about kept

women, the Other Woman was an outcast from society, a misfit. Today, with all our values shuffled, nothing is black and white. Many of my extremely successful unmarried career women clients are involved with married men, men who either can't get divorces or simply feel they are too old to make the effort and hurt too many people in the process. These aren't really affairs; or if you want to use that word, you'd have to say they are love affairs. Some have gone on for a number of years and are almost like marriages. Often, indeed, it is the presence of an attractive, intelligent mistress which keeps a marriage intact. A man feels he can survive the ennui of a relationship which has gone dead if he has the excitement of romance in his life.

Yet even today, the fulfilled woman who falls in love with a married man finds it difficult to accept the situation realistically. Like Harriet, she keeps hoping for more and eventually, inevitably, she asks him when he is going to get a divorce. The sad ending, which I see again and again, is that if and when he gets a divorce, he feels so liberated he discards the mistress, and marries another woman.

Through my astrology, I am often able to spot would-be philanderers before they hurt my clients. The problem is that most of them, like Harriet, simply don't want to face reality.

I put Harriet's folder away in my top desk drawer and shut it firmly. Then I laid out a chart for the new client. It's always interesting to have a stranger sitting opposite you and explore, through astrology, secrets not only hidden from the world but from himself. For you never know, until the stars tell you, what is behind the dignified Capricorn in his handsomely tailored clothes, the chic Taurus in her high-style clothes—or the lady on the cusp between Pisces and Aries whose problem was so delicate that she had chosen to borrow the name of an eighteenth-century novelist of manners.

Jane Austen—the thought flickered through my mind it could be her right name but I trusted Maggie's hunch that it wasn't—was on the cusp between Aries and Pisces, but her sun was actually in Aries. Many of my Aries clients had suffered problems recently, dissolving partnerships, marriages breaking up. Currently, these people are under the influence of the planet Uranus, which sets off the unexpected and not until 1975 will they be free of these sudden changes. Whatever Jane Austen's problem, I had the feeling it must be serious or she wouldn't be coming all the way from New York to consult me.

At that time, I was still located high in the Marina Towers, in a pie-shaped studio with a balcony looking out toward Lake Michigan. The view changed hourly. In the late February day, it was of the street lights snaking along the avenues and the taillights of cars heading home from the loop. Not too many years ago, the area I was facing was called the Gold Coast; the great mansions of the merchants who built Chicago stood there in gloomy splendor. In my lifetime, some of them still stood, but now they are all gone, and high-rise apartments have taken their place. Expensive still, but lacking glamour.

I was pulled back to business by Jane Austen's announcing herself on the intercom. Pleased by the sound of her voice—Maggie was right, she did have a striking telephone manner—I went out to the elevator to meet her. I don't know what I was expecting, certainly not Mrs. Onassis in person, but the reality of Jane Austen was a bit of a shock. I don't think I would have identified her if she hadn't been the only one getting off the elevator.

She wasn't ugly, nor was she handsome. Nothing that definite. She was, in a maiden aunt way, pretty. A good skin, untouched by cosmetics. Unplucked eyebrows and eyes innocent of shadow or liner. A good figure, maybe, but concealed under a bulky coat and matching dress. Skirt length, midi; not fashionably midi, just maiden lady. Good, sensible shoes; the kind which looked as though they had arch supports. Pale, sand-color stockings. And hair tucked under the kind of felt hat once worn dramatically by Katharine Cornell as Iris March—but now favored only by stage governesses.

I had to remind myself she wasn't a mouse, she was an Aries. Only her polished voice, carefully overlaid with charm, hinted of the power and determination which must be hidden in the lady. For, in a way, Maggie had been right. Any woman who went out of her way to hide her light under a bushel was a mystery.

She said, defiantly, "I've never been to an astrologer before."

I thought, OK, Aries. I'll meet your challenge. "We're quite respectable, really. You must have heard of Evangeline Adams, our greatest American astrologer. She came from Boston and was related to the Adams family. Does that make you more comfortable?"

"Do I still sound as Boston as all that? I came from the Middle West but I went up to Boston as a child. My mother insisted I learn a proper accent but I've tried to lose it. I guess when I feel strange, it comes back."

The smile was soft, winning, absolutely charming. It asked for protection. I wasn't fooled. The Pisces might be the soft velvet glove, but it couldn't hide the Aries battering ram from me. I led the way into my office and took her coat. As I had suspected, the dress was equally unattractive. She sat down primly in my visitor's chair, her gloved hands—cloth gloves, naturally—clenched tight.

I said, "Relax, we have an hour and a half. Take off your gloves and hat, Miss Austen."

"That isn't my real name. I'm sorry I couldn't tell your secretary who I am but—I am protecting someone else. I'm going to have to ask a question so personal and important about him that it would be very wicked of me to tell you his real name. And, of course, if you knew my real name you might know who he was." She smiled again.

I smiled back. "Then what may I call you? I'm a Jane Austen fan and I would keep thinking of her heroines if we kept up the Miss Austen. But maybe you are like Emma. Is that one of your favorite books?"

The hands, gloved, stayed clenched. "I'm afraid I don't have time to read fiction, Miss de Jersey. It's just—I noticed a book of hers on a desk when I was going to call you, and it seemed a coincidence because my real first name is Jane. You may call me Jane, if you like. That sounds better to me, too."

I picked up a pencil. "What time were you born?"

The taut little hands reached for her bag (real alligator?) and clung to that, as though I might try to snatch it from her. "I gave your secretary the date. March 21, 1920."

"Can you tell me the moment and the place? If you don't know the hour, I'll have to rectify your horoscope by checking out important events in your life. It takes longer but—"

"That is the problem. I didn't come here to ask about myself. There is another person. A man. He is the one who has to be protected. He doesn't even know I'm here. I came on the three o'clock plane and have to get back tonight before he gets home from a board of directors dinner. He thinks I'm attending the meeting of a club I belong to. Sort of a woman's organization."

"What do you want to find out about him?" Please, God, I thought, don't let this be another one who wants to know if he'll divorce his wife. She didn't look the type, but you never could tell.

"Oh, dear." Her face didn't change color but she gave the impression of blushing. It really was quite remarkable. "I really don't believe in astrology. But my secretary doesn't do anything without reading her horoscope in the newspaper. She keeps after me to have mine done by an expert, for she says the newspapers are very superficial, they have to be. So I pretended to her I was getting interested and I asked her to give me a list of names, some in New York, some outside. I didn't want her to know whom I finally selected because of—Robert."

"What is his birth date?"

"October 23, 1898. In Kansas City. I'm afraid I don't know the time. You'll have to—"

"Rectify," I said automatically. "Do slip off your gloves even if you want to keep your hat. This may take a little time."

"I have one idea which might help." She slipped off her gloves. Her hands were thin, with long competent fingers and short unvarnished nails. The only jewelry she wore was a plain gold watch, neat but far from chic. It probably wasn't even expensive. Yet she had come from New York to spend an hour and a half with me. She was obviously the kind of woman who had been trained to spend her money carefully. And I suspected that the one who had taught her was Robert, her hearty father, seventy years old and "important," a Scorpio on the cusp of Libra. The sweet Libra smile, the boyish appeal, and underneath the driving ambition, the tremendous will to be the best, be first.

"His birth time," she said finally. "A lot of people in business used to call him Chick. I once asked him why. He said it was because of a joke his uncle made about him, before he was born. His father died in a railroad accident the summer before Robert was born. His mother went to her sister's to have the baby, because she had almost no money and her sister was married to a banker. Every morning, at breakfast, the uncle would ask Robert's aunt, 'Has the chick been hatched?' One morning, after breakfast, when his uncle was already at the bank, Robert was born. His aunt called the bank and said, 'The chick is hatched and it's a little rooster.' His uncle always called him Chick after that and so did a lot of the boys he went to school with in Kansas City."

"Did his mother ever marry again?"

She shook her head. "She and Robert were very close. She always called him Robert and so do most people, these days. I've never thought of him as anything else."

"Is his great asset in business the kind of personality which charms birds out of the trees?"

That lovely smile again. It was obvious that, whatever he had taught her about money, she adored him. "Absolutely. I've heard him on the telephone with a stranger, talking estimates. By the time he had finished, he was calling the other man by his first name, and I guess the other man was calling him Robert. He's an absolutely marvelous extrovert. His uncle sent him to college, the first year but he worked his way through the other three. Yet he was president of his class, of the fraternity, everything."

"He didn't have much money as a boy?"

"Oh, no. He worked as a shoeshine boy, he delivered newspapers, to help out. When he finally made good, the first thing he did was build his mother a big house in Kansas City, a show place."

That explained a great deal. His frugality, yet a desire to make his money show, when he spent it. Apparently he didn't feel his daughter needed a showcase. Perhaps he even wanted to keep her for himself. A strong-willed Scorpio sometimes does stake out a firm claim on his womenfolks.

Jane added, "He always went back to Kansas City every weekend while his mother was alive. It still is his legal residence even though his factory is in New Jersey and his—he's lived in a New York hotel for many years."

"When did she die?"

"More than twenty years ago, in 1948. He took her around the world with him that last year of her life. It had always been her dream and he took two months off from business to make it come true. She was crippled with arthritis at the last and he used to carry her around the house. She died in his arms. He's a big man, you know. Not tall, but very strong, with a big chest and shoulders. He doesn't look—his age."

"Do you have a picture?"

The deft fingers disappeared into the alligator bag. "Your secretary suggested I bring a candid picture. I don't have many. Mostly, the pictures he liked are the formal, posed kind, the sort he sends when he is making a speech."

"Does he like to make speeches?"

"He's crazy about it. I think he might have been an actor, if he had gone into the theater. He used to grab a plane and fly out to California and back the same day, just to make a speech. Now I make him do it in two days and I go with him."

All right, Robert was nearly seventy; but a young seventy. I wondered if he appreciated a dutiful daughter tagging—perhaps nagging—after him. I reached for the snapshot.

Jane hadn't been too prejudiced. He was still a handsome man. The picture had been taken on a boat. He was wearing slacks and an open shirt, leaning against the rail. There was a woman on either side of him and he had his arms around them.

"I took the picture," Jane said. "It's the most recent one I have, taken when we were on a cruise last fall. May I have it back?"

I returned it. "I've asked you a lot of questions which may seem irrelevant. They really weren't, because everything you've told me helps me figure out Robert's hour of birth. People who were born between eight and ten in the morning tend to enjoy being in the public eye, making speeches. Add all these things together with the story you told me of his nickname and I think we can take 9 A.M. as the approximate birth time. Now that I know that, I will have to consult my ephemeris"—I showed her one of the reference books astrologers use—"to find out the sidereal time of birth, that is the time by the stars."

She watched me intently. Because she seemed more relaxed, I continued talking as I worked. "A horoscope is a chart of the heavens showing the positions of the planets at the exact moment of the person's birth. The constellations always stay in the same relation to each other and so are called 'fixed stars' but the earth and other planets move constantly. Since it takes about 26,000 years for all these planets to return to the same spot they were in at the moment of your birth, you can see how individual a scientifically calculated horoscope really is. Even twins have different horoscopes because, in the revolution of the earth on its axis, a new degree of the zodiac comes up every four minutes, what we call your rising sign.

"When Robert was born, the sun was on the cusp between Libra and Scorpio. And these cusp people, born on the borderline of two signs, as the sun passes from one to the other, are especially influenced by their rising signs. Sometimes you will find a client really belongs more to the zodiac classification of his rising sign, his ascendant, than to his sun sign."

"What is Robert's rising sign?" She looked inquiring.

"Sagittarius. Difficult, charming, trying. It's been called the bachelor sign, although sometimes Sagittarians marry several times. We also often find a Sagittarian who never divorces his wife, but who has a girl in every port, so to speak. I've just talked to a client who is in love with such a man. He comes right up to the point of divorcing his wife, he sincerely thinks he has found the one woman in the world—and then at the last moment, he flies home to mama. Each woman he plays around with seems to be the perfect creature, his ideal—but the instant she is captured, she loses her luster."

"Robert only married once."

"But many women find him attractive?"

She returned the snapshot to her wallet. "Of course."

"You are an only child?"

"Yes, but—"

"When did your mother die?"

"Six years ago. But I don't want to talk about myself. There is something I need to know about him."

"Let me describe him a little to you first. Because he is on a strong cusp, Libra-Scorpio is a blend of gentle, fair-minded, charming Libra and strong, secretive Scorpio. He is independent, passionate, determined. He has many acquaintances but few close friends because he is hard to know, a blend of apparent contradictions. The Libra in him will sometimes procrastinate, postpone decisions. Yet his Scorpio pushes him into snap judgments. When he is being a Scorpio, he will fight to the finish, stubbornly, sometimes ruthlessly. Yet the Libra in him will walk away from trouble, forget insults, ignore opposition. Does this make sense?"

"I sometimes can't understand him myself. I've seen him remember a little thing which was done to him years ago, and eventually get his revenge. You wouldn't dream he was capable of such pettiness. He looks like such an innocent. There's a boyish side to him which is deceptive."

"Johnny Carson was born on the same cusp—the TV Tonight Show man. He has that same endearing manner, but I suspect anyone who has ever worked with him knows that beneath it is intense pride and drive. A Libra-Scorpio cusp is often capable of ruthless ambition. I know one former child actress who was born on this cusp. She looked like an angel and was famous for her long golden curls. But she had already been married four or five times, each time to a richer and more prominent man."

"He works very hard. He enjoys making deals. But there is another side of him, too, Miss de Jersey. He is far more involved with causes and world affairs than the average man. He is terribly young and curious about everything."

"He has his moon in Aquarius. These are high-minded people who care deeply about the world. They will espouse causes, frequently unpopular causes, simply because they want what is right. And they are open-minded. They are always willing to listen when someone brings in a new idea. Many brilliant business people are Aquarians, the ones who look beyond the trees and see the forest."

She nodded, frowning. I smiled at her. "But I know you came to see me because you are worried about him. His chart shows he has a heart condition. He's had at least two heart attacks, perhaps more."

"Will there be another one—soon?" She looked down at her hands, clenched tight again.

"I'm afraid so, my dear. Scorpios tend to be vulnerable where the heart is concerned."

"Will it be the end?"

"He has Saturn and Mars in the eighth house of death, which suggests a sudden seizure."

"When?"

I shook my head. No astrologer of experience will predict death. There are too many planetary aspects to be considered. And even then, when we think we see death, we cannot be absolutely certain whether it is a physical death or a spiritual regeneration on this plane. In Robert's chart, the solar eclipse coming in the Fall would affect his eighth house of death. There were other ominous planetary influences and Uranus would parallel Pluto. This might mean a sudden, violent heart attack. Whether it would kill him is a question. The shock of being near death might bring about spiritual regeneration.

"Please tell me. I need to prepare myself. He is all I have in the world."

"I just can't be certain. So many aspects are involved."

"Then tell me what you do see. Whatever time remains, I want to devote myself to him. I'll quit work. I want to be with him night and day."

"Are you sure that's wise? When he is gone, you will have your own life to live, you have to go on. And you might frighten him. Or he might not want you to know. Eleanor Roosevelt once was asked what she would do if she learned she had a fatal disease. She said—quite rightly, I believe—that her choice would be to go on as usual as long as she could, so as not to disturb her relation with those she loved."

"I happen to feel differently. I would never forgive myself if he died sometime when I was not with him. So if you are holding back because you think you are being kind, you are wrong, Miss de Jersey." She lifted her head. I could see tears in her eyes. But her eyes were defiant; after all, she was an Aries.

I said, "If he lives through Thanksgiving, there will be time ahead. If he doesn't—"

"In other words, I have almost a year."

"For sure. Maybe more."

"It's enough. Robert has had two serious attacks. One was at a professional football game. He couldn't get his breath. I kept him at home in bed for nearly six weeks. The next was in California. He called and had me fly out. The cruise we took was partly for his health."

"What do his doctors say?"

"They won't predict. I never let him travel alone. Even when it is just a dinner meeting, as it is tonight, I arrange to have someone there watching him, being sure he doesn't drink too much or over-exert himself. It's hard on him. And me, too, because sometimes I feel like a policeman. Now that I know how much longer he has, I can relax. Don't you see?"

I did see. I couldn't imagine anything more irritating or humiliating for someone with a chart like Robert's than being constantly watched. Nor was it fair to Jane.

"It may come a little before Thanksgiving," I told her. "Shortly after his birthday."

"And it's the end?"

"I'm afraid so. But it need not be for you. You're a young woman."

"I'm forty-nine. And an old maid. That makes me pretty hopeless in the eyes of the world, doesn't it?"

I got out another chart. "You weren't born in Boston?"

"No. Oklahoma. I told you I went up there as a child. I'm March 21, 1920. My secretary tells me I am an Aries."

"Actually, you are on the cusp between Pisces and Aries. Often, I find that in a close-knit family relationship, the parents and children will all be cusp people. In your case, the cusp is very strong, like Robert's, so there is the double attraction and under-standing. Pisces is soft, feminine, yielding, submissive. A Piscean like Mrs. Nixon prefers to stay in the background, behind her man. It is painful for her to be in the limelight, although, again, she will endure it if she feels she is helping him. On the other hand, an Aries loves adventure, anything challenging. You have a job, you say. An Aries woman frequently has a career. Sometimes she will go out and after a man, if she wants him. Sometimes she gets him, too. But marriage can be difficult because she likes to dominate, wear the pants. Often Aries women don't marry until late in life, when they have learned to bend a little, not to be always on the aggressive. Again, your rising sign is going to be very significant. Do you know your time of birth?"

"I'm not finished asking about Robert." Again Aries fire flashed in Jane's soft Piscean brown eyes. "I need to know one more thing about him. I don't want to hear about myself. I don't matter."

"All right." I turned back to Robert's chart. "What do you want to know?"

"Is there any sign of—mental disturbance?"

"Not a bit. His mind is as keen as it ever was. He'll be that way until the end."

"Is there—any indication of a new romance? A—woman?" She almost gagged over the last word.

"I don't see remarriage. Remember, however, he has Sagittarius rising. He will always be attracted to women. He has never liked being tied down."

"And I've been doing that."

"I had a client, a Virgo, who was married to a Sagittarian. She got a valentine from him once which said, 'You're so nice to me it's almost as good as not being married.' Being a circumspect Virgo, she was not amused. I tried to explain to her it was meant as a compliment."

"I think I'd better tell you something. I've always taken care of his checkbook. Recently, there was a check missing when he handed me the statement. And he had crossed out the stub. But the account was over $5000 off. I called the bank. They told me the missing check had been cashed. I finally had to ask him. He said it was a private matter and none of my business. To drop it."

"Did you?"

"No. I couldn't. He finally told me the check was made out to Tiffany's and it was none of my business for what."

"So you think there is a woman."

"I don't know." She sounded dim, subdued. "It doesn't seem

possible. I'm with him all the time. And the doctor has warned him against any kind of—sexual activity. It could be fatal."

"Does he follow doctor's orders?"

"I don't know. He lets me think he does." She got up and walked over to the window. The lights of the new high-rise building were brilliant and festive in the clear, cold night. "I suppose it could be a lie, about tonight. He could be with—her."

Poor girl, I thought. All the fierce Aries devotion wasted on her father. Suddenly, looking at her, I had another thought. "You aren't worried about money, are you? What would happen if he remarried?"

"Miss de Jersey, I didn't come here to talk about money."

All right, I thought. We had another fifteen minutes left. And we had about exhausted Robert as a subject, if I had to be tactful. "Let me do your horoscope, quickly. Do you know your birth time?"

"My mother always insisted it was 6:29. I don't know why she got the idea about the exact instant. In the morning."

People born between 6 and 8 A.M. frequently live outside the pattern of a monogamous society. Sometimes this even means a double life, a liaison. In Jane's case, I was sure it was her determination to remain single, out of devotion to her father. For she was not doing anything to make herself attractive, or desirable to other men.

"Why do you dress the way you do?" I said.

"What's wrong with it?" Aries fire again. Temper on edge.

"Your skirts are too long. You should wear bright colors. And make-up."

"That's my own problem, isn't it? Why should I?"

"Because you're a woman. I think you could be beautiful. You're deliberately hiding yourself."

"Really, I don't care to talk about myself." She stood up.

"Your time isn't up yet."

"I've found out what I needed."

I shrugged, said, "I hope so," and put the two charts—Robert's and the beginning of hers—into a folder. Probably the reason Robert had been able to live this long was his intense strength, his love of power and life. People who have this zest often live beyond medical indications. So, in a way, astrology can be more accurate and exact than doctors because we take into consideration the personality, as well as the health prognosis, of the patient. And it was understandable how a girl, an only child, could attach herself with such devo-

tion to a man with his personality. I've encountered some astrologers
—mostly those with their suns in earthbound signs—who mistrust
the brilliance and power of Scorpios. I don't, because once a woman
has become involved with a Scorpio man, all other signs—with
the possible exception of the enigmatic Gemini—seem dull by
comparison. And add to this, the overwhelming charm of ever-
seeking Sagittarius, and you have a man who is hard to duplicate.

We stared at each other. Finally she drew on her gloves and
picked up her bag.

"When Robert dies, I will die, too. That's why I have no interest
in myself."

"Perhaps you are wrong. Sometimes a horoscope brings out
surprising information. And also your chart would show the death
of a loved one, a loss. I'd be interested in finding out what it indicates for this autumn. If your father—"

"Please keep still." She swayed against my desk. Her face was
white. I regretted my frankness. There are times when you must
use tact and extreme caution so that the truth the client asked for
is cushioned, will not penetrate until the client has strength enough
to accept it. I had believed Jane when she said she wanted to know
the probable date of her father's death. I was annoyed with myself
for misjudging my client's stamina.

I said hurriedly, "Would you like a cup of tea? Or perhaps we
could drop in someplace and get you a glass of sherry. You don't
seem to feel well. And you're my last client. I'm going home anyway."

She stared at me as though I were some stranger she was seeing
for the first time. "I have to go. I can't miss my plane. I have the
check for your secretary."

But she still didn't move. I went and got her coat and put on my
own. She watched me like a zombie. Finally she opened her bag,
studied a check, and put it back. After a moment, she took bills out
of her wallet and put them down on Maggie's desk. I brushed them
into the center drawer and shut it. She wanted to remain anonymous
to the end, which was all right with me. But the way she looked
wasn't.

"I have a car. I'll drop you at the airport," I said. "It's not out of
my way."

Which wasn't quite the truth. But I didn't like to have her struggle
with the cab situation, at rush hour. The traffic to O'Hare would
also be nasty, but it was what I deserved, a penance to pay for

misjudging a client. And when she still stared vaguely into space, I decided to take charge. "Jane Austen, or whatever your name is, if you don't want to miss your plane, you'd better say yes. Do you want your father to get home and find you missing?"

She turned and saw me, at last. It was obvious she didn't care for what she saw. "Robert isn't my father. There is no reason you should know our relationship but I can't bear you saying 'father, father, father.' Robert is my lover. In spite of what you say about my clothes, I've been his mistress for twenty years."

It was my turn to keep still.

I had made the classic mistake of taking something for granted which wasn't there in the chart. Student astrologers fall into this trap constantly, but I should have known better by now. When I was starting to practice professionally, I made a mistake which should have been a lesson to me. It was a hot, humid day and my young male client was wearing slacks and a sports shirt. In his chart, I saw trouble in the seventh and eighth houses, and surmised his marriage was in difficulty and about to break up. Later I discovered he was a priest about to leave the Church. As a priest's vows are the same as marriage, the mistake was natural. But I felt incredibly stupid. Also, in the early days, I was invited to entertain with capsule horoscopes at a Jewish meeting one evening. I told one distinguished gentleman he was connected with the law. It turned out he was the rabbi, but he graciously explained I was right, because the duty of a rabbi is to administer the temple laws.

It all goes back to one basic observation: the ability to interpret is the difference between an amateur and a professional in astrology. Every aspect of a chart must be weighed in relation to every other and the wise astrologer (but who is wise all the time?) never makes her own conclusions. The ironic aspect was that now, considering Robert's chart, everything had been there for me to see. I had been put off by the difference in ages, of course, but primarily by Jane's appearance. She was the last person I would have selected to be a mistress, much less a mistress of long standing. Yet I do know from experience how little the girls who look like sex symbols can offer to a man. They are invariably far too concerned with themselves.

As I had explained to her, there is an attraction between cusp people, no matter on which cusps they lie. But two cusps are especially powerful. Libra-Scorpio is probably the trickiest of them all. Possessed of a strong ego, personal power drive (sometimes to the exclusion of anyone else) plus the charm to carry off whatever he wishes, the Libra-Scorpio man can be a top executive, as in Robert's case, working constantly, determined to go far. Or he can go to the other extreme and become a high-powered con man, an embezzler taking chances and making short cuts to achieve his goal.

On the other hand, Pisces-Aries is also a fooler. Here you see the insight, intuition and reserve of elusive, talented Pisces combined with the ego-drive of the ram. This is the kind of person who is bored by easy conquests, a routine life. He or she doesn't stay long enough in dull situations to learn whether they are as pedestrian as they seem. Instead, he plunges headlong into the kind of adventure which would terrify any average person. And if the Aries-Pisces cusp is a woman, she is often deep in intrigue—despite appearances, she is a challenge and a mystery. Maggie had not been far wrong in her original impression.

Robert and Jane were a challenge to each other. In a curious way, each had met his match. Suddenly, all the contradictions I had noticed made sense. There was no point in being wise after the fact; it would sound like second-guessing. So I kept quiet. Besides, it had been a long day for us both. I put her into the car without conversation, slid under the wheel, and concentrated on driving. Finally, she said softly, with all the tenderness and sweetness a Pisces can produce when the mood is on her, "I am sorry, Miss de Jersey. I put you in an intolerable situation. I remember when Robert first got sick and went to a doctor, he wouldn't discuss his symptoms. He used to insist on the doctor guessing what was wrong. I did worse. I—misrepresented myself."

I couldn't help laughing at us both. After a moment she went on. "The difference in our ages doesn't seem to matter. Except now, when I realize he is going to die. I can't quite face it, yet. Everything will change. I will have lost him and there won't be any good in my trying to keep my job. It was too tied up with Robert."

"What do you do?"

"I'm his assistant. I handle everything for him."

"Including his checkbook."

Silence. "In the beginning of our relationship, it was different. I knew there were other women. God knows, I took enough of their calls. But it's been a long time since anything like that happened."

"Were you jealous?"

"Not at first. Why should I have been? You see, I had no intention of falling in love with him. That was the last thing in my mind. All I thought, here was a powerful man who could help me in my career."

"What does he do?"

"He owns an enormous factory which manufactures a special kind of plastics. I applied for a job there because I had a tip from one of the vice-presidents in the bank I worked in up in Boston. He said it was going places and Robert was considered a genius. So I applied for a job."

"As his secretary?"

"Mercy, no. In the accounting department. I wanted to be where the money was. You see, I never went to college. All I was able to afford was secretarial training. But I was good with figures. In a million years, I might have had some kind of an executive job in the bank. But I wanted everything fast. I was already an assistant with my own secretary when I met Robert."

"And he fell in love with you?"

"He didn't know I existed. But I saw him and I decided he was where the real money was, not the accounting department. So one day when they needed a secretary to take notes at a director's meeting and they called in to my department, instead of sending my secretary, I went myself. Afterward, there was an obscure point I decided needed clearing up. We talked for two hours. Finally he invited me to dinner. I told him everything that was wrong at the plant. The next time he came out there, he called in advance and made a lunch date with me."

"Did you dress up for it?"

"You think a lot about clothes, Miss de Jersey. As a matter of fact, I started to. Then I realized I could never compete with the sort of women he took out, dancers and society girls, actresses. I'd seen his name in the columns and checked on the girls whose names were mentioned with him. So I wore the same thing I would have worn if I'd carried my lunch in a brown paper bag. The way I sold him was by showing him how loyal I could be, how much he needed an absolutely trustworthy little mouse who would devote her life to him, who would never get married, who would crawl up Fifth Avenue on her hands and knees over broken bottles for him, who would make her life his. Absolutely."

"And he hired you?"

"That noon. At twice what I was earning. You see, Robert is a man who isn't easily fooled. He had to know why I was so interested in working for him so I simply told him the truth. As I believed it then, anyway. That I hated being a woman, that I wanted to be rich and successful, that I would learn a lot from him as his confidential secretary, and after he died, I'd be ready to take over myself."

"When did you fall in love?"

Silence, except for the purring of the heater, with an occasional clank to remind me the car wasn't in top shape. "That changed things, of course. I had no intention of being trapped into an office romance. I'd seen enough of them to know how ridiculous they are, how rough on the woman. But working with him so closely, listening to him talk with those other girls who called up, making lunch dates and dinner reservations for him—I fell in love. It was all against my plans. I decided to quit—I'm talking too much."

"No, you aren't. I'm interested." And I was.

"I told him I wasn't getting ahead fast enough. So he squared off and said it was my own damned fault, I hadn't taken enough responsibility. We had an awful fight. I forgot I was in love with him, why I was quitting. I got a big raise and a chance to take on some of the work with the salesmen Robert had been doing. And he gave me a title: Assistant to the President. No woman had ever had it before."

"Was there gossip?"

"Naturally. A lot of men were jealous when that happened. So Robert and I had a long talk. We decided the smart thing to do was for me to play the old maid, the frustrated female who was married to the business. That meant dressing the part, too. The first real date we ever had was one Saturday when he went with me to shop. Afterward, we went to dinner at one of those restaurants where I'd been making reservations for him with other girls. I didn't feel underdressed because he was in on the joke. You see, I knew I was in love with him but I didn't know how much. I thought I was using him. And I knew he thought he was using me. So—"

She broke off. I took a glimpse of her, a quick look. She was staring straight ahead. She had a sweet, firm little profile. I could see how such a girl could grow on a man.

"So what?" I prompted.

"So one day, when we were working on the annual report, he

was interrupted by a call on his private line. It was obviously one of his ladies, so I slipped away myself and went to the washroom. When I came back, he was off the telephone and standing at the window. We were in the Chrysler Building on 42nd Street at Lexington, high up, looking downtown. He didn't turn around. He just said, 'Close the door and lock it. Pick up the telephone and say we aren't to be disturbed, on any account. I'm going to make love to you'."

How like a Scorpio, I thought. "And you—"

"I was terrified. And thrilled. I was a virgin. That bothered him afterward. It didn't bother me. Perhaps if nothing had ever happened between Robert and me, I would have done something about it, with another man, just out of curiosity. But with Robert —it wasn't great the first time, or even the second. Just the same, I knew I pleased him. And that made me really fall in love with him. So—I have never had sex with anybody else so I can't say I'm an expert—he says we were wonderful together and I know we must be special, too. Otherwise—"

"He has been around. He would know."

"Yes. At first, I didn't know what to do. I offered to quit again and he told me not to be a damned rabbit. Then after a while, being with him began to mean too much to me. I never had to make dinner reservations or answer the telephone when the girls called any more, I had my own secretary and he had another little girl to do the routine things. But I knew he was seeing other women, too. He made no secret of it."

"Were you jealous?"

"No. Yes, yes of course I was. And once in a while, I would go out with another man. Nothing important, one of the salesmen who was buttering me up, occasionally a customer. Robert teased me about my dates. Then one man came along, a widower, a nice person with three little girls. He was a space salesman for a magazine and I persuaded Robert to buy a small campaign in his publication. First he took me out to dinner on the expense account and later on his own. One night he asked me to marry him. I was tempted."

"Were you really?"

"I knew it wouldn't be exciting, being married to him. But I guess those women of Robert's had been bothering me more than I realized. I was ready to get out. I thought about it all weekend and on Monday morning, I told Robert. He—cried, Miss de Jersey.

I've never seen anything like it. He promised he would give up everyone else if I would stay with him. That was about fifteen years ago. Ten years ago he took a furnished apartment in a hotel and I moved in with him as his wife."

"May I ask you a question? You said his wife died six or seven years ago. Have you never thought of getting married?"

She laughed, a good booming laugh. "Miss de Jersey, that was when I was playing games with you. You thought you were asking me about Robert's wife and I told you honestly my mother died six years ago. Robert's wife is still alive. He is still married to her."

"Does she know about you?"

"I have no idea. We've never discussed it."

"Really?" I must have sounded as skeptical as I felt, for she answered sternly, "You can't understand a man like Robert. If he wants me to know something, he tells me. We hardly ever go out. We have dinner sent up from the restaurant in our building and we sit and he talks—mostly. I know a great deal about him. But not from asking questions."

"You're right. You don't ask a Scorpio personal questions. Not if you expect the answers you want. Just the same, it must be difficult. When does he go home?"

"On holidays. And birthdays. Once in a while if his wife or one of his daughters is sick. His daughters are married and have children of their own. His older daughter's husband worked in television in California. I've—met him."

"You travel with Robert?"

"Occasionally on business in the past; now I don't let him go alone. And that cruise after his heart attack."

"You travel as his wife?"

"With business acquaintants, yes. On the cruise, I was his widowed daughter. That way, it explained our passports being in different names. He said we wanted to share a stateroom on the ship because of his recent heart attack. No one suspected anything. Even my secretary doesn't dream I'm living with Robert."

"But his wife—"

"In the early days, I used to talk to her on the telephone. Sometimes, in the hotel, I answer the private telephone and recognize her voice. Then I pretend I'm the answering service."

"She must recognize your voice."

"I don't know. If she suspects, she has never made any trouble. Perhaps she and Robert have agreed on that. Once, before our affair was really serious, his younger daughter visited him in New York. She was very curious about me. She once asked me if I was the woman her mother knew about. Of course I pretended I didn't understand. That was when I was living with my mother. When Robert and I spent the night together, I went to his apartment and left in the early morning, walking down the service stairs, so nobody would see me."

"Your mother must have known."

"I told her everything. Mother and I were very close. As soon as I was earning enough money, when I became Robert's confidential secretary, I moved Mother down from Boston where she was living with her sister. I promised I would always take care of her and I did. She met Robert and liked him. After I moved in with him, he built a house out on Long Island for her. It isn't in a fashionable district—she would have hated that—but it has everything she dreamed of, a washer and dryer, a dishwasher, airconditioner, a garbage disposal. She was proud he built it for her, not for me. I used to go out weekends when Robert was away on business, or in Kansas City. The neighbors all thought I was married. My mother would have liked it if it could have come to pass but—he paid all the bills when she died. It was cancer. She had private nurses around the clock for many months."

"And the house?"

"I still have it. My aunt lives there now. We don't get along very well. She doesn't approve of me or Robert. But she keeps quiet to the neighbors and I use it as my mailing address for the office. It's just an arrangement. After Robert is gone, maybe I'll sell it."

Traffic thickened as we neared O'Hara. Horns hooted and taxis darted in and out. I had to concentrate on driving and Jane, sensing my preoccupation, was quiet. I knew I would be late getting home and Ralph would worry, because he was concerned about my car. But it was wonderful to be married to a husband who worried about me.

Of course, Jane was luckier than most women in her position. She had Robert all day at the office and was with him most nights. She was able to travel with him. But she didn't have the security marriage brings. Perhaps that didn't bother her as much as it would other women. After all, she was on that free-wheeling Pisces-Aries cusp. Just the same, there had to be the doubts and the lonely periods, always on holidays which are family times, bad for women alone. They used to tell me that the reason the early

Romans had their pet astrologers was that men in high positions have little sense of security and few people they can trust. In a way, Jane had done this for Robert. Yet by being his alter ego, she sacrificed a great deal herself. In order to protect him and his family, she had made herself as close to invisible as possible. She had no friends, probably nobody she could call on in emergencies except Robert.

I knew, if she were willing to accept astrology, it might give her a sense of relating, of belonging, to the universe, which she lacked today. But I also knew enough about her to realize you didn't push our Jane, either. However, since I might never see her again, there were questions I wanted to ask.

"He's been faithful to you ever since you gave up the man who wanted to marry you?"

"Oh, yes. I'm sure of it. Why do you ask?"

"Twenty years is a long time." And, I didn't want to add, he had Sagittarius rising.

"Sometimes I've been the aggressor in sex. He likes it that way. Sometimes I see him looking at a girl and I think, perhaps he would be interested. If he could. But I doubt—"

"Then why does the incident of the check to Tiffany's bother you so?"

"I don't know." Her voice was small. "It may be someone—very glamorous. He always told me how he never had any use for those women who go around with diamonds hung all over them. It was one of the things which seem to annoy him about his wife, she wanted possessions. To prove his love for her."

"Perhaps the jewelry was for his wife?"

I could feel her shifting restlessly beside me. She wanted to talk, yet she was afraid to say too much. It was habit, I supposed. She must have discussed him with her mother. But now there was no one—except me, who didn't even know her real name.

"I don't think so. I think he would have told me. Unless—"

"Unless what?"

"He might be planning to go back to her. At the end of his life." Her voice was bleak.

"What about his will?"

"I never asked. Once, he told me not to worry, I'd be taken care of. Of course, I have the house. And some stocks. And there will be severance pay when I leave."

"You'll really have to give up the job?"

"Of course. I wouldn't want to stay anyway. Actually, business has been going badly. We've had new competition and labor troubles. There are days when he threatens to sell the whole damned place. Then there are days when I know it would hurt too much. The factory is like something he created out of himself. More like his own than his children."

"I know you came to Chicago to see me because you didn't want Robert to discover what you were doing. I'm not sure I've been of much help. But I think you would find comfort in astrology, as all of us do, in the next few years. I would like to do your horoscope if you are ever in Chicago. If not, may I try to persuade you to see an astrologer in New York?"

"No," she said flatly. "When he dies, it is all over. There won't be any more and if there were, I wouldn't want it. I came to you with two questions. You've given me the answer to the important one."

After that, we stopped talking. When we drew up in front of United Airlines, and the redcap opened the car door, she gave him a polite maiden-aunt smile which spilled over on to me. "I have no luggage, thank you. I just came for the day. It was nice knowing you, Miss de Jersey."

I watched her go, Jane without a last name. She sailed through doors which flew open at her approach. Her past had been exciting. It had even been great fun, I was sure: the games, the midnight conferences in the stateroom of the ship, the façade kept up for the office. A woman who really is a partner to her man in business has an understanding, far greater than the rest of us, of what makes him tick.

If I never saw her again, at least it *had* been fascinating. I wished I'd thought to have told her so.

Ralph met me at the door. Yesterday I had made us pea soup, a good hot dish for a cold night, and he'd been putting his own touches to it while he waited for me. "I'm not sure it's any better," he said. "In fact, I'm pretty sure it's rather worse. Do you want to go out to dinner or will you chance it?"

"I'll chance it."

"You sound tired. What held you up?"

"I drove a client to the airport."

"Somebody important?"

I looked at him. "I haven't the slightest idea. She never told me her real name. She made the appointment as Jane Austen."

"Maybe her reincarnation." Ralph took off my coat and pulled me into the kitchen to taste the soup. It was different, rather spectacularly spiced. Just the same, it was wonderful to be safely home. There had been a time when, after a bad experience, I was afraid to remarry. I told Ralph I thought we should consider just living together. He settled that by giving me a choice of dates for our wedding; the only thing I had to say about it was to pick the one most favored by the stars.

That night, as I was dropping off to sleep, it occurred to me that since I had Jane's correct birth hour (or the one her mother had insisted was correct), I could work out her chart over the weekend to satisfy my own curiosity. But a number of things interfered. One big thing was my nephew's one-man art show, for which I had loaned him my studio. He had invited a number of people who were important to him for the opening on Saturday afternoon and had spent a great deal of time selecting what he wanted to hang. On Friday night, when the family had gathered to help, it started to snow. Snow? By midnight a blizzard of pretty big proportions had moved in on us.

My sister-in-law began casting long looks at me; at my nephew's request I had selected the date of the opening by astrology so astrology and I were on the spot. I promised everything would be all right. My sister-in-law called weather on the telephone and heard different. When we parted to go to our separate homes, the atmosphere was pretty tense. But on Saturday morning when we woke up, the sun was shining, the snow had stopped. And by afternoon the weather had warmed enough so that the roads were cleared and even people who lived in the suburbs could get into town easily. Everybody who mattered came, the exhibition was a success. And I, the astrologer, was a prophet with honor in the bosom of the family.

Maggie came back from Mexico the next Monday, and I had saved up stories for her, the kind she'd appreciate especially. One was a letter from a movie producer, a Capricorn born December 23 (also on the cusp of Sagittarius, oddly enough; or maybe not oddly because very often I run into a rash of clients with similar signs) who told me he would ask his ninety-one-year-old mother, still bright as a button, about the hour he was born. He repeated, "My mother said of course she remembered, it was around dinnertime. I said, 'What time did you have dinner?' She paused and thought, 'Oh, sometimes in the middle of the day, then sometimes in the evening.' So you figure it out, Miss de Jersey. What happens in my stars depends entirely on whether dinner was served at eight, at noon, or three o'clock in the afternoon on that (to me) memorable day."

Actually, I had written and explained to him my clients often didn't have the correct birth hour. Parents forget. I remember once I sent a young man back to his mother twice because she insisted he had been born at 5 P.M. and I knew, from everything about him including his appearance, it couldn't be so. At my insistence, she suddenly remembered it was his little sister who had the 5 P.M. time. Of course, anyone new in the practice of astrology isn't equipped to make these judgments. Only years of experience with thousands of clients plus almost an intuitive understanding of different birth times, can give this kind of insight. There's no mystery about it. But to the novice, the person who is approaching an astrologer for the first time, this kind of experience often astonishes.

Maggie held up the cash she had found still locked in her desk drawer. "And who dropped this?"

"The woman who called herself Jane Austen. I suspect she was afraid to give us a check because she didn't want us to know her right name."

"She's that important?"

"No, it's the man in her life. She says. He's Sagittarius rising."

"And she has her sun in Aries."

"Aries tends to be a bit overpowering. Our Jane is assistant to the president of a concern which does something in plastics."

"What about her father?" She held up Robert's chart.

"He's her lover. I made the same mistake."

"Wow."

I nodded. "Double wow. You wouldn't think any of it to look at her. Almost dowdy. Butter wouldn't melt in her mouth, as my mother used to say. But, as my grandmother put it, still waters run deep. She practically engineered their romance."

"To a Libra-Scorpio cusp with Sagittarius rising?"

"Yes, indeed. Of course he's almost seventy years old now. But it started when he was a dashing fifty, with eyes glittering at every female."

"Married?"

"Of course."

"I'd like to know the wife's sign."

"So would I. But he's dying. I give him until Thanksgiving at the outside."

Maggie mock-moaned. "Why do all the marvelous clients always come when I'm away?" As an answer, the telephone rang to announce a Chicago grande dame who, at eighty-eight, was still looking for romance in her future. Well, you had to give her credit for hoping.

As I was going over her chart (sun in Aquarius, Capricorn rising, at least a change of pace) I thought about Jane again. If I'd seen her twenty years ago, I would have been pretty green at astrology but not so green that I wouldn't have taken a dim view of the combination of her and Robert. In my opinion, the real secret of their rapport was in the fact that they had never married. If they had really been man and wife, Jane would have tried to wear the pants, inevitably. Now she didn't quite dare. In addition, her position as assistant to him at the office, kept her as automatically number two. To gain her own way (which I'm sure she had most of the time), she had to use her Pisces wiles, put her man first—or seem to.

Often Aries women marry weak men, but with their moon in Aries, reflecting the power of their wives. This isn't a hopeless situation if the man doesn't object to her taking the initiative in sex relations and acting like his mother in other ways—telling him how to get ahead in business, to wear his rubbers, to have his hair cut and shoes shined. A little-boy sun-in-Taurus type even enjoys this. But when a strong man and woman are living together, one (and in our society this must be the woman) must choose to allow herself to be second mate, out of strength, not weakness. In Jane's case, she had deliberately chosen Robert. Because of the age difference, she cast herself in the role of a daughter, but a daughter who took on the functions of a devoted mother who worried about his health, who fussed over him, who adored him.

In exchange, in lieu of marriage, he accepted her devotion but made none of the demands a husband tends to make on a wife. They lived in a hotel. She had no housework to do, no meals to cook, no servants to direct. In her position, coming from a background of little money, she undoubtedly equated domesticity with being a servant. She was not his servant, in any sense; not even in the way a wife occasionally feels she is being used. If there had been a legal tie between them, it might have been different. After all, he had Sagittarius rising and his sun in Scorpio. And Mars was in Scorpio in her chart, showing powerful attraction to a Scorpio man.

When my grande dame had left, I found Maggie still studying Jane's chart. Above it, she had Robert's. One of the most fascinating elements of astrology is the comparison of charts. You can never tire of it.

"He has Saturn on her midheaven," she said.

I joined her. "I'm not surprised. I once heard a marvelous old man, an astrologer who died years ago, tell a group of us youngsters that when the other fellow's Saturn falls on the midheaven of your chart, run! It means he has control over you."

"Jane isn't the running type."

"But she did try to escape, several times. Anyway, I think that advice is wrong. First of all, in that situation, it won't do you any good to run, the karmic link is so strong. Second, it is like trying to run away from life. Your relationship with that person is destined and you are meant to learn from it. Of course he has power over you—you're under his spell, so to speak—but if you understand, and make the most of it, instead of trying to resist, you will gain in the end."

Maggie had blocked out Jane's chart. She had Uranus on the cusp with Venus in the twelfth house of secrets, which means an unconventional arrangement. Venus, love, in her chart was opposed to Saturn, which meant she was attracted by a father figure.

It was all there. If I'd done her chart before Robert's, there would have been no question about their affair. Her mother had undoubtedly been right about the birth time. People born between 6 and 8 P.M. are under the influence of the twelfth house which means something secret, hidden. The arrangement of planets, particularly Mars and Venus, in her chart, might have hinted at scandal, an unsavory relationship. But they were supported by Pluto in Cancer. Pluto means healthy, normal sex which strengthens rather than destroys the bond between two people and Cancer shows a warm, close, family feeling. Of course, there was a strong Saturn tie between their charts. There can be no lasting relationship between two people without this destiny pattern. I've known of charts which matched like pieces of a picture puzzle. Women and men seemed made for each other, soul mates. But when the Saturn bond was missing, they could not sustain their engagements, or marriage.

Maggie said, "It's going to be a terrible thing for her when she loses him."

I nodded. "And it's there, the loss of someone deeply loved, this fall. There wasn't any real doubt when I did his horoscope. Now I am sure. It's always hard for a woman to lose the man in her life; more difficult in a way than it is for a man to lose a woman because, although he is physically dependent on a wife, he is much more in demand socially than a woman. But in her position, it is going to be doubly rough. She won't have the support a widow has, from friends. She won't even be able to express her grief publicly. The years ahead are bad. But she had that wonderful basic strength. And during the difficult days, she will be exploring herself, learning why she had the long affair with Robert, why she made it work, but finding out"—I put down the chart—"finding out the most important thing a woman can learn, that no matter what her age, she can fall in love again. People with Saturn joining Venus tend to make late marriages. And this time it will be different. She will have learned from all her experiences, good and bad. She's going to marry and be happy."

"I wish you could tell her that."

"It isn't the right time. Not now. She's concentrating on Robert. But I suggested she consult an astrologer in New York when things get tough."

"She'll be fifty-five in 1975."

"Aries women find happiness late. They need maturity in order to cope with marriage, accept it instead of fighting it. Remember Jenny Price, the decorator? I always told her she'd marry late and someone out of her past. When she retired at sixty-five, as a sort of joke, she brought me a list of the men she knew who were unmarried, widowed, or divorced. I went over it and said no, not one of them. She retired to Arizona and met a man she'd dated as a young woman. They had stopped seeing each other because they were falling in love and he was married. His wife had died of cancer and he and Jenny got married. They're happy as larks."

The doorbell rang. Maggie opened it for my 11:30 client. I put Jane and Robert back in the folder. Common sense said for me to tell Maggie to put it among the inactive charts, for why would she come to see me again, what reason would she have for making the trip to Chicago? But my ESP said no. I wrote "active" on the folder and went to take my 11:30 client.

Winter melted into spring, and then to summer. In the old days, summer, especially August, often was a slow time for astrologers. I used to plan to take a vacation then. But today no time seems to be slow; even Christmas isn't uninterrupted. So I worked hard all during August and by early September, when it was time to start on my public appearance tour, I was tired. In addition, I had moved from the Marina Towers to a new suite on the 53rd floor of the new John Hancock Building. I hadn't yet had time to decorate it properly. However, my beautiful new view, dipping right into Lake Michigan, compensated for unhung pictures and lack of furniture. And I had room enough so that when Ralph and I decided to stay in town and go to dinner and the theater, we didn't feel we were camping out.

So on a Friday night in September, Ralph and I had decided to give ourselves a night off, alone, go to dinner, the theater, and maybe dancing or listen to jazz later. I was in the middle of a long, lovely hot shower when I thought I heard the telephone. I jumped out, then back, deciding firmly that nothing and no one would interfere. It kept on ringing. I wrapped a towel around my middle, telling myself it might be Ralph.

I had trouble placing the voice, but it was distinctive, and vaguely familiar. It said, "Thank God. Miss de Jersey, I need help."

I took a deep breath. "I'm just leaving. Who are you?"

"You won't remember me. My name is Jane Grisson."

"I'm afraid I don't."

"I came to see you last winter. I told you my name was Jane Austen. You were kind enough to drive me to the airport. Now I need help again. Desperately."

"Where are you?" I clutched the towel, annoyed with myself for having weakened to the ringing telephone.

"Chicago. The Ambassador East Hotel. Could you come here? I know it is a lot to ask but we have no friends in Chicago."

I repeated the fib, "I'm just going out the door. I have an important appointment. Can you call me Monday? I'll manage to fit you in, somehow, if it's vital."

"Miss de Jersey, I need a doctor. Now. I think Robert has had another attack. Remember, you told me—"

I remembered. And thought, oh, God. Our family doctor was away at a medical convention. I knew no heart men. Surgeons, yes. Eye men, yes. But this was Friday night and I had no possible way of getting in touch with them. I said, "Can't the hotel help?"

"I want a specialist."

"Why don't you get in touch with your doctor in New York? He must know someone here to whom he can refer you."

"I've tried. He's on his way to Europe. The doctor who is taking over his patients is away for the weekend. I can't reach him until Monday, the answering service says. Please help me."

"I don't know what to do, honestly." Then I heard a key in the lock. Ralph. Early, thank God—unless I was late. I said, "Hang on. Maybe my husband has an idea. Otherwise—"

Of course Ralph did. A beautifully obvious one. A client of mine, a nurse, is engaged to a co-worker of one of the country's great heart specialists. In a matter of minutes Ralph had calmed Jane, contacted the nurse, talked to the young doctor, who wangled a bed in the intensive care unit of the hospital and ordered an ambulance to go to the hotel. He needed the name of the patient. Ralph looked at me.

"I only know his name is Robert."

"Well, get on the other phone and find out his full name."

Jane, after a moment's hesitation, said the name was Robert Folsom and I suggested it might be simpler if she told the hospital they were married. Then I hung up and gave the information to Ralph and rushed to dress. While he zipped me up and I struggled with the second false eyelash, I said, "I never heard of Robert Folsom. Did you?"

"No." His hand paused on the zipper. "Wait a minute. Is his nickname Chick? He was a big man in the sports world. Owned a race horse and a piece of a football team, a pro team, some years back. He used to be interviewed at half time. A big, good-looking guy. Does that sound right?"

"It does indeed." Flying blind, I finished the second eyelash.

He completed the zipper. "If this is the man, he dropped out of sight. I seem to remember there was always some blonde hanging around in the shadows. Who is this Jane?"

"His assistant. She was his confidential secretary."

"Oh?"

"For twenty years she's been his mistress."

"All right, let's go. I have reservations at Jacques and we're already one martini behind. How long has this mistress been your client that she gives you a call on Friday night in an emergency?"

"I've seen her just once."

"Then tell your answering service to take all calls until you pick up the phone tomorrow and announce you are alive. I made a reservation at the College Inn for the midnight show and invited Carmen McRae to have a sandwich with us after she finishes working there."

We had a night on the town, ending delightfully with a long late supper. Carmen reminded me she was an Aries. The last time I'd seen her, I had told her she was going to change her manager and move into another apartment; she had assured me, in best blunt Aries fashion (sun in Aries, moon in Sagittarius, Leo rising—what we call the grand trine of fire signs) she had no intention of doing either. Now she admitted both things had happened, and she wanted to know about the future.

When Ralph wasn't looking, I had slipped her chart and my ephermis for her year of birth into my handbag. So I was able to tell her big things were right around the corner in her career; Jupiter was not only smiling, he was beaming. Then she wanted to know about Venus. She was tired of "dating kids young enough to be my sons." She wanted someone mature. I left her with the information she was going to have to wait a couple of years, maybe more. Things at that moment were rough all over for my Aries clients in their love lives.

When we got home, I checked the answering service. Jane Grisson had called. So had a Mrs. Folsom. I said I wasn't to be disturbed until I called in, maybe around noon, maybe later, and asked Ralph if he would like some coffee. He said yes, largely because neither of us wanted a good evening to end. While we sat drinking it, he said, "Did you see me in your chart?"

"I knew I was going to meet someone. And when I found out you were a Gemini—"

"You said you didn't want to get married. You'd live in sin but you wouldn't marry me."

"It wasn't you. It was the aspects which were bad for marriage in my chart."

"Then what happened when I put my foot down and gave you a choice of dates?"

"By then, the aspects had changed a little. I couldn't resist."

He nodded.

After a while I took the coffee cups to the little kitchen and we left the sleeping city to go to bed.

At noon, Ralph brought me the newspapers and orange juice. No matter what time he turns in, he gets up early, cheerful as a bird. "It's a magnificent day. I have an appointment with my tailor at noon. Come along and I'll buy you a huge lunch and then we'll go to the Art Museum."

"I should call Jane Grisson."

"OK, but don't let her bug you. Or spoil our day. You've done enough."

I half-promised. Which was just as well, because Jane was at the hotel waiting for my call. "Something terrible has happened. I have to see you, Miss de Jersey. Can I come there?"

I looked at Ralph. He nodded resignedly. "I'll go to the tailor alone. Then I'll pick you up about two. No later."

"Is it Robert?" I asked Jane Grisson.

"Yes. Not what you think. The heart specialist is coming in to see him this afternoon. I'm going to try to reach Robert's doctor in Europe and have a conference call. Robert says it's all non-sense. He's feeling better and wants to be moved to a private room where he has a telephone. But he said something last night and I did something—when may I come?"

I told her one o'clock. Then I got up and looked at the view of the lake from my window. The boats were out and the water was a dazzling blue. Although it was too cold to swim (and, I regret to say, too polluted to be safe for more than wading) people in bath-ing suits were sunning themselves on the beaches. It would have been nice to have joined them. But I had just time to fix us a quick breakfast and walk Ralph to Michigan Avenue, where he hailed a cab to take him to his tailor.

Jane was waiting in the lobby of the building when I returned. Her white linen suit was still too long but she was hatless. Now that she wasn't hiding her beautiful ash-blond hair, she was better-looking. She was also tanned, which did much for her. I told her so.

"Robert and I were away all summer. We went to India, then to Turkey and Greece. Places I've dreamed of seeing. We've talked about going to the Orient next year, but—"

"You didn't tell him what I told you?"

"Of course not. But I had to admit I consulted you. Robert is a strange man, Miss de Jersey. I have never tried to hide anything from him before and he knew I was lying. I had to tell him and he suspected why. So—" She lifted her shining head. Her hair was pulled into a knot on top, a style my mother had fancied when I was a little girl and one which, to my surprise (and even greater to Jane's, I suspect) came into high fashion a little later on that winter, with the maxi coats and dresses. "So I told him he was going to live to be an old, old man. Afterward, I wasn't sure I had said the right thing. He doesn't fancy getting old."

"None of us do, but a man like Robert must hate the idea. However, it is better than having him know how little time is really left. That's the burden you asked for. Is it worth it?"

She nodded. "I've quit working. I told the office I was going to retire and travel. With Robert already semi-retired, they weren't surprised. Once in a while I pretend he has asked me to come in and do a special job, which would explain anyone seeing us together, near the apartment."

"You're happy?"

"Until last night. The nurse said he was under sedation and didn't know what he was doing. But never in his life has Robert been less than in control. He—"

I glanced around. No one seemed to be paying any attention to us but I don't believe in talking in lobbies, or in elevators, either. "Let's go up to my studio and discuss it. We've done your chart. Things aren't all bad ahead."

In the two elevators which we had to take to get up to my 53rd floor studio, I had the chance to study her. She was an attractive woman. Now that she didn't have to play a role in the office, she had relaxed some of the stiffness in her dress. But she was still in disguise. And there was something missing, a quality which had impressed me at our earlier meeting. It was almost as though something had happened to soften and erode that stiff little Aries backbone. And I suspected it wasn't entirely the fact she knew Robert's end was near. She had already faced up to that.

Her folder was in the active file. Otherwise I knew I would have spent too much time finding it, and eventually had to call Maggie at home to ask where. I put both charts on the desk in front of me.

"You and Robert were meant for each other. Everything points to it astrologically. Even the similarity of your backgrounds is significant. You both lost your father at an early age and had to work. In each case, this meant you became deeply attached to your mother. You became involved with him partly to replace his mother; despite the difference in your ages, you wanted to take care of him, as she had, and he needed your unquestioning devotion. On another level, you were his daughter. This ambivalence often occurs in childless couples. You were both a daughter and a mother. He was a father and a lover. Both of you felt free of the restrictions of marriage."

She was silent.

I went on to give her some astrological reasons for their compatability. They both were strongly influenced by Aquarius; that was her rising sign and his moon was in Aquarius. This meant that although they were two independent souls, self-reliant, self-made, there was respect between them. And they shared a beautiful balance of planets in the water and fire signs. Scorpio and Pisces are both water signs, meaning emotion, affection, depth of feeling. Sagittarius and Aries are fire signs, which indicate zeal, enthusiasm, action.

"Robert is secretive, a man of mystery. He likes to do things himself, not lean on others; that's the Scorpio-Sagittarius. You sense this with Pisces wisdom. And your Aries pride has made it possible for you to live side by side with him without ever asking questions. In some women this would be a sign of weakness. In your case, it was strength."

"I'm not so sure now. I feel—"

"Tell me about it."

"How long is he going to live?"

"He will survive this crisis. The danger period now seems to be around his birthday. I'll have to watch carefully."

She walked over to my sweep of windows. Her back to me she said, "I don't like to burden you further with my troubles but there is no one else I can talk to. You say we were made for each other. I agree we've been happy. I think for the first time in his life he knew what it was to relax and have fun. I gave that to him and I learned about myself at the same time. It has been a rewarding and wonderful twenty years. But what good are memories going to be after he's dead?"

"You have learned a great deal from him. You're not the same woman who decided to use him to help you achieve your ambitions."

She turned around. "I'm not sure I wasn't better off when all I wanted was a career, to be important. I've been important to him but I haven't gone as far in business as I might have. I have no friends at all. My only relative is my aunt and we really don't like each other. Through Robert, I met some of the wives of his business associates. They were nice to me, but I think it was because they felt they had to be. They didn't like me for myself. I wish I'd never met him."

"It was your fate. Did you ever hear of the Saturn cycle? Every twenty-eight years, Saturn returns to the place it was when you were born. Because Saturn is the great teacher, we astrologers believe no person is mature until he has completed one Saturn cycle. The decisions made between twenty-eight and thirty-one are the ones which shape your life. That is when you met Robert and decided not to use him for your own ambitions, but to join forces with him and make yourself a whole person. You couldn't have avoided your karmic destiny. It is there in your chart."

"You think I had no choice?"

"Very little. In some charts, I see indications that a woman could have gone both ways. Not yours. You and Robert were inevitable."

"And is our break inevitable?"

"There is a loss of a loved one in your chart. But in your next karmic cycle, when you are fifty-five or fifty-six, you are going to have your greatest happiness and reward. You are going to be married, probably to a man with grown children, who will love and appreciate you."

She sat down, her slim tanned hands gripping the corner of my desk. For a moment, I saw the beauty, the fire which must have challenged and held Robert. "I think I've already lost him. Last night, at the hospital, I did as you suggested. I said I was Mrs. Folsom. So they asked me to wait, after he had been taken into intensive care. For almost an hour, I walked up and down the corridor. Then the nurse came and told me it was all right, I could see my husband for a few minutes. He was dozing and I didn't want to disturb him. So I just touched his hand lightly and was going to leave when—"

Her shoulders sagged. I waited. After a minute, she went on. "He talked in the ambulance. He held my hand while they gave him oxygen. He even made a little fuss when he found out he was going to be in intensive care instead of a private room. The young doctor explained this was the only bed available in an emergency and he would get more care than if he'd had private nurses around the clock. Finally he agreed but insisted he wanted the first private room available. I told him I would talk to the hospital, but it was really up to the doctor. I suppose this annoyed him. He didn't tell me good-bye when he was taken into the care unit. The nurse saw how upset I was and I guess that's why she asked me to wait."

I turned and looked out of the window myself. The speedboats were making patterns of white foam on the water. But I really didn't see them; I was merely giving her time to steady herself.

And her voice was clearer when she continued. "He opened his eyes when I touched his hand. I smiled and whispered he was going to be all right and I'd be back first thing in the morning, as soon as they would let me see him. And he—he stared at me as though he had never seen me before. Then he said, 'Get out. Go away.' The nurse heard and came over and whispered to me to leave. I wanted to die. She told me this often happened, he was disoriented. I didn't believe it. I didn't sleep all night. This morning, when I saw him at eleven o'clock, he seemed all right. Neither of us mentioned what had happened. But it has been burning a hole in my mind. Is this the break you see in my chart, the loss?"

"I don't think so. Actually, he must have been sedated. Strange things happen under drugs."

"The young doctor told me that this morning. I had to explain my true relation to Robert. There was no point in lying and saying I was his assistant, traveling with him. Because—do you know what I did last night? I must have been out of my mind. I called his wife and told her who I was and asked her to come to Chicago."

"Have you told him?"

"Not yet. I asked the doctor to do it."

"What are you going to do?"

"I don't know. Last night I packed. I didn't plan even to go to the hospital this morning. Then I decided I had to say good-bye. And this morning he was so bright, so happy to see me. It was as though he'd never told me to get out."

"When is his wife coming?"

"Today. She may be at the hospital now. I've told your young doctor friend to have the specialist talk to her, and have her sit in on the conference call. Did I make a terrible mistake?"

"Perhaps not. How does he feel about his wife?"

She shook her head. "In California, when he was so very low, he told me that if he died, I was to ship his ashes to his wife without a word. I wouldn't have done anything so cruel. But sometimes I don't understand him. He hated me last night, I felt. I—I wanted to die. I wanted to kill him."

"It may not be such a bad idea to have his wife there. Then she will understand you haven't tried to interfere. If he wants to go back to her, then you must accept that, too."

"Will he?"

"I don't think so. If I could do her horoscope, I could be certain. How would you feel if he did decide to keep her here with him?"

Her deep breath was a groan. "Empty. Lost. But I would go away. I'd move out of the hotel and back to Long Island."

"How about his will?"

She shook her head. "He hasn't changed it, to my knowledge. Not since we have been together."

"Then you will—"

"Forget it, Miss de Jersey. I wanted success, yes. But I didn't go with Robert because he had money and I expected a reward. You do understand that, don't you? Once when we were watching the President on television—Nixon—he said, 'I'm richer than he is and one day you'll have a lot of it.' That's all I know. Last night, I tried to reach you. I wanted to ask if I should call his wife. When you weren't at your studio—"

"It's up to him now to decide what he wants. You've set the wheels in motion and you just have to wait."

"Should I stay here or go home?"

"How are you off for money?"

"I have plenty. Robert likes to have plenty of cash around."

"I mean for the long pull."

"I don't know."

"You've talked frankly to his doctor. Why don't you talk just as frankly to his lawyer?"

"The only lawyer I know of is the one who takes care of the company affairs." She sounded hopeless. We stared at each other. It isn't my job to be a nursemaid to my clients. Most of the time they wouldn't welcome it if I tried. Just the same, when you become involved in a tragic situation you have to be human. I couldn't leave Jane Grisson sitting alone in a hotel room all weekend eating out her heart. I couldn't. Yet I couldn't take her home with us. There are limits to every man's patience.

Suddenly, I thought of my once-a-year client, Harriet. I could see her sitting home on a lovely Saturday afternoon, brooding over her cat or whatever. I hadn't seen her since our last appointment but Maggie had been on the telephone to her with some regularity and reported Harriet was still carrying a burning torch and hoping, each time the telephone rang, that it would be David, returning to the fold.

I found the number in Maggie's book. Harriet picked up the phone on the first ring. I said, "Sorry, it's only Katie. But I do have a favor to ask of you. I have a friend in town, a client, who is alone and pretty miserable. Her boss is in the hospital with a heart attack. Could she come over to your place for a little while?"

Harriet was delighted and unsurprised. It was exactly the sort of thing which came naturally to her, taking care of strangers in trouble. Then I gave Jane the address on Superior Street, adding, "What you tell Harriet is up to you. Everything, or nothing. She's had a similar experience recently. Only in this case she never belonged to him as you do to Robert. This man has run away from her."

I almost dropped my pencil when Jane said, "The bastard." But she looked better. The spine seemed less eroded.

"No, honey, the fault lies not in ourselves but in our stars. Remember? Harriet's man is a Sagittarius, too. Call me Monday and let me know what's going on. Or if it's urgent, there is my home number. I'll be there tonight and all day Sunday."

As it turned out, the telephone didn't ring for me either that night or Sunday. But on Monday morning, when I was having my second cup of coffee after Ralph left the house, Maggie rang me to say, "Katie, a quick question. A dame named Mrs. Folsom wants an appointment. She says she is leaving town tomorrow so it has to be today or Tuesday. I told her it was impossible, you were booked solid and had clients climbing the walls for the next month. So she suggested I check with you. Is it a pal?"

"No. Or maybe yes, by this time. Do you remember Jane Austen? The one who came from New York while you were in Mexico? She came to town with her lover and he had a heart attack Friday night. Ralph and I got him in a hospital. Her real name is Jane Grisson."

"But this female says she is Mrs. Folsom."

"That's Robert's name. She uses it sometimes. You'd better try to fit her in."

"Monday is impossible. You have a TV show to tape, in addition to everything else. But I just might do it on Tuesday, in late afternoon. If you're sure it's necessary."

"It's necessary, all right, poor girl. The wife—the real Mrs. Folsom—is here, too. She—I mean Jane—is in a pretty bad way. I called Harriet to ask her if she'd mind doing some baby-sitting over the weekend with Jane. I'm afraid this means the wife has won and he doesn't want Jane around."

"Listen, Katie, this is funny. I thought Jane was an Aries. We went over her chart together, didn't we?"

"Of course. Her folder is in your top drawer right now. She's on the Aries-Pisces cusp."

"Well, this Mrs. Folsom is on the Virgo-Libra cusp. I asked her birthdate because I thought she was a new client. It's September 23. Do you think it could be the real wife? What do we tell Jane? And what exactly are the ethics involved about having the mistress and the wife as clients?"

"Who sent the wife?"

"I didn't ask. Should I call her back?"

"No, don't ask. Just make the appointment. I think I'd better alert Jane as to exactly what is going on."

As it turned out, Jane didn't mind my seeing Mrs. Folsom at all, particularly when she found out Robert's wife was leaving town. The young doctor, suddenly turned reticent, had only reported her arrival and the fact that Robert was improving and being moved into a private room as soon as one was available. Meanwhile, Harriet and Jane seemed to be good therapy for each other. They had even been to the Art Museum on Sunday and Jane was planning to go with Harriet on an assignment to photograph a folk singer in a fur-lined bathtub for a cover for his latest album. Then she added, "Harriet's been shortening my skirts. She says I look like a Do Do. I either should drop them to the floor or put them above my knees. Which do you think?"

"Great," I told her absent-mindedly. I must admit, it was the legal Mrs. Folsom who was occupying my thoughts, right then.

She, too, was on the cusp. It is almost uncanny how cusp people are drawn to each other. But her Virgo-Libra cusp was far less dynamic than Jane's Pisces-Aries, or Robert's Libra-Scorpio. However, he was certainly attracted to his wife at one time and probably still felt affection and consideration for her. Otherwise, why hadn't he obtained a divorce?

I could understand why a wife with her chart had accepted her husband's having a mistress. She was on the borderline between analytical, pristine, critical and sometimes material Virgo with harmonious, fair-minded Libra—who backs away from any direct confrontation, who would procrastinate rather than take a definite step for good or bad. This is a combination of signs which produces a person even more complex than most cusp people. For he or she often seems not to belong to any zodiac sign—until you begin to dig a bit more deeply. Often the outward appearance, the side the world sees, depends on the rising sign and the moon supplies the clue to her secret self. Yet, because I have as clients a number of Virgo-Libra cusps, I have discovered one thing they all seem to have in common.

We usually think of Virgo people as cold, lint-picking. I know of one astrologer who manages to irritate his Virgo clients by always referring to them as "Virtuous Virgos." Actually a Virgo woman is often misunderstood in emotional situations because she seems distant and matter-of-fact (Garbo is a Virgo), yet she can be marvelously exciting as a sex partner, especially if there are planets in Cancer or Scorpio well aspected in her chart. The appeal, however, first has to be cerebral. A Virgo woman is not the type to fall in love at first sight; a man's mind is more exciting to her than his body. I remember a Virgo client once told me, "I fell in love for the first time when I met a man who was more interested in exploring the book I read than he was in investigating my body. It was a challenge."

Intellect is the keynote to interesting a Virgo. They grow bored with the kind of partner who lacks imagination. Yet there are also two negative aspects connected with Virgo and sex. Virgo men, fastidious to the extreme in other ways, sometimes can be aroused only by women they find inferior, girls they don't mind connecting with the animal side of sex, or people with handicaps, cripples for whom they feel sympathy. And it is not uncommon to find a Virgo a kept woman, or an expensive call girl; Virgos can concentrate on sexual skills and turn off their emotions so that sex, like everything else, becomes a job.

Yet when you find a Virgo on the cusp of harmonious, gracious Libra, the cool mind is often at war with the luxury-loving body. A Virgo-Libra is a woman who will go all out in sex if the approach is right—and can turn cold as ice and disconcerting when it isn't. All of this can be hidden under the pretty Libra face and rounded body. Which means, although she may not be as frankly passionate as a Pisces-Aries, she still is an intriguing woman. She stands back and looks at herself looking at herself, a wonderful thing.

Even before I was in the door to my studio, I asked Maggie, "What does Mrs. Folsom sound like?"

"A lady. Detached. When I called back to confirm the appointment, she explained it wouldn't take long, she was just coming to please her husband."

"Do you believe her?"

"Yes and no. There isn't anybody in the world who isn't curious about his horoscope, given a chance to have it done without admitting he cares."

"Is she that sort?"

"Well, if what you are asking is, is the real Mrs. Folsom as exciting-sounding over the telephone as the phony one, the answer is no. Just the same, I'm eager to see her. And why does her husband want her to see you? Are you getting beyond yourself, my friend?"

That made me think because you do have to tread softly when you are advising people who want—or think they want—the same thing. In my time, however, I have had as clients all three people involved in a divorce action: husband, wife and Other Woman. I don't take sides—I can't. My only aim is to show all the parties concerned why the situation arose and let them decide what to do about it. Once, by just such a process, I was able to persuade a young wife she was much better off if she simply let the Other Woman take over; the wife was fast becoming an alcoholic just to escape his pressure, and the Other Woman had the harsh strength to handle him and make him like it. On the other hand, I have prevented divorces simply by pointing out to both women involved that the man wasn't capable of fidelity and never would be.

However, I had to stop thinking about Mrs. Folsom because Monday was its usual wild self. There were emergencies and crises, no lunch except for a milkshake Maggie smuggled in to me while a client was repairing his unwilling tears in the washroom. Maggie had a dinner date with the TV producer in charge of my taping so she went with me to the studio. After we were finished, Ralph picked us all up and took us to dinner at one of his pet restaurants, Gene and Georgetti's.

On our way to Ralph's favorite table in the corner, Maggie touched my arm and cocked her head in the direction of a booth. There were Harriet and Jane, with a pair of bearded not-so-young men in velvet suits and ruffled shirts. I gave Jane a sharp look to see if anything had changed. Other than the fact she was smiling, she was the girl I'd seen Saturday, in the depths. Certainly, it was the same white linen suit. Yet I was pleased at my inspiration for combining the two. Jane's heart might be aching but she was making her face behave. And having Jane as a responsibility had at least pushed Harriet out in public, although she didn't seem very happy about it.

Maggie and I exchanged one quick glance in which we agreed to stay out of it. But I was seated facing the room when Harriet and Jane got up to leave. To my astonishment, Jane was wearing a miniskirt. Then I realized someone had shortened her white linen suit drastically, perhaps a bit too drastically, for although she had good legs, it didn't go with the rest of her.

She hadn't seen me. And I heard nothing more from her. On Tuesday morning, Maggie suggested calling her to warn her to keep away from the office at the time Mrs. Folsom had her appointment but I decided against it. The temptation to get a look at Robert's wife might be too strong and one thing I didn't want was a confrontation.

Tuesday droned on, uneventfully, except for the usual minor crises. Maggie left at one o'clock, reluctantly; she was having a party for her youngest daughter and had no choice. Finally it was time for my four o'clock appointment: Mrs. Robert Folsom.

Virgo-like, she was early. I interrupted my conference with my three o'clock to seat her in the little glass-enclosed room which I used for waiting clients. It offers the most spectacular view of the lake and city, and, although I had been tempted to use it as my office, I had to reject the idea simply because the view was too distracting. Mrs. Folsom was properly polite about what she saw and I was properly apologetic about having to make her wait a few minutes. But it was obvious she'd come early because she was as curious about me as I was about her. And I found us eying each other like a pair of unintroduced dogs.

She was chic, as naturally chic as Jane Grisson was plain. Tall like many Virgos, rail slim, the kind given to plain little dresses which cost a fortune and do all sorts of great things to the female figure. Or maybe it was just a naturally great figure, flat stomach, high rounded little bosoms, slim waist, remarkable for anyone, much more for a woman of her age. I was impressed. Granted that Jane Grisson was twenty years younger, and undoubtedly a far more efficient secretary, Mrs. Folsom didn't exactly look like the deserted wife. On the contrary. If I hadn't known better, I might have picked her as the potential home wrecker.

My three o'clock, a Capricorn executive, ran a few minutes over. I had to give my full attention to a complicated problem of his, but I was aware of Mrs. Folsom's eyes on my back instead of the view. And when I was ready for her at last and opened the soundproof door, she didn't move. She simply sat smiling at me from one of my bucket-seat chairs.

"I suppose you wonder why I came to see you. It was Robert's idea. He thinks you are pretty remarkable, after what you told his secretary. I must say, I'm amazed at him. A hard-headed business man getting fixed on the stars."

"Plenty of them are. That man who just left—"

"Oh, I know!" Quickly. "It's just that Robert has always been so conservative. Although not in every way, I guess. And if you are worried whether I suspect something about his double life, you can relax. I've known about this little girl for a long time. And there were others before her."

"Why did your husband want you to have your horoscope done?"

A little gesture of the shoulders. "I think he's scared."

"Of dying?"

"What else? She told him you said he had a long life ahead of him. I think he's sent me here to check up. He knows I wouldn't lie to him. I never have and I'm not going to start now. Why should I?"

"I don't look for death unless I am sure a person really wants to know, for an important reason. Do you think he does?"

"I think he knows he is going to die, if that's what you mean."

"How is he?"

"Tanned. He's raging to get out of intensive care so he can get to a private room with a telephone. The doctors are of two minds about it. He gets marvelous nursing in the special care unit. But he isn't used to being surrounded by people, especially some patients worse than he is. He says it's depressing and I agree. So he'll probably be moved. I'll be gone by then, and his devoted Jane can take over."

She was seated and I was still standing. I walked over to my desk and glanced at her. She didn't move. Finally I said, "I prefer to do my chart in here. If you wouldn't mind moving—"

She said, "What is she like, Miss de Jersey? That's really what I came here to find out. What does she have, to hold him so long? My daughter said she was nothing, a mess."

"That isn't quite true. But she has no feeling for clothes, and you obviously do."

"Strange. Robert always took an interest in what I wore. I remember my first ball gown. I wore it to the reception, after we were married. It was very proper with insets of lace back and front so it wouldn't be too revealing. Mother helped me picked it out. Robert grabbed a pair of shears and ripped them out. My mother was shocked. That was—tell me, Miss de Jersey, where did my marriage go wrong?"

"The time you were born, the hour, and the place, might help me to find a clue."

"Atchison, Kansas. September 23, 1899. Early afternoon. My father broke out champagne because he thought it was a boy. When the doctor finally broke the news I was female, and mother couldn't have any more children, he drank it anyway and got drunk."

I sat down and pulled a blank chart toward me. She still didn't move, although she raised her voice to reach me. The words tumbled out in a rush (again—Sagittarius rising, I thought). "Of course he was spoiled. His mother. Do you know what she did to my trousseau? One afternoon when I was out at a party, she went through all my nightgowns and cut off the sashes. I guess she hated the idea of my looking pretty in bed."

I didn't answer, for I was busy doing calculations. The chair opposite me was suddenly filled. I said, "Your Sun is on the cusp between Virgo and Libra, which you probably know. Your rising sign is Sagittarius with Capricorn intercepted—like your husband. Your moon is in Taurus."

"What does that mean?"

"You are both Virgo and Libra—extremely critical, always appraising, yet charming all the while. Your sun sign is backed by quiet, determined Taurus. You loved pretty things. You have never divorced your husband because you didn't want to give them up and because it would hurt you in the eyes of the world. You are part Capricorn too—which means you dislike divorce because it is a confession to the world of failure. Your marriage is a sign of security to you, and one of the great worries of your life has been your fear of financial loss. Possessions mean too much to you."

She said, "That's ridiculous. Robert started his business with my money. My father was rich. His father was dead and his mother didn't have a dime. She lived on the charity of her relations."

"You've always been frustrated even though you were spoiled; your birth hour signifies that you wanted to express yourself but never did. You said yourself your father was disappointed because you weren't a boy. After you married, you lived in the shadow of a mother-in-law who took charge of the house. Is that true?"

She nodded. "Mother Folsom lived with us. Then after a while, when I couldn't stand it any longer and even the children complained, he built her a house of her own. When he came home, he spent more time in it than in his own."

"How long has she been dead?"

"Over twenty years. But I can still close my eyes and hear her voice. 'Maddy, you spend too much money on clothes. Maddy, do you use peroxide on your hair? Won't it all fall out? Maddy, Robert was all I had, my little baby. You have your two beautiful children. Why can't you share him?' It made me sick. Share him? I never had more than a corner of him."

"That's not quite true. It was a love match, wasn't it?" Her Mars was in Scorpio, his sun sign, just as Jane's was. And in his chart, his Venus was side by side with Saturn, which showed his overpowering devotion to his mother, plus the fact that he had married someone, in his mind, as close to her as possible.

"You and your husband have exactly the same ascendant—23 to 24 degrees of Sagittarius. Unusual though it is to find a man and wife sharing precisely the same ascendant, I have seen it a few times. In each case, they were basically much alike, with very similar values, ideas and ideals—attitudes and reactions. You both have Neptune in the seventh house which means you both over-idealized your marriage at the beginning. Neither of you could face the realities of marriage when it was necessary so you could meet the problems head on and communicate with each other."

"The first years were wonderful, in spite of everything."

"There is a change in human relations every seven years. We never stay the same. The bond either strengthens or it weakens."

"In our case, it weakened frightfully."

"You wanted children badly."

"So did he. But in my case—I had to show her I was more of a woman than she was. She used to hint, indirectly, I wasn't built to have babies, I was too narrow hipped. I would have gone on having them by the dozen but—something happened. I'm not sure what."

"Your sex life went sour."

She stood up. I had the feeling she wanted to leave, get out. She compromised by going into the reception room, where she had left her handbag. She took a long time lighting a cigarette, obviously a delaying tactic. Finally she came back to my desk with an ashtray in her hand. "How did you know that? Was it a wild guess?"

I indicated the chart. "It's here, in the charts. His Mars squares your Mars—a problem in sex. His Mars in late Cancer makes him extremely sensitive to the environment during intercourse—your Mars in early Scorpio makes you, unconsciously, quite demanding. Anything short of perfection, ecstasy, could seem unforgivable to you. The result could be tragic."

"I don't suppose—I've never mentioned that to a living soul. I couldn't say anything to him. It was too painful, I'm sure he hated it as much as I did. He couldn't make love to me while his mother lived with us. For a while, I went on trips with him, leaving the children at home. But after a while, that didn't work, either. Once in a hotel room, I started to cry and couldn't stop. He got mad and yelled at me and the house detective came to tell us to be quiet. That was the last time we tried."

His Mars, the planet of sex, was in Cancer, representing the maternal influence. It all made sense.

"Yet you never divorced him?"

"He never mentioned it. Nobody knew anything was wrong. Including his mother. We stopped quarreling. What was there to fight about? He was away a lot, traveling. After he built the plant in New Jersey, he was in New York more than he was home. I had no choice but to go along and pretend we were happy. He put every cent my parents left me into his business."

"And gave you what in exchange?"

"I have 51 percent of the stock. When I die, it goes to my daughters."

"And if your husband dies?"

Our eyes met. "I think I will sell the business. It has no interest for me now. Earlier, it might have. Even without sex, we could have made a business team. I needed something to do after the children were grown, away in college. But by that time she came along. His mother died and the next thing I know, there is that girl."

"Jane Grisson?"

"What does she have, Miss de Jersey? Nothing, my daughter says. Yet he's been more faithful to her than he was to me. We've split his life down the middle, I had half and she had half. But she had the best half, after his mother died."

"I think, oddly enough, she was a substitute mother for him, just as he was a father to her. This happens more often than people think and there really isn't anything unnatural about it."

"I had my own children. They came first. I couldn't be a mother to him."

"She had no children. She had no father. Her mother, the only one she felt close to, died. Robert is all she has."

She put out her cigarette, mashed it out, over and over. "You can't expect me to weep over that."

"No, but you asked me to explain it. I'm trying. She also found out that the way to live peacefully with a Scorpio is never to ask questions, make demands. She was never a nagging mistress. You have no idea how unusual this is. After the first glow is over, mistresses are often more demanding than wives. Perhaps it's because they have more to complain about."

"And I was a nagging wife."

"Possibly, because you have Mercury in Virgo adversely aspected to Saturn. And your Moon in Taurus makes you a bit possessive. But there is a bond between you and Robert which is extremely powerful. Both of you had Saturn falling on the other's ascendant. This is destiny. You are really very much alike, so you couldn't live together, yet never actually break the bond. He never really wanted to divorce you. He is proud of you, the mother of his children. He was glad to see you, wasn't he?"

"In a way. Yet she was the one who telephoned me." She was on her feet again, moving restlessly around the room, straightening pictures, adjusting pillows. She turned to add:

"I don't know. I don't think I have ever really known him. He had these girls. But I don't think he ever had any fun. Do you suppose he had fun with her? When he sees me we talk about old times like old friends. But I tire him, I know I do. I guess she doesn't."

"Has he given you any presents recently?"

"Presents? Miss de Jersey, he never was able to give a present in his life, a real present. I used to go down and pick things out for birthdays and Christmas, for me and later for the children, and send him the bills. He paid, but not without screaming. He's wildly extravagant in some ways, but when it comes to giving presents . . . Did she ever get anything from him?"

"I don't know. Very little, I suspect. But may I ask you one question? You don't have to answer."

She paused, in midflight. "All right, since you put it that way."

"Is she in his will?"

"No." She had a pillow in her hand and I thought she might hurl it at me. "No, he promised Bobby, my oldest daughter's husband who is executor, he would not embarrass me. If that is why Miss Grisson called me, you can let her know it's no use. Robert has given Bobby his word and he wouldn't go back on that."

She put down the pillow and emptied her ashtray into the wastebasket. Still bending over, scrubbing it with a Kleenex (tidy Virgo!) she said, "I think the first time I found evidence there had been another woman, I wanted to die. Yet I didn't hate her. I hated him. I hated him for giving some cheap thing what belonged to me."

"Did you talk to him about it?"

"Never. Remember, nice women didn't talk about sex in those days. It was something which happened in the dark, under the bedclothes. OK if a woman enjoyed it, otherwise it was her duty. My mistake was I found it wonderful. Then it was taken away from me."

As an astrologer, I know that many marriages do break up in the bedroom; even today, among our brutally frank teenagers, just talking about sex isn't enough. For women too often fail to realize that a man needs encouragement and appreciation in bed as well as in business. Failure to him is humiliation and a woman who helps him recover confidence after failure is of rare value. So often, when families or wives object to a man's so-called philandering, and particularly his choice of object, they do not take into consideration the value of simple kindness and expressions of pleasure, of spontaneous giving. Sometimes the most loved and loving mistresses are not voluptuous or even pretty, just women of insight and understanding.

Perhaps, if Mrs. Folsom had come to me years ago, I might have been able to help her. But now it was too late. She went into the reception room for her handbag. "What shall I tell my husband about his glorious future?"

"Just what I said."

She pulled on gloves. "And have you any private word for me?"

"You are going to travel, I think. Perhaps live in a foreign country for a while. There is a new moon coming up in your progressed chart, meaning a new beginning. Because it is joining your husband's Saturn and about to cross your own ascendant, this means that at last your tie to each other is finished, in this life. The chapter is closed. But your life is far from finished. A new one is starting."

"No tall dark strangers? No, Miss de Jersey, I'm not laughing at you. I'm just trying to keep it light. I'm a mess and it's too late to do anything about it. My children don't need me, certainly my husband has found his perfect companion and, whatever my destiny was, I've missed it. And I'm too damned old to change."

After she left, I sat watching the boats coming in for the night. Another year was almost on us. Robert Folsom wouldn't be here to see it. His wife would come into a great deal of money. Jane Grisson would be left with a house on Long Island full of modern equipment, a few clothes, and her job severance pay. It hardly seemed fair. Yet in a strange way, I felt sorrier for the wife than I did for Jane. Mrs. Folsom had everything—and so very little.

Maggie received a check from Robert Folsom which took care of both Jane's and his wife's visit. After that, we heard nothing for nearly two weeks. Once or twice, when we had a moment or two to spare, Maggie and I wondered who was wearing the Tiffany jewels Robert had bought. Then Jane slipped out of my mind. Other problems became more pressing. I had almost forgotten that time was running out for Robert, when Harriet appeared at my studio door early one morning looking, as Maggie put it later, like the-widow-wore-red. Her eyes were swollen from tears, which we had seen before, and she was wearing a bright red pants suit which accentuated the pale, tragic face.

"He's dying. Where is Katie? She must look at his chart."

I was in South Dakota on a personal appearance and definitely out of touch. Maggie, who had been through crises with Harriet before, found her file and studied David's chart. "He isn't dying so far as I can see nor do I think he's getting a divorce."

"Who are you talking about?"

After some confused moments, Maggie finally cleared up the fact that it was Robert Folsom that Harriet was inquiring about. He had been getting along very well, there had been talk about his leaving the hospital with a nurse if Jane could find a furnished apartment and his son-in-law had been here and gone back to California. Last night, there had been a turn for the worse. No one had called Jane so when she had stopped in at 8 A.M., as she regularly did to bring him the newspapers, she had been horrified and had called Harriet.

Maggie said I would be back the next day and Harriet burst out, "But it may be too late!" Maggie reluctantly studied Robert Folsom's chart—Mars had been adversely aspected in the eighth house, but it seemed to indicate a brush with death rather than death— and said she thought he would recover, but this was just the opinion of a student. So when I finally arrived home late the next day, after traveling most of it, Ralph met me at the airport with, "There's a bunch of rattlesnakes hissing at each other in your office. Jane and Harriet and some of their new hippie friends are camping in until you come home. Maggie wasn't going to leave them alone there so I took over yesterday evening and finally cleared them out by promising I'd drive you in from the plane so you could study Robert's chart."

He had not been exaggerating. My studio, my quiet little studio, looked like a sit-in at a dean's office. Harriet and her friends were in faded, not-too-clean blue jeans, and assorted beads and wild shirts. They were gathered around Jane, who was more conservatively dressed in a long blue sweater and a very short blue skirt, with panty hose to match. I suppose, in this age of fancy dress, no one would have stopped to look at Jane twice on the street; just the same, for Jane, the change was extraordinary and I wasn't quite sure I approved. By contrast, I, of course, felt square.

One of the young men, a rather sweet-faced boy with what I can only describe as a Dutch bob, took my coat and brought me coffee; whatever the looks of him, I was glad to note later he had left my little kitchenette tidy as the proverbial pin. There was a note from Maggie saying she had left Robert's chart in my top desk drawer and locked it. Unless the client gives permission, no one except the client and astrologer ever see an individual's horoscope. There are two reasons for this; first, it is confidential, and second—a little knowledge in astrology is a dangerous thing. One planetary aspect considered out of context of the whole (remember, over 1700 factors are involved) may be very misleading. The art of interpretation requires years of experience, insight and understanding, and consequently is the province of the professional.

There was complete silence as I unlocked the drawer and found the folder. There was more silence as I started to study Robert's chart.

Finally, I said, "It's all right, for the moment there is no crisis. Maggie was exactly right. But if the rest of you don't mind, would you wait downstairs? I'd like to talk to Jane alone."

They went meekly enough. When they were gone, Jane said, "I can tell by your face you think I'm being pretty silly. I suppose I am. You see, I never had a normal childhood and I guess I'm going overboard. But they are sweet and they've made me feel one of them. Robert is amused by my stories about them. It's come to the point where we have so little to talk about that if I didn't have the kids, I wouldn't know what to say."

I said, "Jane, he is already removing himself. His progressed sun and moon are coming close together in the sector of death and regeneration. There was an aspect of violence the night before last, Uranus paralleled Pluto, when the attack came. Now I think the end will be quiet. He'll slip away. Every day he will remove himself a little more from this plane. You must be prepared."

"Is it soon?" She was crying quietly.

"A few days. Perhaps on his birthday, when the planets are in the same position as when he was born. He is ready, isn't he?"

"I think so. He seems tired, but happy. The nurses all talk about his smile. I've never seen him smile so—radiantly. I cry so much these days, when I'm not with him. I'm not crying over him. I'm crying for myself. All these silly clothes, and the young kids, are just to pass the time. Underneath, I'm lost."

"I know." And I did. Jane would never change fundamentally. Someday another man would find in her just what fascinated Robert. "But this isn't the end of your life, even though you think it is. You're going to be happy again."

"His son-in-law is coming. He's going to sell the business. When it's all—over—I'm going back to New York with him and help him."

"And then?"

"I guess I'll look for another job. Harriet suggested we might both of us move to California. I'm not sure. She is younger than I am and she might get bored."

"She needs someone strong to lean on. It might work, for a while. But don't let her leaning become permanent."

Jane rubbed her eyes. There was already a smudge of black mascara underneath each one. Strangely enough, it made her look younger. "But I'm the one who has been leaning on her. She's done everything for me."

"Just wait. She needs direction. She must find a man too, and you can help her in her attitude toward men. Like so many Taureans she is too possessive, men are frightened away. You know how to love without making demands, asking questions. It is your great charm. Never forget that."

"In other words, lengthen my skirts."

"That doesn't matter, either. It is fancy dress for the moment. But when his son-in-law arrives—"

"I know. He wants me to look respectable. Isn't that funny? Bobby is older than I am, and he treats me like—like a stepmother." I could see another bout of tears was imminent so I sent her downstairs to join her friends.

In the days which followed, she stopped seeing Harriet and the hippie group and spent most of her time at the hospital. There was no pain, no sudden deterioration. But Robert was dying and knew it. Once he smiled at her and said, "Your Miss de Guernsey, or whatever her name was, was wrong. Or did you lie to me?" Another time, after his son-in-law arrived, he called them together to say, "I want you to know each other. Without Jane, I'd have been dead long ago. She has kept me well, made me happy." Then he gave instructions for Bobby to give Jane a settlement after the factory and business had been sold. He had left one third of his estate to his wife, and he wanted his daughters to have the other two thirds. But he asked his son-in-law to make sure Jane had enough to live comfortably the rest of her life.

I was doubtful about these arrangements and I tried to urge her to have him make some specific bequest, in writing. Because Robert had Sagittarius rising, and so many planets in conflict with each other, I was afraid he would neglect to make any arrangements definitely. He had never asked to see his lawyer; even when Bobby asked about the will, he was told Robert would "see to it himself." Yet he didn't.

Like other men with the curious combination of Libra-Scorpio and Sagittarius, he was a strange mass of contradictions. For many years, his wife and children had resented his preoccupation with business, considered him cold and methodical, without any sense of fun. Then came the blondes—and, later, Jane. And even with Jane, he was two men. One was the man who loved to travel and laugh, yet had wept at the thought of her leaving him, the big boss who locked the door and made love to her in his office, who had spent hours planning the dream house for her mother. Another was the man who never altered his will to include Jane, who wanted his ashes sent to his wife without a word, who had virtually neglected his wife and children—yet never obtained a divorce.

He died early in the morning after his birthday, on October 24, at 1:55 A.M. Central Standard Time.

Jane and Bobby were with him. Bobby made arrangements for the body to be cremated and took the ashes to Kansas City for burial beside Robert's mother. Jane came in for a minute at noon to say good-bye to me.

I asked, "What are you going to do?"

"I'm going to close the apartment in New York. Bobby says to take anything I want. Then I'm going in and help him close the office and sell the business. There are things I know which nobody else has any ideas about."

"You trust Bobby?"

"He's a dear. Rather blunt and outspoken and he stutters a bit. But he is so friendly! He reminds me of Robert, in a way."

"Do you know when he was born?"

"I know a lot of things about him, but not his age. But his birthday is December 20."

"Sagittarius again! But this time on the Capricorn cusp. Be careful, my dear."

"I don't know what you mean. I don't care if I don't get a cent of Robert's money. I've always worked, I don't know what I would do without a job. I can't sit still and feel sorry for myself. Besides—"

Her voice broke and her face fell apart. I offered the box of Kleenex but she shook her head. "No, I just wanted to tell you what happened. I don't care about anything else for he left me the best part of himself. Do you remember that check to Tiffany's I was concerned about? I thought it was for jewelry for another woman?"

I nodded. I remembered well. It was the one unsolved mystery in the whole case.

She said, "He bought a diamond pin for me. He sent it to Bobby and asked him to keep it, and give it to me with his love after he died. To show me how much he had cared, always."

Jane reached for the doorknob. Tears stung my own eyes as I watched her straight little back go down the corridor. In a strange way, it was a happy ending, after all.

3

Is Life Worth Living?

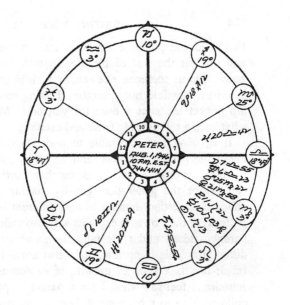

MAGGIE says I am a pushover for the younger generation. I will admit I keep my fees lower than many astrologers of my experience and I do it for one simple reason. I don't want to shut out youngsters who can't afford to pay more, and I refuse to confuse myself and everyone else with a sliding scale.

But I feel we were all put on earth for a purpose, and my purpose right now is to do what I can to help young people understand their role—which, hopefully, is to keep the world from blowing itself up before we reach the year 2000. I don't know whether this makes me an optimist or a pessimist. However, in my state of mind, I can communicate with young people.

For one thing, they accept astrology because they aren't afraid to explore concepts which have roots in ancient mysticism. They understand far better than our generation that the wise men of previous eras might have had knowledge on which we, in our frantic pursuit of science, stupidly turned our backs. They also, like all young, challenge the clichés behind which parents, often in desperation and fright, hide.

I really don't feel terribly sorry for the mother who comes in to me weeping, saying she doesn't understand her son or daughter. Why should she? Just because she has been the medium by which that child was put on earth doesn't mean she should know him in and out for the rest of his life. In fact, I believe that complete knowledge of someone else—either a child or a husband or wife—is neither possible nor desirable. Having someone tucked in your hip pocket becomes a bore for you both. Mystery, surprises, are what keep a relationship fresh and exciting.

It is, of course, desirable to understand as much as you can about the people you love, and why they react as they do, which is where astrology comes in. Better than anything I know, astrology can bridge the generation gap by making a parent look at his children as distinct human beings, different from himself, with life patterns of their own. It explains why two children, born of the same parents, raised under virtually the same circumstances, react so differently. This is normal. It is also normal for young people to rebel; that is a state of growth, of exploration, flexing of mental muscles. I feel sad when I see a parent so permissive he gives his child nothing to rebel against, because aggression is there in all of us and must find an outlet. I also am apprehensive when a smug mother or father tells me, "My son [or daughter] and I are very close. He tells me everything." This isn't possible, it isn't reasonable, and, most important, it isn't right.

So I'm never very alarmed when a father or mother asks me to see a child, nor am I unduly flattered when he or she calls afterward to say how impressed that child was with me. At a certain age, a child won't listen to his parents, but he will sit impressed and enraptured when a stranger says virtually the same thing. It's the noninvolvement which does it.

Which is why, on a chilly February day in 1964, I deliberately canceled a business engagement that might have meant a good bit of money to me, and took a cab out to a hospital in Evanston to visit Peter N., seventeen years old, who had just "totaled" his new Jaguar outside Calvary Cemetery.

"I can't understand it," his father told me. "The kid's a superb driver. I gave him the Jag for Christmas. He took care of it the way he always did of his toys. He's not the type to smash things. Yet the cops said he was going like a bat out of hell and heading deliberately for a lamppost. I know that kid like the back of my hand. He wouldn't do a thing like that."

I didn't much care to point out to Arthur N., a TV personality on whose talk show I appeared with some regularity, that the boy had indeed done it, that he hadn't been drinking, and that none of our actions, ever, are irrational. Although Arthur had never been my client, from time to time on the show we had discussed his horoscope briefly (he was a Scorpio, with his moon in Virgo, an interesting combination) and off camera I had tried to tell him a little about his relation with his son, Peter, a Leo.

When Arthur and his wife had divorced, the custody of the two children, both boys, had naturally been given to Frances, the mother. But Peter had so obviously preferred his father—there is often a strong attraction between Scorpios and Leos because they share a mutual respect and admiration for the ambitions and high standards characteristic of both signs—that his mother, almost in revenge, had focused her attention on the younger boy. So long as his father had no inclination to remarry, this had worked out. Peter had spent vacations and every weekend with his father and they had done things together, sharing a man-to-man closeness which, I had tried to tell Arthur, was good, but too good to last.

And, of course, it hadn't. For Arthur had decided to remarry. He had picked the woman with Peter very much in mind. She had never been married, although she was thirty-six; she was no kid, yet she was young enough to "speak Peter's language"; and they were "crazy about each other—you should see them, they spend hours talking on the telephone, just gossiping."

The woman Arthur had chosen—or who, in my opinion, had chosen him—was his long-time secretary, Sandy Rolfe. Sandy was a character in the industry. She'd been with him in New York, when Arthur was riding very high, and she and her devoted Irish Catholic family had transplanted themselves to Chicago when Arthur was transferred. Sandy had once been fat and jolly, known for her good humor and her pretty face. When Arthur divorced, she had taken herself in hand, dieted down to a size 10, and become less jolly and easygoing. In fact, I'd heard the story from a newspaper woman that Sandy had made no bones about wanting to marry Arthur. She'd even told casual acquaintances she was out "to get him."

Which was OK with most people, because Sandy had always been loyal to Arthur and no one in the industry had cared much for his first wife. Only Arthur seemed to have missed the fact he was being manipulated. And, in my opinion, he was being particularly dense in not realizing what was happening to Peter. Peter had liked Sandy in the past. Perhaps, as a small boy, he had almost loved her, because she was the one who fussed over him when he visited his father's office. I think there had even been some kind of a story about her baby-sitting with him when Dick, his little brother, was born.

But a devoted secretary-auntie type is one thing; a jolly old thing who remembered your birthday and kept candy in her desk for you. A prospective stepmother is quite another, especially when a boy had clung so desperately to his father since the divorce.

When I had tried to hint at this, tactfully, Arthur had laughed. "Katie, my God, Peter and I are friends. There's nothing we haven't discussed. Dames, sex, drugs, the whole bag. He knows it isn't right for a man as virile as I am to be without a woman. And Sandy has always been nicer to him than his real mother. Why, we're even going to have his own bedroom in our new apartment, a great big room fixed up so he can entertain his friends."

"Has he many friends?" I'd asked. Arthur had looked sheepish.

"Well, no. He and I have sort of been best friends. That won't change. But wait until he has Sandy to cook up big pots of spaghetti for him and his pals, make them welcome. You know as well as I Frances never would do anything like that. This marriage is going to be just great. Wait and see."

I said I would. Meanwhile, Peter had smashed up his new car and, what was worse, didn't seem to care one way or the other. In fact, he treated it as a kind of joke. He was sitting up there in a North Shore hospital flirting with all the nurses, especially a dark-eyed little thing named Mary Bates who was "pretending to teach him astrology."

Which is another reason I was called in. I was to go as a friend of the family, find out what Mary was up to, discover what brand of astrology she was teaching and—incidentally—find out what was bugging the boy.

"All in one hour's session at my regular fees?" I had teased Arthur. For once Arthur, who was quick to tease himself, didn't laugh. He insisted he was going to pay me double, triple, anything. At which point I had to spell out to him the fact that there are some things money can't buy. I was going as a friend, not an astrologer. I would even take a small gift to prove it.

So there I was, sitting in a hospital in a chintzy visitor's chair on a lousy day in February, visiting a patient who was far from pleased to see me. What had started out as a light snow had turned into steady accumulation and, although it was only shortly after noon, the sky was so dark every light in the hospital was on. My present, a book on very basic astrology, was on his bedside table unopened. The television set bleated away at top volume, turned to a quiz show he wasn't watching. A beautiful little Japanese dietician was hovering patiently while he checked the menus for the next day.

I had, indeed, tried. I had shouted my name in his ear, knowing full well that his father had told him who I was. He had been unimpressed. The remote control for the TV was pinned to his pillow, but he made no move to turn down the sound, or shut it off.

He was an insolent young Leo, self-absorbed, self-important, imperious. Leos don't need to be rude. They can be utterly charming. Only when a Leo has been badly handled does he react in such a negative way. Peter, despite his arrogance, could be a lost kid. The car crash might have been a desperate bid for love and attention and, if he had killed himself in the process, it would have been worth it. Leos are like that—they love drama, so much they will settle for all or nothing. Right now he was making a big thing out of being incapacitated and I must admit, he was getting away with murder, Leo fashion. Even I, a very busy woman, was sitting on the edge of my chair waiting for a glance from the young lion prince.

Eventually the dietician left, not without a sweet apologetic smile in my direction. Peter and I and the TV set were left alone together. He made a pass at unwrapping the book, then tossed it away when he saw the title, and leaned back wearily against the pillows. He was a handsome young beast. Where Arthur N. was short and sandy, Peter was magnificently tall, with a bush of gold-blond hair, the shade his mother tried to achieve through her hairdresser, and the high color which belongs to only the young and healthy. He bloomed against the white hospital pillow.

I said, or rather, I shouted, "Is your friend Mary on duty? The astrology student?"

No answer. Or maybe he hadn't heard me. My impulse was to walk out. Then I remembered you were supposed to practice what you preach. I reached over and touched his hand. I smiled at him. I remembered what I had told my astrology students, "A Leo is the easiest person in the world to manage. All you have to do is tell him, at regular intervals, how important he is to you. But you can't challenge or try to put him in his place. He'll react by becoming utterly impossible."

Peter turned off the set. "What did you say?"

"I asked if the astrology nurse was on duty. I'd like to meet her. That's my profession, you know."

The silence was almost shocking. Outside aluminum lunch trays were being replaced belatedly on noisy carts. I continued to present my hand. And smile.

"Her name is Mary Bates. She works a split shift. She won't be on until midafternoon, unless she comes early to give me a back rub. She does, sometimes."

"She sounds like a nice girl."

"I suppose so." The indifference was too much, a little too much. I gathered Mary had the key to Leos. She let Peter know she came in early, on her own time, to rub his back. So he talked about her to his father. It was the back rub, not the astrology, he was really mentioning. It was Mary's devotion he was tossing in his father's face, like a challenge.

Then suddenly, Leo-like, he challenged me, too. "Miss de Jersey, what do you think of Camus?"

At that time, plenty of my young clients, the Brains, were talking a lot about Albert Camus, French writer and philosopher of despair. They kept quoting to me his philosophy that in order to live a man had to be totally committed to life. Somehow, from his father's description, I wouldn't have put Peter in the Brain class. Yet you never can tell.

He had challenged me, so I challenged back. "Have you ever considered suicide?"

Peter understood. "Camus decided life was worth living. Then he was killed in an accident. Does that make sense?"

"It was a car crash, I believe. Yes, to an astrologer it does make sense. The pattern of our lives is there when we are born. Yours. Mine. Perhaps the accident to Camus seems like irony but it was meant to be."

No answer. Outside the room, the voices of visitors, padding feet of nurses. Something which sounded like a stretcher creaking down the hall. Far away, the faint sounds of the quiz show on the sets of other patients. Then, "Twice when I was young, I tried to kill myself. My father used to kid me about it. He'd tell visitors how funny I was when I got sick on the sleeping pills and had to be walked around like a drunk. I was only five."

I thought, oh, dear, Arthur's Virgo sharpness and Scorpio sarcasm at work. Often a Scorpio, in his need for independence and privacy, will slam the door on those he loves best, especially if he feels they are trying to demand too much, become too possessive. I couldn't imagine what devil drove Arthur to these tactics on a small

child, a child he loved very much. And it was particularly stupid
to make fun of a little Leo. Yet I could see him doing it.

"That is just his way," I said. "A Scorpio tries not to show how
deeply he feels about anything."

"Don't kid yourself. First he left my mother and me and Dick.
Then he started taking out young dames. Chicks. And dropping
them if he got to first base."

"Let me tell you something, as an astrologer. Scorpios have great
pride. So do people like you, born under the sign of Leo. Neither
of you seem to think you have to bend to the rights of other people,
to try to understand them. The difference between you and your
father is that, while a Leo will admit to his feelings, a Scorpio tries
to hide them. I know he loves you very much. He's talked to me
about you many times."

"Is that how you knew I was a Leo?"

"Why not?"

"I wish he'd mind his own business. As a matter of fact, Miss
de Jersey, I wish you'd mind yours. I know why he sent you up
here. He wants you to spy on me, to find out what is going on
between Mary Bates and me. Well, I'll tell you what to say. You
can tell him it's none of his goddamned business. Just because he
produced the sperm which made me doesn't give him the right to
interfere in everything I do. If you were my age, I'd put it even
more bluntly."

"Why don't you? I'm not easily shocked. Even if I am over
thirty."

He turned away from me. I decided I'd wasted enough time, for
one day. I stood up.

"So I've hurt your feelings." His tone was taunting. "It's surprising, how people will kick little kids around. But let the kid
get out of line and they can't take it."

"You aren't exactly a little kid. And I didn't come here to spy
on you and Mary. I came because I thought you were really interested in astrology and I might be of help. That's why I brought you
that book."

"OK. Thanks. But I know what the pitch is. Mom was giving
the head nurse a bad time last night about Mary. Saying she was
spending too much time with a young, impressionable boy and all
that crap. Would you call me impressionable, Miss de Jersey?"

"I don't know. But I gather Mary has been kind to you and you
aren't returning the favor. Your mother could hurt her very much

if she complained to one of the doctors. Maybe they would believe her and maybe not. It wouldn't be good for Mary's record no matter what happens."

"Is that true?" He sounded genuinely worried. Then the sullen arrogance came back in full cry. The prince looked down his full leonine nose at me.

"What can I do about it if she is in love with me?"

Damn, I thought. Damn all men and all Leos who have had their paws stepped on. "How do you know she's in love with you? A girl who takes up nursing should have warmth and sympathy. She cares about her patients." I wanted to add that maybe she felt sorry for Peter, but instead I changed it to, "And I suspect you might be rather building up her devotion to annoy your parents. Particularly your mother?"

"Why should I do that?"

"I've met your mother. Beautiful as she is, I am sure she hasn't always been the ideal parent. And of course you are a Leo. Leos have certain ways of doing things. I have a client, a Leo, a beautiful girl. A man she'd been going out with rejected her. Although she didn't really like him, although she recognized they weren't suited, she went out of her way to win him back. Then, of course, she told him she never wanted to see him again. You take the device of showing your mother other women find you attractive, to make her jealous."

"That's crazy." The TV set clicked on. I thought, OK, I've done it. But I could report to Arthur what was going on, even without seeing Mary. It was all so obvious, it was almost sad. Suddenly the noise stopped. Peter said, "Don't go, not for a minute. She's talked about you a lot and when I told her you were coming, she almost flipped her bird. She thinks there's a lot of truth in astrology. Can you really see what's going to happen to a person when you do his horoscope? Is it all cut and dried? If it is, why worry?"

"It isn't quite that simple. You see certain lines of behavior, yes. Patterns."

"For example, can you tell if someone is going to kill himself?"

"Not really. Sometimes you see the possibility. If in a chart, several planets are badly aspected in relation to other planets in the sectors of the chart which refer to death, or self-undoing, you will be alerted that there might be some attempt at self-destruction. But only one, or two planets, if they are badly aspected, don't necessarily mean a suicide attempt. Let me put it this way. If you have one

bad character in a room holding a gun on you, it isn't as bad as
though you had three gangsters threatening you. But even with
three, it doesn't mean you will die. The Marines might come and
rescue you."

I smiled. He didn't return it. "Have you ever known by a chart
that someone was going to kill himself?"

"You can seldom be sure in advance. After the fact, it's easy to
be wise. Take Hitler's chart, for example. His Mars squared Saturn
—that is, made a 90-degree angle to it—which meant he would rise
and fall by his own hand."

"If you had seen this in his chart when he was born and warned
somebody, could you have stopped him?"

"Maybe. If the other portents weren't too strong. In his case,
they were. If I find a grouping of planets in certain houses of a
chart and feel they are adversely aspected, I do try to alert rela-
tives and point out certain periods of danger, when the movements of the stars, what we astrologers call the progression, might
trigger an attempt."

"But what if the parents don't care? Or are badly aspected themselves astrologically?"

I said, "You catch on fast. Or has Mary been telling you more
about astrology than you pretend?"

"Did you ever have a client kill himself? And don't treat me
like a little boy whose nose should be kept out of the jam jar, like
Sandy does."

"I thought you liked Sandy."

"Do you know her?"

"Everybody does. Everybody who knows your father, that is."

"Do you think he's going to marry her?"

"Would that be so bad?"

"I don't know. I honestly don't know." At last he was just what
must have charmed Mary Bates, a confused, unhappy youngster.
"Dad insists I must be prejudiced, that she's a wonderful woman.
And I must say, when I was a kid, she couldn't have been nicer.
I know Mother can be a bitch and you were right just now when
you accused me of telling her about Mary to make her mad. If
Dad could find someone who would really be nice to him, that would
be OK by me. Mom was always having at him. I think she blamed
him for making her quit show business when I was born. She was
jealous of his being such a big shot, while people forgot she'd ever
had a career. I asked Dad about it once and he laughed. He said

she never was that great; he just put her on the show because he was making a pass at her and she was a good-looking babe with a big pair of boobs. But it was a blessing when she got pregnant with me because she was getting worse all the time. Of course maybe that wasn't quite true but—"

"Your mother is an Aries, if I remember rightly. Aries women need outlets besides domesticity. Perhaps if there had been some kind of a compromise . . ."

"Well, believe me, there wasn't. I used to lie in bed at night, listening to them scream at each other, tearing each other apart, and wonder if I should call the police. Miss de Jersey, they *hated* each other."

"Unfortunately, a lot of married people do. They stay married because they don't know what else to do, they don't believe in divorce or they can't afford two households. It isn't like the story-books. Once the guy puts the ring on your finger, you don't neces-sarily live happily ever after. For you never really know much about another person until you are married to him. And both of you have to work hard to make a marriage succeed. Living with another person can have its joys but it also can be very irritating."

"Do you think Sandy is right for Dad?"

I hesitated. It was the moment for complete candor. Anything else would be wrong. Heaven only knows Sandy adored him. She was loyal. Someone once said she would have gone out and mur-dered in cold blood if he had asked her to. There was no question of there ever having been an affair between them. For one thing, until recently, she had been anything but glamorous, twenty pounds overweight, with good features and nice skin, but looking much older because of her fat. For another, she was a Catholic and came from one of those close Irish families who cherish the virginities of their daughters, no matter of what age. Her devotion, dedication, to Arthur was obvious, in sharp contrast to the way Frances had treated him.

On the other hand, I had found her annoyingly possessive. There had been times—once, I remember, I was trying to deliver a really important message to him from Phyllis Diller, whom I'd met on his show—when I just couldn't get through. He never was available and didn't return my call. I was just about to decide I had done something to make him angry when, on impulse, I dialed his number around noontime and he answered the telephone him-self. He hadn't known I wanted to talk to him. After that, as a matter of policy, I had bypassed Sandy. If he happened to be out, too, I'd leave the message with the switchboard and he'd usually call back in person.

"At this point," I said carefully, "I suspect he needs someone whom he can trust completely. Who won't compete. That's Sandy."

"That's Sandy," he agreed. "She wants to stay home and make babies. She's a virgin, you know. Dad told me rather proudly. I don't think he's ever known many virgins."

"You're too young to be so cynical."

"I was just reporting facts." But he laughed, a good, deep, rumbling boy-laugh, genuine. I joined him. Without putting anything into words, it meant we liked each other. I said, "One of these days you'll be getting married yourself and be glad your old dad has somebody like Sandy taking care of him. You wouldn't want to be worrying about his being there alone."

"No, I suppose not." He sounded dubious. "I don't think I'll ever get married, though. Believe me, listening to Mother and Dad, I've had it. You are so right when you say it takes a lot of work to make a marriage even bearable. I've watched people. Even kids not much older than myself. When they get married, they get nasty. The girls whine and the fellows snarl and sleep around and—oh, hell."

"It will be different when you meet a girl you love."

"You sound like Mom. A mass of clichés. Nothing is ever wrong that a good cliché won't fix. She used to dither around about childhood being the happiest time of your life. She used to pretend those suicide attempts of mine were kiddie pranks. Honest. I took a whole bunch of pills belonging to some sick old guy who was staying overnight. When he found out, I'd already passed out and they hadn't missed me. But it was an accident. Such a little kid doesn't know what he is doing, was how they put it. The other time I thought I'd make sure. I hung myself in the attic. Dad heard the stool I was standing on go bump when I kicked it away and raced upstairs and cut me down. He knew sure as hell that was no accident. But they kidded me about it afterward like it was all a big joke."

"Are you sure you really wanted to die? Weren't you just asking them to notice you and love you more?"

He shook his head vigorously. "You're like all the rest. You think kids don't know what it's all about. I didn't want to live any more. I wanted to be dead, dead, dead."

"I'd like to do your natal chart sometime."

"Mary's already done it. She says I'm going to be a great artist."

"Has she studied astrology?"

He shrugged. "She reads a lot of books. I don't know. Would my suicide attempts show? She didn't see them."

"Probably, if you were serious. Many young people, even young children, get depressed and think they don't want to go on living. This doesn't mean they are going to kill themselves, unless a suicide attempt backfires. You can see whether a person is really seriously intent on suicide from a chart, usually. But remember, that doesn't mean he will succeed."

"Do you think only cowards commit suicide?"

"In my opinion, the answer lies in that pattern of life I was talking about. Some people have stronger patterns than others. It's the answer to why you have a person who had every reason to kill himself—he is dying of a disease for which there is no cure, he is in great pain, his family is running out of money so he can't have proper care—and still goes on, until he dies a natural death. Yet other people commit suicide with what to most of us seems no reason at all." A silence. A long silence. I turned and studied the boy. Finally I said, "If you like, I'll do your chart."

"No. It's all crazy. Besides, I don't want to know what is going to happen to me. What's the use? Let it be a surprise."

"Knowing the pattern helps you to cope better. If you understand that you are going to go through a difficult period, but it will end at a certain time, you can endure it. I once had a serious eye infection, so serious my doctors weren't sure I wouldn't lose my sight. I told them it would clear up at a certain time and it did. The knowledge helped me stand terrible pain and discomfort."

"But what if you see in the chart that it won't end? That you'll die?"

"Each one of us is going to die sometime. That is a part of the pattern, too. But when is seldom sharply indicated. All we can see are indications."

"And you tell the person so he can guard against them?"

"Sometimes. It depends if it will help."

"If you'd seen in my chart that I was going to make a suicide attempt when I was five, and another time, at ten, would you have told my parents to watch out?"

He was challenging me again. I said, "I would have told them you needed more attention and perhaps I could have pointed out periods of danger."

"I tried to hang myself the day Mom came home from the hospital with Dick. I hated the little bastard."

"Your father must have suspected it. He must have been concerned about you or he wouldn't have found you so fast in the attic."

"Maybe. I remember he made me promise not to mention it to Mom. Not that she would have cared. My brother Dick is the one who is going to make her proud, in her old age. He's a genius. He's going to be a writer. It isn't that I don't have talent, too. But I'm too lazy to work." He sounded proud, but I could see him watching me for the effect.

"I'm not surprised. When you want attention, instead of working at something which will make your parents proud of you, you hurt them and yourself by cracking up a car. Does that make sense?"

"You really think I'm no good, don't you?"

"I think you're right about being lazy. I'll have to see your chart before I can tell you anything else about yourself."

"My doctor is always kidding Mary because she reads our horoscopes in the paper every night. He says it's nonsense."

"That kind of thing usually is. It's an amusement, because the writer can only talk in broad generalities about a certain sun sign. I can't say, for example, that on a certain day all Leos will have trouble with Scorpios because it makes no more sense than saying on a certain day all blue-eyed people will have fights with brown-eyed people. I can tell you, however, that in a general way a Scorpio, like your father, will have ambitions and goals which appeal to someone who has Leo strongly in his chart—subject, of course, to all the other aspects."

"It sounds crazy."

"Unless you think about it. Our bodies are vast electromagnetic fields. Doesn't it make sense that, if many diseases, both physical and mental, are caused by chemical imbalance that our behavior can be influenced by the position of the stars when we catch our first breath and become part of the universe? A very famous biologist, Dr. George Wald of Harvard, once said, 'I tell my students, with a feeling of pride I hope they share, that the carbon, nitrogen and oxygen that make up 99 percent of me and you were cooked in the deep interiors of earlier generations of dying stars.' So why shouldn't we be affected by our relation to stars which now exist?"

"Why did Diana Barrymore kill herself?"

"I only saw her once. She wasn't really my client."

"You were on Dad's show one afternoon when some other guests never showed. You got on to suicide. You said you could see certain suicide portents in some charts. Dad asked you about Diana and you said yes, you had seen a bunch of stars, or something, which meant a bad time."

"I guess I did. I remember I told her if she stayed on the wagon through a certain period, things would clear up for her."

"And she didn't?"

"Perhaps she couldn't. It wasn't in her basic pattern. She really tried to destroy herself in many ways. I'm not convinced her end was really suicide. It might have merely been the result of many other attempts to hurt herself. Including sleeping pills and drinking sprees. And turning up drunk when she did get a good break in the theater."

"Tell me about her."

"I only saw her once. I don't remember anything else. Really."

"Don't be nervous, Miss de Jersey. I'm not going to kill myself. You aren't putting ideas in my mind. Mary says I'm going to be a famous artist. I have to stay alive to show my folks how wrong they are about me."

Just then, to my relief, there was a knock at the door and, immediately afterward, a bright-faced girl with a smooth head of dark hair under a ridiculous white ruffle which was a nurse's cap, came in with a wheel chair. She said, "I've just come on duty, Peter, and I noticed nobody had taken you down to therapy today. Were you a bad boy and refuse or did they just forget?"

Peter said, "Mary, this is Katherine de Jersey, a real flesh and blood astrologer. Miss de Jersey, this is Mary Bates."

Mary drew back. "Oh, my Lord, I've heard you talk, Miss de Jersey. I've longed to meet you but if I'm in the way—"

"Of course not. Come and sit down a minute and then I have to go and you can take Peter to therapy. He tells me you've done his horoscope."

Mary's pink face grew pinker. "Oh, my God. No. I just had a book and tried to work out something from it, the way I do for myself. I'd be ashamed to let you see it. Besides, nobody knows just exactly when he was born. Neither his mother nor his father can remember."

"Those things happen. That means we'd have to rectify his chart using events in his life. It's fairly complicated, even for professionals."

"I know. I feel embarrassed you know about my trying, even. It was just to amuse Peter, those first days when he was feeling lousy and had trouble sleeping." She looked at Peter and got pinker still. I thought, she is in love with him. But she's a nice girl and won't do anything about it. In a way, I was sorry. Because it was obvious she had so much love and sympathy to give, and Peter was in such need of it. However, it was none of my business. I said goodbye and left them together to settle the question of whether he was going down to therapy or not. My bets were on Mary.

As I entered the elevator, I had an odd feeling; the psychic side of me was flashing little red warning lights.

That night, by mistake, if anything is ever really by mistake, I took home Diana Barrymore's chart instead of that of another client who was going to call me next morning about a date for surgery. So I studied Diana's chart. Ralph teased me, saying he had heard that Toscanini always went to bed with a good musical score, instead of a book. But I begged him to let me keep the light on long enough to recheck something. I wanted to find out exactly what I had seen on a spring day in 1959, when I'd left Diana Barrymore's hotel room and gone down the corridor with the same odd feeling.

Diana's chart had been worrying me. I've seen worse, in my time. But in her natal horoscope I had noticed bad aspects, a gathering of planets which is called a stellium, opposite the eighth house, which is associated with death or regeneration or transition. Her eighth house was in the sign of Virgo, of which the ruler, or associated planet, is Mercury. Mercury was in the first house of self-expression, side by side with Uranus and the sun. Uranus often stands for something sudden and involuntary and the sun, of course, represents the life force. Saturn (the inevitable destiny) was beside Jupiter, which in this position indicates accident, something unforeseen. And, as the eighth house is almost opposite the first house, the various portents were, as we say in astrology, "opposed to each other."

To astrology students, I explain simply that you have to get opposite another person and look each other in the face for a real quarrel—or real communication of any kind. Under certain aspects, opposed planets mean marriage between opposite worlds. Sometimes it indicates trouble, direct confrontation. And the conjunction of planets indicates the extent of the problem.

No astrologer, no reputable astrologer, would ever say that any combination of signs means death, especially death by your own hand. Any astrologer who is a real professional feels very responsible toward a client and knows that he can either be helpful or very destructive. You have to know exactly what to say, how much, and how, no matter what you see in a chart. You also must put it in a way so that the client will respond positively, act on the suggestions, not wait for things to happen. Also, you have to be careful, if you mention negative trends (and I think you usually should), not to create an atmosphere where the client will dwell on them and, perhaps, exaggerate their significance. If there is one fault which is more common than any other among all clients, it's a tendency to dramatize the situations in which they find themselves, rather than try to improve them.

Certainly, the pattern in Diana Barrymore's life had been self-dramatization, rather than much effort toward correcting her flaws. In her progressed chart—that is one which looked into the future— her moon was moving into a critical period the last part of December 1959, and most of the next month January. But up near the end I could see daylight. So, in dealing with her, I concentrated on hinting at a bad period, but assuring her if she worked hard at it, better times were ahead. In other words, I had said to her—the words now came back to me vividly: "If you stay on the wagon through Christmas and New Year's and then through January, everything will be better. Your long period of frustration will be over."

At that point Ralph turned out the light.

No astrologer should take problems to bed. When you don't sleep, you are no good to the client you worry about, or anybody else, the next day. I have trained myself to clear my mind so I can fall asleep practically instantly. But once in a while I can't help waking up in the middle of the night and reliving something which has happened. In a curious way, this doesn't exhaust me. It's like watching a late, late movie and when it is all over and I see the end, and understand from a fresh point of view (because I'm learning every day) why it had to happen, I fall asleep promptly again.

That night, Diana came back to me as vividly as though I'd been watching her on television. I had heard from her in May of 1959.

I was still in my studio in the Italian Court Building. It was one of those days when the moon is parallel to Neptune, which means in my case, as I'm highly influenced by Neptune (I'm intuitive, an ad-libber, quick on the trigger when the aspects are good) that I was feeling indecisive, absent-minded, frustrated. Maggie had left for the day and after that everything seemed to fall apart. I lost charts, the telephone pestered me with wrong numbers. Even the evening ahead loomed as a problem. Ralph was out of town on business and I couldn't decide whether to stay at the studio and try to work, or go home and spend a lonely evening.

The telephone rang. My quick reaction was to let the answering service take care of this wrong number. But Neptune must have been bugging them, too. They didn't pick up the telephone so, to quiet it finally, I did. A familiar voice said, "I'm told I can't leave Chicago without seeing Katherine de Jersey."

The voice. Low, husky, a kind of whisky tenor, as our grand-mothers would put it. Diana Barrymore was appearing in Tennessee Williams' play *Suddenly Last Summer* in Chicago. I'd been wanting to see it, but Ralph had been tied up with a series of sales conferences. I said, "Where are you, Miss Barrymore?"

"At my hotel. We only have another week to go and the last week is always so hectic—could you see me now? I'll grab a cab and come right over."

Have you ever felt low one instant and fine the next? That's the moon moving ahead into better aspects. Suddenly, my sluggish depression vanished. I stopped being vague. "No, wait. I'll come to you. I need the exercise and to get away from the telephone. Let's say I'll be there in twenty minutes."

So I walked down toward the Blackstone Hotel in the dying sunshine of a warm afternoon, feeling pleased with life and looking forward to meeting Diana. I'd heard good things about her performance in *Suddenly Last Summer*. She was on the wagon, at long last. She was also in love again, this time with Tennessee Williams, not anyone's conception of Mr. Right in a matrimonial venture. He was a person as haunted and obsessed with loneliness as you could find; whatever Diana's problems, and I was sure they were many, I couldn't see them solved by an association with this troubled, albeit brilliant, man.

I announced myself from the desk and she told me to come up. When I got off the elevator, she was waiting for me. I'd never seen her in person and was startled to find out how tiny she was—dark, small-featured, with inprobable dyed hair. She was wearing pajamas of flaming cerise chiffon; I think we called them lounging pajamas in those days.

She told me—punctuating her simplest remark with four letter words and expressions so vulgar I should have been horrified but somehow wasn't: "I want you to level with me. None of that business of trips across the water. I've had that. And husbands, too. I want to know if I will ever find a man who will make me happy and if I'll ever be a great actress. If not, why should I bother going on living?"

Although she was just thirty-eight, she'd known death at close hand. Her father, John Barrymore, had, according to legend, drunk himself to death. Her mother, Michael Strange, the poet, had died of leukemia. A beloved stepbrother, a homosexual, had killed himself with sleeping pills, alcohol and pep pills; she had cradled him in her arms the night his lover had jumped from the top of a New York skyscraper. Recently, her third husband had died of a heart attack. If ever a woman was disaster-prone, it was Diana. Yet "they" said she had brought much of her trouble on herself—"they" being her best friends. Time and time again, she had ruined herself by getting drunk before important appearances. She had inherited money from many sources and run through it. Her taste in men was odd, to put it gently. She was never too much in love for a casual affair, a quick romp with a taxi driver or anyone else who crossed her path.

All of this she had reported in her biography three years back. Supposedly, it had been a purge and the turning over of a new leaf. But she was still plagued by fear of failure. She said to me, "I want something different from this man. I want friendship, companionship. I want him to write plays just for me, and to be brilliant in them."

Diana had been born on March 3, 1921, close to dawn, in New York. She had her sun in Pisces, joining Uranus in the first house, which means a rebel who insists on her own way, despite any odds. Her rising sign was six degrees in Aquarius. Aquarians tend to be rather detached in individual relationships, interested in the welfare of the world but not especially in people close to them; if you'll study young people who consider themselves part of this age of Aquarius, I think you will find this a fair description—they worry about the fate of the natives of Kenya but are casual, even carelessly cruel, with their contemporaries, their lovers, their parents.

Pisces people, unless they are altered by the influence of other strong planets, are sensitive, artistic, sometimes even in the genius category. But they are moody; and in low moments, no one can feel sorrier for himself than someone whose sun is in Pisces. Perversely, they will overextend themselves in all directions to help people, sometimes to the point of interfering. Then they will decide their efforts aren't appreciated and accuse the reluctant benefactors of all sorts of ingratitude. I've seen Pisceans go out of their way to alienate the people they love best in this way. Unfortunately, too, these people can carry this same attitude into love affairs and even casual sex.

A sun-in-Pisces may seem promiscuous; deep down underneath, it is an insecurity with sex which drives him or her from one bed to another. If you find Pisceans marrying several times, it is because they tend to make the same mistake over and over, they can't seem to learn through experience. In addition, Diana's six degrees in Aquarius indicated sex problems. A person in this degree seeks different bed partners because only novelty can arouse. In the old days, we called this promiscuity. Now we realize it is usually the insecure nature which demands variety, fresh excitement, constant stimulation.

In addition, the planet Mars, which symbolizes sex, was in Aries, a somewhat masculine sign, side by side with Venus. Poor Diana, quick to respond to sex, aggressive in her choice of partners, was doomed to the chase. I feared she never would be able to form a lasting relationship of any kind and in her search for thrills might turn to sadism and masochism; whether she had arrived yet at this point physically, I didn't know. A few nights later, when Ralph and I attended the play as her guests, and went backstage to thank her afterward, we heard her laughing cruelly at one of the young men in the cast. When she had finished and he had slunk away, she actually seemed happy, pleased with herself.

From the standpoint of environment and heredity, Diana had been badly used. Her father had been a lover and a drunk; her mother an egocentric poet given to dressing in mannish clothes. She had been indulged, neglected, and ignored. Yet, given a different astrological pattern, she might have survived. For it was all there. Her moon 2½ degrees in Capricorn, indicated rejection by both parents, abandonment in both senses of the word, loneliness and aloneness.

Comparing charts of people who are related, or who want to be, is one of the most fascinating aspects of astrology. It's like sitting down with a real life mystery story. In some ways Tennessee Williams, who has been called the lonely man of the American theater, was not ill-matched with Diana. His moon was in Pisces on her sun. Under ordinary circumstances, this isn't an ideal arrangement. It is more apt to work out if the woman's moon (the moon, being feminine, is the reflector) is on the man's sun. But this relation is not unique in many love affairs. And his ascendant, Aquarius, was the same as hers; his preoccupation with the underdog, the rejected, matched hers.

They both had Uranus in the first house of self-expression, which means neither of them were conformists. He had Mars, sex, in the twelfth house of secrets, joining Venus. Both planets were in Cancer, a sensitive, rather feminine sign. His sun was on the cusp of Pisces, her sun sign.

"There can be a good relationship here," I said, "if you don't demand too much."

"What do you mean too much?" She was on the defensive, fast. I tried to explain what I meant. His success was all over the chart: Jupiter in the first house, Mercury in the second house (money and writing). Even Venus not too well aspected in the twelfth house, which was under the sign of Cancer, was a benefit; it showed his ability as a writer to deal with all kinds of sex, including morbid sex. In her horoscope, however, I could see nothing more than talent, and rather moderate talent—plus sexual aggressiveness, her acute self-pity. Of course, despite her demand for frankness, I tried to soften my description of these aspects. Instead of saying, "It won't work," I tried to tell her, "Keep him as a good friend. Enjoy him. Take what is there. But don't push him into a corner."

She was barefoot. The angrier she became with me, the more rapidly she paced the floor. I said, "There's an astrological axiom. You cannot put into a chart what isn't there. Nor can you remove something you see."

She stopped, her back to me. "Am I ever going to be a great actress?"

I stared at the badly aspected planets clustered in her first house. Yet there was that break, around the end of January. And the eighth house, which stands for death, can also mean regeneration. I used to tell astrology students the story of a dancer, an amateur astrologer, who saw her own death in the chart. She prepared for it, transferring all her property to her son, in his early twenties. On the night of the full moon, which she expected to trigger her own death, her son was killed in an accident. What she had seen in her own chart was the spiritual regeneration she would go through in seeking help after the death of her son.

I wanted to give Diana something positive. So I delivered that message: "If you stay on the wagon through Christmas and January, your period of frustration will be over."

Of course she didn't. Her play closed in Chicago, she went back to New York. Casting around for something else to do, she became restless. A close friend, a Sagittarius who, like many of that sun sign, tended to be a bit of a hero-worshiper, trailed Diana around trying to keep her off liquor. On Christmas Eve, he wrote me, she embarked on a gigantic bender. From that time she went downhill. On January 25, she was found dead. Presumably this was the release from frustrations I'd seen in the chart.

The next morning, I wakened, determined to try to do something about Peter N. All the way driving down in the car I turned over different approaches: to Peter, to his father, even his mother. And then, as often happens, the solution was waiting for me. Maggie's first words were, "Your ten o'clock appointment canceled. Flu. So I put in Arthur N. He phoned asking when you could possibly fit him in as a client. Wasn't that luck?"

It was more than luck. A famous New York physician, Dr. Virgil Damon, once wrote that whenever he needed the help of some expert badly enough, he would turn the corner in the hospital, and there was the man or woman he wanted. I believe this happens, so long as your demands aren't selfish. At any rate, at ten o'clock on the dot, Arthur N. announced himself from downstairs. His first words as he came in the door were, "I want to talk to you about Peter."

"I'm glad," I said. "I like the boy. And you have no reason to be concerned about the little nurse, Mary. He isn't in love with her. He was just teasing his mother. I don't know what Mary feels about him but she won't be any problem. Primarily she feels sorry for him."

"Sorry!" He banged his fist on my desk, hard. "What in hell is wrong with everyone? I've reached the limit of my patience. Everybody feels sorry for poor Peter. He cracked up a new Jag I gave him for Christmas. He is rude to his mother and Sandy. Last night he told me he's decided to drop out of school and become an artist. He wants to go to New York and live in a loft. I said if he wanted to paint, he could paint right here in Chicago, where there are plenty of good teachers. He said he didn't plan to paint right away. He wanted to meditate. Meditate!"

"Arthur, take off your coat. And don't go on like that or you'll have a heart attack. I think I understand now what is happening between you and Peter. Would you let me explain it astrologically?"

He looked at me. "God damn it, Katie, don't treat me like a child. I am older than you and I know damned well what is wrong between my son and me. I have spoiled him rotten. I know you're going to bleat about the poor little rich boy who was given a Jag and no love. Katie, I love that boy and I've gone out of my way to prove it. Ever since the divorce, I've spent 80 percent of my free time with him. And don't ask me what I did with the other 20 percent because I'm human and I'm a man."

"If he wants to go to New York to see if he can paint, why don't you let him?"

"Katie." He pulled off his coat roughly and threw it across the room. Maggie tiptoed in, picked it up and escaped. Arthur had a formidable temper. Angered, he forgot he wasn't still the network big shot who could pick up a telephone and have almost anybody fired. "I have knocked myself out for that kid. So has Frances, oddly enough. She has custody legally, but she hasn't peeped when he decided he wanted to spend more time with me. I know, I still give her the dough for child support. Just the same, she could have raised hell and she didn't. And Sandy has been an angel. Nothing less. What he needs right now is a good hard shove. And I'm the one who is going to deliver. Either he does what I say or he never gets another dime from me. Ever. Now don't argue with me."

"I wouldn't dream of it. What else did you want to say?"

After a minute, the infectious grin which once had grandmothers—and plenty of other much younger ladies—drooling over him, spread slowly across his face. "OK, I'll come off the boil. It isn't your fault Frances and I produced a monster. And I thank you for going to see him yesterday. He enjoyed the visit."

"He isn't a monster. He's a Leo, a young lion. He needs special treatment. He can't take your sarcasm; it hurts him. He feels rejected by his mother, mostly because of Dick. So he behaves badly. I think the divorce hurt him more than you and Frances will ever know."

"Katie, I am fond of you. But you are talking nonsense. I know how to handle my own son and the time has come for me to assert myself. And don't you try to butt in."

"If you aren't here to talk about Peter, what do you want? I had half-hoped you'd let me do his horoscope in relation to yours. It might help both of you."

"If you don't mind, let's wait until he becomes a second Picasso, the way that little nurse of his promises. Sandy and I are going to be married very soon. We drove all the way up to the hospital last night in that lousy weather to tell Peter. All he did was talk about living in a loft and being an artist. I wanted to hit him, broken leg and all."

"He's afraid of losing you."

"Katie, stop it. We made it perfectly clear he is welcome in our home at any time. Sandy is fixing up a room for him. Whenever he comes to visit, he can go in there and shut the door and it's his castle."

"The word which bothers me is 'visit'."

"What? Well, his mother does have custody. But the room is his if he decides to live with us. Then he goes off on the loft business."

"Can he draw?"

"The kid's always had talent. But he sits on his can and listens to records. I think I could forgive him if he even cracked a book once in a while, or played good music. His stuff is all by groups with names like Cow Tit who have no discipline. Katie, maybe I'm square but I'm not musically illiterate. Some of these rock groups aren't so bad and I'm all for them. Others are nothing but noise. The problem is, he doesn't know the difference and he acts superior if I complain because I do. Now stop laughing at me."

I said I wasn't, really. "But you're a sophisticated man. And right now you sound like all the suburban mothers. Tell me about Sandy. How does she feel about being married outside the Church?"

He smiled. "She's a good kid. Her family isn't too happy, naturally, but Sandy agrees it would not only be damned expensive

but hypocritical for me to try to get my marriage to Frances an-
nulled, even if I could. Besides, I'm not getting any younger. I
don't want to wait months, maybe years. We'll just have a few people, and the immediate family, at some hotel and a judge I know
will say a few words. Quick and easy. You'll come, won't you?"

I thanked him, adding, "I'd like to help to pick the date by
astrology, if you'd like me to. I'll compare your birth dates and
then call Sandy. All right?"

He seemed pleased. I already had his—October 23, at 5 P.M., in
New York. He was nearly fifty years old and Sandy was thirty-six,
some difference but not too great. She'd been born in Brooklyn on
March 26, what hour nobody was quite sure, as she was one of
eight children, but I had known Sandy over the years and I was able
to make an educated guess about her moon and rising sign.

Her sun was in Aries, not surprisingly. Time and time again, a
man choses women in the same astrological sign. But there was a
vast difference between Frances and Sandy. Frances was a double
Aries, very strong and determined to take the lead even in matters
of sex. Sandy had Scorpio as her rising sign and her moon in
Capricorn.

I said, "She'll be a lot more of a wife than Frances, I can promise
you. She has that Capricorn stability. Capricorns want marriage to
succeed; they dislike divorce intensely. So her Aries ambition will
be directed toward helping you. Frances had to resent your career
because she didn't have one of her own. And Sandy's Scorpio ascendant is on your sun. Very good, in all."

Immediately, he relaxed. Arthur was a complicated man. Along
with his sun in Scorpio—which means ambition, strong ego—he has
the moon in Virgo and Saturn was 30 degrees in Cancer. All of
this added up to a keen, quick mind, the tongue often too sharp
and sarcastic, and enormous pride. Although he hid his feelings in
Scorpio manner, that pride had been badly battered when he lost
his network show. I had only known him casually in those days,
and Frances not at all then, but it was possible he had taken some
of his hurt out on his wife and children. Certainly, I had heard him
be cruel, if amusingly cruel, on the air. Once he had virtually de-
molished a poor old comedian who, in his fright, had tried to
upstage the master. I could imagine his caustic teasing of Frances,
when she tried to revive her singing career. I could also imagine
his retelling of Peter's suicide attempts, with comedy angles.

In the past, I had tried to point out to him that there are two sides to every story, just as there are two sides to a coin, and he couldn't always be right. He didn't like to even sniff failure and, since he had Taurus as a rising sign, he could be unbelievably stubborn about facing up to reality.

With anyone who has his sun or rising sign in Taurus, the bull, you have to be even more tactful than usual. Taurus people are often so charming and attractive and seemingly without quirks you forget how they resist pushing, like the bull. You can lead them, you can entice them into doing almost anything you want. But you cannot push, and you regret it if you try. Taurus people also tend to resist change. Once the mind is made up, you're stuck. I have a charming Taurus client who is beloved in her neighborhood because she mothers everyone and everything: children, puppies, old ladies, invalids, priests, rabbis, ministers, birds, cats, even rabbits. No one guesses how set she is in certain ways, because she is always darling, always ready to do anything for you. But recently her oldest daughter told me that Mother has never allowed any of her children to wear yellow because it was her unlucky color. When her daughter's fiancé turned up wearing a yellow shirt to ask for her hand, my friend considered it a personal insult.

So I couldn't tell Arthur that, as I saw it, his life with Sandy wasn't going to be unadulterated bliss. But, because he had come to talk about his future marriage—without really coming out and saying he had vague doubts—I had to approach the subject from out in left field. Sandy's moon was 13 degrees in Capricorn in the third house, which is the mind, the environment. So, in her own way, she was going to be extremely conventional and stubborn once she had his name and was Mrs. Arthur N. instead of Sandy, the good-natured, loyal secretary. She would still be loyal, of course, but her innate inflexibility would inevitably begin to show. It wasn't for nothing that she was a virgin still at thirty-six; at heart she was an extremely rigid and conventional person, fearful of scandal and of offending her parents' standards. And, as that particular degree in Capricorn indicated, she was capable of attaining almost any goal if she set her mind to it. No one would have ever guessed that fat Sandy would ever marry Arthur, back in the New York network days. But she had bided her time and accomplished a miracle.

Of course, the easygoing Sandy of those days had been a façade. Probably long before anybody else, she had recognized how essentially weak the marriage of Frances and Arthur really was. So she had made herself a family friend, good old Sandy who kept candy in the desk for the children and would baby-sit in an emergency. Arthur had always been surrounded by girls on the show; babes, chicks. Sandy had outsmarted them all. At the propitious moment, she had gone to health and exercise classes, shed those extra twenty pounds like an old coat and emerged as a desirable woman. She was even aware of Arthur's weaknesses. Being a true Scorpio so far as women were concerned, he never thought of marrying any of the women he had romanced while he was married. He wanted someone new and fresh. Sandy was so fresh she was even a virgin.

I said cautiously, "Not that Sandy is a cipher. She's a very strong woman. She has a mind of her own, you know."

Arthur beamed. "She's nuts about children. Really, she's more like a sister to Peter, but she would love to have Dick with us, too. You know how close Dick and Frances are, but I bet Sandy could break him down."

I wanted to say, "Amen." Of course I didn't. Arthur would soon find out for himself about the iron fist in Sandy's white glove. Maybe he would even like it. I didn't know. So far, he only knew how efficient she was in the office. He wasn't even aware, because the office was run for his convenience, how jealous she was of her power. My experience in having difficulty reaching him was a minor example, but significant. I'd heard that in the old days, the quick way to Arthur was to keep high in Sandy's good graces.

Arthur said, "It's going to be great to be able to have somebody really wanting to take care of me. Frances always acted as though it was unreasonable of me to expect her to take care of my laundry or send my suits out to be cleaned or pressed. As for entertaining, forget it. Even if I told her I wanted to have a few friends in on a certain date, I never knew what I'd come home to. Sometimes it was great and everybody said what a lucky guy I was to have such a fascinating wife and hostess. Other times there would be nothing to eat or drink and the place would look like a pigsty. Once I got home and she wasn't even there—and she'd never told the maid I'd invited fifteen people for cocktails."

"Sandy will always be there," I said. Which was true. Yet there was something in their charts which gave me pause. Her Saturn, which ruled the house of marriage and marriage partners, was right on Mars, in his chart—"in conjunction" in other words. This isn't a good aspect. Although it explains a strong attraction before marriage, it means trouble afterward, often in sex relations. It would be irresponsible not to hint at this. Yet I knew he wouldn't listen if I were too blunt. So I went on, carefully watching his reaction, "Sandy will be fine as a hostess and she already knows how to take care of you in many ways. But, since we are both adults, let's admit more marriages break up in the bedroom than any place else."

Abruptly, the sunny Arthur vanished. "I'm not sure what you're driving at, Katie."

I took the plunge. "I'm concerned about your sex life with her."

"That isn't your business, is it?"

"You came to consult me for some reason. You don't want to talk about Peter. Won't you let me tell you what I see in comparing your chart with Sandy's?"

A typical Arthur grunt. I took it for consent. "She is an Aries but she has Scorpio rising. I'm not sure in exactly what degree yet—I am still rectifying her chart for the precise moment of birth. Scorpios have the reputation of being extremely interested in sex. Some of them, however, fear and reject it. I've had a number of Scorpio priests and I am convinced that several have welcomed the celibacy vow. As a good Catholic, I am sure she wouldn't consider going to bed with anyone except her future husband. But as you are going to be married soon and are both mature people—wouldn't it be better if you are sure everything is good before you take what for her will be an irrevocable step? Even if she isn't married in the Church, the idea of divorce is repulsive to her; it's there in her chart."

"You have nothing to worry about." His voice was firm.

"I'm glad. I see these damned aspects and I have to mention them. You've had one bad marriage and I'd like this one to be great."

"It will be. But just for your own information, Katie, Sandy prefers to be a virgin on her wedding night. That's OK by me. In fact, after spending most of my life in a profession where the girls all have round heels, it's refreshing. For once, I know exactly where I stand." He stood up and looked around for his coat.

Maggie obliged. I shook hands with him instead of exchanging the usual show-business kiss. When the door closed, Maggie looked at me speculatively. "The great man was annoyed."

"He's marrying Sandy any day now. I offered to pick a date by astrology. But when I compared their charts, I found her Saturn joins his Mars."

"So you said it wouldn't work out?"

"Not in so many words. I did ask about their sexual rapport and was told to go stand in a corner and wash my mouth out with soap. He's a Scorpio and she has Scorpio rising. If either of them were younger, there might be a chance of success. But he's going to use tricks instead of tenderness to rouse her and she's never going to be able to tell him it doesn't work. In a year, maybe two—"

"She'll leave him?"

"No. Never. It will go on looking like a perfect marriage from outside. She'll do all the wifely things except gratify him in bed. He may start wandering again but he'll never divorce her, he's too old. And she won't want the world to know the marriage is a flop. I just wish Peter had courage enough to clear out and live in a loft, away from the whole bunch."

Maggie groaned ostentatiously. "So you're back on the youth kick again. Next thing I know you'll be offering to support him."

And I had to face the fact Maggie was probably right about me and Peter. I had seen him only once but already I was more involved than I'd ever been with his father. So I said, "Let's forget Peter." And didn't quite mean it. Fortunately, the telephone rang just then to announce my next client was downstairs.

I was getting ready to leave the office when Sandy called. She was jolly as always, her professional telephone manner. She thanked me for going to see Peter. She had been interested, she claimed, in my comparison of her chart with Arthur's. Then, her voice chilling rapidly, she said, "Arthur told me you'd like to select a proper time for the wedding, by the stars. Actually, if you don't mind, I would prefer to pick my own wedding date. It's bad enough for me, a Catholic, not to be married properly in a church and my parents would think I was really around the bend if I juggled the time according to astral portents. Flipped my wig, as Peter might say."

I said I understood completely before she had a chance to disinvite me to the wedding. I had no intention of going now, anyway; I was sure I would be an embarrassment, if her family found out my profession. Besides, I should have realized this would happen. For in her chart, Saturn opposed Mars in the houses of self-expression and marriage. Sandy had always been interested in people for what they could do for her and this marriage was for position, not love. Poor Sandy, I thought, she'll never know what she is missing. Bad as Arthur's marriage to Frances was, at least there had been love and good sex part of the time.

Since everything was clear now between Sandy and me, I had no hesitation about letting Maggie send Arthur a bill. Ordinarily, I would have skipped it. My visit to Peter had been something I had done for a friend and our session this morning had really added up to very little. But from now on, I wanted Sandy to know whatever contact I had with her or Arthur would be on a professional basis. And I dashed off a note, all flags flying, which I wanted included with the bill:

Just one suggestion, which I hope you won't mind. I haven't done your son's chart and he doesn't seem eager to have a horoscope. I suspect he is a little afraid. However, for the sake of your marriage—and for the sake of Peter, too—I wish you would let him try living away from home, on his own. I think he could make it, if he wasn't always in your shadow, fearing he would seem ridiculous. And it just isn't good for honeymooners to have a third person around. Think about it.

When I signed the note after Maggie had typed it, I told her not to bother keeping Arthur N.'s folder. My secretary, however, knows me better than I know myself. A week later, I came in to find a clipping on my desk from one of the gossip columns, describing the marriage of Arthur N. and "Sandy Rolfe, his elf-faced secretary." The wedding, held in a penthouse at the Ambassador East Hotel, had been a bang-up occasion, with celebrities awash. I wondered if Peter had enjoyed it.

I was about to toss the clipping in my wastebasket when Maggie removed it from my hand. "Arthur's file," she reminded me.

"I told you not to keep one on him."

Maggie shook her head. "You never know. I put everything under 'J,' in case you're searching for it when I'm not here." I stared at her. "J," she said, "for 'Just in Case.'"

Of course it is a small world, as we all know. My path didn't cross with Arthur and Sandy, in what presumably was their gay social whirl after marriage. But I did run into Frances N. one evening in early September. She was a member of a small club in Chicago which has its headquarters in a near North Side discothèque. About once a year, I lecture there, discussing the various zodiac signs. Afterward, as door prizes, I do mini-horoscopes. Since many of the same people attend year after year, I find the tenor of my lecture growing more serious, and some of the questions I am asked are very knowledgeable, indeed.

I didn't see Frances N. in the audience. In fact, I had forgotten she was a member. About three years ago, when she was on the entertainment committee, I'd had the feeling the door prizes hadn't been selected just by chance, for all her pals happened to win. However, when I found she had declared herself in on the group, I couldn't help suggesting perhaps it would be more tactful if she disqualified herself and let someone else be a winner. She flew into such a temper I promptly told her to forget it. But I did make her wait until the end, although she complained bitterly. Afterward, I heard she had been reprimanded. And I hadn't seen her at a meeting since.

Now, however, here she was, wearing a silver-gray wig which changed her remarkably. She was still an arresting woman, although everything about her was underplayed, in comparison with the old Frances. Her dress was dark, and simple. Her jewelry was modest. Her make-up had been applied deftly.

She had waited patiently until I had finished the last mini-horoscope. Then she asked, with unexpected humility, "Would you have time for a cup of coffee? I have rather a favor to ask of you, an odd favor. You don't have to say yes but I think you might be interested in my reasons for asking it."

Ralph was waiting at the Pump Room for me, and we were going out for a late supper. However, I was intrigued. I hurried through my farewells and joined her in the dining room.

"Of course you think I am a bitch," she said.

I looked at her in astonishment. Frankly, I had never been that concerned about her. Arthur had complained, yes. And Peter, come to think about it. And there had been the incident of the door prize. But I've long since learned people are seldom what they seem, on chance acquaintance. And Frances was a double Aries. It is hard for a woman, in this world, to be so fiercely ambitious. No matter how much she achieves, it is never enough. If she doesn't marry and devotes herself to a career, she inevitably suffers because she seldom gets the top job. Usually she does the work and a man, a figurehead, gets the credit. On the other hand, if she chooses to marry and tries to gratify her ambition through a man, she invariably suffers from jealousy of his freedom and his power.

Suddenly, she smiled, and I caught a glimpse of the swashbuckling devil which had fascinated, and infuriated, Arthur. And had held on to him, long after he knew their marriage was doomed. "Of course I've played around. And got away with it, which most women can't endure. But I have my excuse. I have my moon in Sagittarius. I can't be tied down."

"I never thought Arthur tried very hard."

She made a face. "You do think I'm a bitch. All women do. I don't mind."

"Your moon in Sagittarius doesn't make you a bitch. It only means you are an idealist. You're looking for something you will probably never find."

"Don't be silly. I've found it. I'm getting married tomorrow. He's an American businessman living in Brazil. But I'm not keeping you here to talk about myself. I know how much Arthur admires you. He's always quoting you, chapter and verse. You once told him something I'll never forget. He and I always had great sex after a quarrel because Scorpio in my chart squared his Saturn. I have no idea what it means but I always remembered because it sounded cute."

I shook my head. One of the discouraging things which happens to an astrologer is that, by the time your words get quoted back to you, they are so frequently distorted. This is why, unlike some astrologers who don't even want their clients to take notes, I encourage mine to bring tape recorders so they have an exact record of everything I've said. I had once told Arthur, in those "cooling down" conversations we often had after an exciting show, that there was a 90-degree angle between Mars in Scorpio in her chart and Saturn in his, a "square," as it were. This explains why they sparked each other but at the same time, quarreled. This sort of astral aspect isn't bad in a business arrangement, when you can separate and go home and forget the problems of the day, or put them in perspective. But when it occurs in the charts of married people, it always makes for quarrels—and, of course, charming reconciliations. After a while, however, the charm of the reconciliations wears thin. That's when the marriage breaks up.

"Arthur and I talked about a lot of things, back in the days when I was on his show often," I said. "But I don't remember discussing your sex life."

"Oh, Katie! Arthur discussed our sex life with everyone. Then he used to come home and tell me what people said. It was one of his pet parlor games."

Thinking back, I wondered exactly what, if anything, he had told her about a conversation with me that had stayed in my mind, mostly because in it he had said things I wish I didn't know. I hadn't been able to stop him. He'd been in one of his black moods during the show. Sometimes this made for much better entertainment than usual, because he made you mad and you lashed back at him. That afternoon, however, he had been glum, rather than sarcastic. I'd carried more than the usual load, with him sitting beside me, sneering. And I'd been annoyed. When we got down to his office afterward, I told him I wasn't going to continue as a guest on his program unless he was willing to do his part.

"More than your part," I had added. "After all, you get paid and I don't."

He'd gone to his metal file cabinet and brought out a bottle of whisky. Usually he drank very little, but he made two very strong drinks and pushed one toward me. "I'm through with Frances," he said. "I'm getting a divorce."

In the past, he had tried to tell me about her affairs with men. I had always stopped him. For one thing, I never was sure he was telling the truth; he might have been inventing them to explain why he had so many girls, why he traveled flagrantly with the singers on his show. In addition, this kind of conversation neither interests or shocks me. It is merely boring.

Yet that night, he had blurted out one thing which had shocked me. Frances had used Peter to make him jealous, sexually jealous. She would call the boy into their bedroom, and in front of Arthur, have him unzip her dress or unfasten the hooks on her brassiere.

"She's been doing it since he was a little kid. One night, when Peter was about eleven or twelve, I stopped her. I took a swing at them both."

I shuddered. "Why didn't you stop it before?"

"I don't know." He drank almost his whole glass in one swallow and poured himself another. I hadn't touched mine. After what he told me, I couldn't. It would have gagged me. "Maybe I liked it. How should I know?"

"Didn't you ever wonder what it did to the boy?"

"No. I figured it was her business and I still do."

If she had come to talk about that, I was going to run. Fast. But apparently Frances had other things on her mind and was in a bit of a hurry, too. She put out her cigarette as soon as the coffee arrived and asked for the bill. When the waiter was out of hearing, she said, "I'm taking Dick with me to Brazil. My future husband has three daughters from a previous marriage who'll be with us in summer which, of course, is winter down there. I figure he owes me Dick. I'd take Peter, too, if he'd come. But he won't even talk to me on the telephone."

"Why not?"

"He's furious. I had that little nurse in the hospital transferred to another floor. With cause, believe me. She was drooling all over him, coming in to visit him on her days off. Disgusting."

"I thought she was a rather nice girl." I kept my tone mild.

"You would. You're not his mother. Anyway, he's living with his father and Sandy. What feeling he had left for me has been stamped on in that sticky home atmosphere. I suppose I shouldn't care. I have Dick, who is everything a mother dreamed of. But just the same—"

I looked at her. To my amazement, she was dabbing roughly at her eyes with the napkin. "Don't laugh. I know I wasn't a howling success as a mother. But you must remember Peter was always a bone of contention between me and Arthur. Arthur made me quit work when I was pregnant with Peter. Afterward, I wondered if that was why he made me get pregnant. He didn't want me working. He wanted me there, a little housewife, while he played around with everything in skirts. I got a maid who was willing to take care of Peter and was offered a spot on another network. Arthur wouldn't let me take it. I'm sure he talked to my agent and saw to it I never got another chance. In those days, he could do almost anything, you know. I always felt he ruined me. He told me he was ashamed to have me singing professionally, his wife. I think he poisoned Peter against me, too. They were always doing things together, man to man. And Sandy, now I come to think about it. She was always hovering in the background, waving diapers."

There are, of course, always two sides to every story. Just the same, she perplexed me. "Are you sure you wanted Peter?"

"What do you take me for? An unnatural mother? Here I am, spending my wedding eve chasing around trying to get someone to help Peter, when I could be in bed catching up on my beauty sleep. Or out with an old beau, being toasted in champagne. Don't think I didn't have the chance."

"I believe you." I put down my cup. The answer was easy: she wanted someone to be responsible for Peter. I was a little shaken. She was shockingly sure of herself and, incidentally, of me. She had either sensed my weakness for young people—which I doubted because in my book she wasn't a very perceptive person—or Peter had talked to her about me. My heart sank. Here I was, vulnerable again. "But how do you imagine I can help Peter?"

"I'm not sure myself. But he needs someone to keep an eye on him, besides Daddy and the new bride. I know I haven't seen him much recently. But when he was in the hospital, I went down every day. We started to communicate. And even afterward, he knew I was always there if he needed help. I don't trust Sandy and Arthur is jelly in her hands."

"Arthur and I don't see much of each other any more. I'm not sure he would welcome my keeping an eye on Peter. Since Sandy—"

"Oh, everybody knows what Sandy is like. Maybe by this time, even Arthur. Peter is seventeen, so old I don't have much say about him. But I do about Dick. Sandy tried to get Arthur to take Dick away from me, when she found out I was getting married. She wanted to send him to an aunt of hers, on a farm in Kansas, the good life, she said. Actually, what she wanted was to get Dick so Arthur wouldn't have to pay me for his support. Thank God I took a hunk of money in a lump sum instead of alimony. Otherwise she'd be in there circling like a vulture trying to extract her pound of flesh."

"I still don't see what I can do about Peter."

She wiped her hands on the napkin. "Neither do I, not right now. He's a strange kid. He hasn't any friends. He never seemed interested in girls, until this little chippie turned up at the hospital. Ten years older than Peter, at least. It was disgusting."

"He liked her. I think he was just trying to get your attention, pretending it was anything more."

"Well, I fixed her wagon. Now, listen, Katie. I just want you to hang in, in case he needs you. I tried to talk to Arthur. But he's no use at all in a crisis. He runs and buries his head in the sand and quivers."

"Is there a crisis?"

"Of course not. I wouldn't dream of leaving Peter if there were. It's just—I guess I'm a sentimental woman. I can't leave without having somebody I can trust." Her hand flew up. The waiter came promptly. She looked at the check, left five dollars, and stood up. "Now that Sandy is pregnant, it might make a lot of difference. She's going to be willing to take her clammy hands off Peter, once she has a kid of her own. Meanwhile, she is just holding on to him for marriage insurance. Don't look so surprised. I know that dame."

I followed her out of the dining room. At the cloakroom, I asked, "When was Peter born?"

"August 1, 1946. Right after the war. Impossible as it seems, he turned seventeen this August. We were all having babies, then, like crazy. It was the reaction from fighting and killing, maybe. Arthur wasn't in the Army but he made a lot of trips overseas entertaining, so he considered himself part of the effort. And then it looked good to all those little goons who were his audience for him to have a baby right at that time. It made him one of the common people. And, believe me, I had that kid like one of the common people. There were so many of us producing that we delivered like an assembly line up at Columbia-Presbyterian."

"What time was he born?"

"Honey, I don't know. I was drugged to the eyeballs. All I remember is that I took a taxi to the hospital sometime in the evening, all alone. Arthur was busy doing a show, naturally. The next noon, he told me we had a boy. He woke me up and made me put my hands on my belly. I had no memory of anything. Then I went back to sleep again. That's all I know. Ask Arthur. He might have more of the details. Although I don't think he bothered to ask questions, either. After he found out the kid didn't have two heads."

We walked out together. She apparently had nothing more to say to me. She was off in another world. But when she had one foot in the cab, she seemed to remember I was there, and half-turned. "Don't worry about it. But if Peter gets in trouble, he might call you."

"Why me?"

"He liked you. And he just doesn't have friends. I guess he could find you in the telephone book, couldn't he?"

Then she was gone. Leaving me Peter. Maggie had been right, filing Arthur's chart under J for "Just in Case." Only I didn't want Peter. I didn't want the responsibility. It wasn't fair. And, besides, as I hurried down the block to the Ambassador East, I had that peculiar feeling again. I was ashamed to tell Ralph and Maggie what had happened. I kept it all to myself.

And then, one Saturday afternoon when Ralph and I were sitting at home, doing nothing and loving it, I switched on Arthur's four o'clock show. He looked awful, tired and beaten. Usually, no matter how exhausted he was, even when he had gone without sleep, he would pull himself together for the show so that he looked okay. My instinct was to call him. Then I remembered Sandy, and didn't.

But a few days later, when I was sitting in the Cleveland Airport waiting for a plane which had "in-flight difficulties"—which means, in case you haven't been through it yourself, that it never arrived— I put aside the paperback I'd bought for the ride and began to toy with Peter N.'s chart. Usually, when I know as much about a client as I did about Peter, I have no difficulty arriving at what seems an approximate birth hour. But somehow, nothing came out even reasonably right, which exasperated me further. Finally, I put my figures away. They lay in my green alligator travel bag for a week, then two. One morning I woke up with a sense of urgency. I put the beginnings of Peter's chart in my purse and decided the time had come for action.

One person might help me. All the way in from La Grange, I tried to remember her name. Mary was easy. The last part was harder to come by, but suddenly it was there, in a flash. I opened my studio door and said to Maggie, by way of greeting, "There's a nurse at the Evanston Hospital, or used to be, by the name of Mary Bates. See if you can find her."

"Mine not to reason why," Maggie said pertly. But she knew why and must have recognized the urgency in my voice, for I heard her working away at the search when my first client arrived. And at noon, when I took a break, she came in with Mary's telephone number clipped to Arthur N.'s slim file.

"She'll be at her residence club any time after five o'clock and stay there until she hears from you. She began to cry when she found out you wanted to reach her. She said it was like an answer to a prayer. Now tell me, why are you getting a head of steam up about Peter all of a sudden?"

"It isn't sudden. It's—is Mary still at Evanston?"

"She switched to Presbyterian. It seems that Frances N. complained about her and Peter. The supervisor took it with a grain of salt, but Mary decided she wanted to be in Chicago, anyway. To be near Peter, do you think?"

"I suppose so."

"But you take a dim view of that combination. Is that right?"

"Not exactly. I just don't want to see her hurt. And, no matter what happens, I'm afraid that's inevitable."

My last client left at 6:15. The door hadn't quite closed when I reached for the telephone number clipped to Arthur N.'s folder. And Mary Bates must have been standing by the telephone, for she answered on the first ring.

"Miss de Jersey, your call seemed like fate. I'm worried about Peter. I haven't seen him for two weeks. I don't like to call the house because his stepmother always answers, so I had a friend, another nurse, telephone and ask for him. Mrs. N. said he had moved but, as he didn't have a telephone, she would deliver the message. Peter hasn't tried to reach my friend. I don't know whether he even got the message."

"Probably not," I said, remembering my experience with Sandy. "Do you think he's gone to New York?"

"No. He simply doesn't have the money. Anyway, he's decided to give up art. For a while he thought he would like to be a photographer, and I will say that his father bought him an expensive camera and a lot of darkroom equipment. I fixed it so Peter could go out on the ambulance one night and take pictures. But Sandy complained about his using the guest bathroom, stinking it up with developing liquid and the like, so he stopped taking pictures. The last time I saw him he said he'd decided to be a perpetual dropout. Of course, he's only eighteen."

"Then he isn't going to college?"

"He may never graduate from high school. He missed the last semester because of his accident. It makes me sick to see anybody with his brain just throw himself away. His father told him he'd pay his tuition and give him an allowance if he went back to school and finished his education. But he won't support him if he doesn't."

"So what is he living on if he's moved out of his father's place?"

"I have no idea. Miss de Jersey, I'm seven years older than Peter and I have never had his opportunities and I wouldn't marry him, even if he asked. It wouldn't be fair. But I do wish—"

"Did you ever find out his birth hour?"

"His mother thought it was midmorning. And his father said he thought it was like after midnight. But they were both wrong. I have a pal who is connected with obstetrics at the hospital and he wrote to the Columbia-Presbyterian Medical Center in New York and we found out it was 10:13 in the evening, Eastern Standard Time."

Suddenly, I knew why I'd been having such a problem rectifying. I had assumed—although I knew better than to jump to conclusions, ever—Peter must have been born after midnight. "And you did his chart?"

"Miss de Jersey, I'm just an amateur. I've read books which tell you how to set up a horoscope, but I can't read what I see."

"No wonder. Interpretation is something you keep learning all your life. Could you let me see what you've done? I'll help you."

"I—I wanted to ask you. But the girls at the hospital told me you're booked four months in advance. And I probably have it all wrong, anyway."

I took a deep breath. "Mary, what did you think you saw that frightened you?"

"It's ridiculous to say this to an expert. But—"

"But what?"

"I'm afraid he might do something silly. I'm afraid he might already have done it."

"Like commit suicide?"

"Oh, God, Miss de Jersey."

"He talked about it to me. But it might have just been what psychologists call a cry for help. I see many people who have troubles and nine out of ten, at some time or other, have talked to me about killing themselves. But I know from their charts they won't."

"I wish you would look at the chart I tried to do for him."

"I'd like to. When do you get off work tomorrow?"

"Tomorrow? Same as today. I'm on the eight o'clock shift now, eight in the morning until four. But if that isn't convenient, I'll exchange with someone else. Do you think you possibly could take time to see me?"

"I'm going to make time. Come here at five. Do you know where I am?" She did, and almost cried again in her gratitude. I wondered what Maggie would say when she saw the note I was going to leave her insisting that she, by some alchemy, free the hour at five o'clock. But I felt strangely apprehensive.

The only way Maggie was able to clear the last hour of the day, a time-slot always the first to be taken, was by bringing that client in at noon. So I skipped lunch, and drank Tiger's Milk and orange juice at my desk. And, being completely busy, I didn't have time to worry about Peter. But Mary obviously hadn't been so lucky. She arrived promptly and had to wait a few minutes; I was running late. I studied her as she sat in the outer office. She looked older than I remembered, and she seemed pale, subdued. Even when I was ready for her, she didn't brighten. She came in quietly, took off her dark coat. She was still wearing her nurse's uniform.

She said, "I told you last night I wouldn't marry him. I'm not sure I told the truth. If Peter needs me, I am willing to devote my life to him."

I put my hand on hers; it was cold. "What sign are you, Mary?"

"I'm Pisces with Libra rising. I know Pisces women like to look up to their men and enjoy serving them. So I guess I can't fight fate. And he's so intelligent and wise he doesn't seem young. He's very deep. When we've had discussions about life, I'm overwhelmed by how much he knows."

"Would he marry you, do you think?"

She withdrew her hand as though mine had burned it. "I don't know. He might. He needs terribly to have someone he can trust."

"And who doesn't tire of telling him how wonderful he is."

"You're making fun of me."

"I'm not, really. Have you compared your chart to his?"

She nodded. "I brought them both with me. Not that I expect you to look at mine. But just in case it might be of any use. If you thought he needed me."

I studied the chart she had done on Peter, and then rechecked it with my reference books. She had done a complete and loving job but what she had missed were, of course, the nuances. Peter was born with the planet Saturn in 29-plus degrees of Cancer in the fourth house. Saturn is our fate, the planet of destiny, problems, trials; on the positive side, it represents the difficult experiences which, in a way, are good for us because they make us mature through adversity. The fourth house represents childhood and parents. Cancer, too, governs the family and home. So Saturn in Cancer in the fourth house means that there is a strong need for the emotional security provided by the sanctuary of home and family —and 29 degrees in Cancer means danger. In other words, all Peter's life he would feel denied the love he needed from his family, particularly at crucial times. And Saturn, sitting as it was in a position where it was adversely aspected also by the moon, corroborated this. Peter would never really feel secure in his relationship to either parent—and would suffer because of that.

I pulled out Arthur N.'s chart and put it beside Peter's. Then I looked at Mary's. She had Libra rising, and his moon was in Libra. Naturally, she adored him, was blind to his faults. (He had Aries for an ascendant, which meant he could be opinionated and domineering, and Neptune as well as his moon in Libra. He was a procrastinator who preferred to substitute charm for hard work.) But, because his moon shed light on her rising sign, which represents her personality, she looked up to him, glorified everything about him. Instead of stubborn, she found him wise and intelligent. His self-will seemed strength, to her. And Jupiter in Libra in both charts explained the mutual attraction. He needed to be adored and, in his own way, was good to her and for her. He also had Saturn in Leo, close to his sun. This not only suggests attraction to an older woman, but gave him a serious nature which responded to Mary's sober thoughts about life in general.

"Your marriage to him might not be such a bad idea," I told her. "You'd be the one who would have to give the most."

"I wouldn't mind that. Miss de Jersey, I expect to work the rest of my life. I don't even care if I have children. I'd be willing to let him explore what he wants to do and do nothing for a while, if that is what he needs. He hasn't had a very happy childhood."

"And he has Venus and Mars in Virgo, the sign opposite Pisces. Did you know that a person with planets in one sign—especially Venus which stands for love and Mars for sex—is often attracted to someone born with the sun in the sign directly opposite? We call this the Law of Polarity."

She said urgently, "I know I could make him happy. He needs to get away from his father and stepmother. He needs a place he can really call his own. Really, in a funny sweet way, he would like it, too. He loves nice things and he takes care of them. You should see how neatly he hangs up his clothes."

My heart ached for her; she was reaching hard to find good qualities in Peter. But she did love him. "He won't appreciate you, my dear. You have to face that. With Leo and Aries in his horoscope, he will accept everything you give him as his right and enjoy feeling superior to you."

"I know. He doesn't love me the way I love him. That's all right."

"Perhaps he will improve when he gets away from his father. I like Arthur, but it isn't easy having him as a parent."

"Peter adores him."

"Could you take that? Most women want to come first in a man's life."

"I wouldn't mind. I have my work. Actually, I never expected to get married. Nursing is so important to me, because I feel needed. It isn't like some of the girls, who are just marking time or trying to find a husband."

A true Pisces, I thought; that is why they make such wonderful nurses. "Have you ever talked about marriage?"

"Sometimes. I'm a lot older, and I used to tell him what he wanted was a mother. But we are good for each other. He gives me books to read. I've learned a lot from him."

"And you give him adoration."

She crossed her arms as though she were chilly, although the afternoon sun pouring in the window made the room—to me—almost too warm. "Miss de Jersey, you are being sweet. But you know he'll never marry me. I have that feeling in my heart. Don't you know it, too?"

I shook my head. "Not really. He needs help and you are the only one—"

"Miss de Jersey, tell me what it means, Pluto in Leo. In one of the books I read, it said it meant—"

Peter had three planets in Leo—his sun, Mercury, and Pluto. Pluto, in his case, was the ruler of his eighth house, death. And Pluto is a tricky planet—it can be the catalyst for good or evil, depending on the aspects. Adversely aspected, Pluto is the knife in the back, the planet which pulls the rug out from under you. Grouped with the sun, which of course indicates the life force, and Mercury, which represents the mind, Pluto was, obviously, the question mark.

I glanced up at her. She had started to tremble. "Look, my dear, it's not good but it isn't that bad. I would say simply that, as a Leo, he finds the subject of death and suicide dramatic. You and I already know that. He's talked to you about it, I'm sure."

"He tried to kill himself when he was a little boy. Twice."

"To get attention. Suicide threats are always a way to frighten and impress people. He's found out he can make people sit up and notice so he's going on playing with the notion throughout his life."

"You don't think he is serious?"

"I didn't say that. He plays with the idea, yes. At times, when he is feeling especially low and rejected, it seems like a promise waiting, a kind of peace, an easy way out—and Leos are always fascinated by the easy way. He might kill himself. But he doesn't have to."

"How can I help? I'll do anything, anything in the world. I'd give my own life for him."

"I know you would, my dear. But that isn't the way to save him. I think it might be a good idea for you two to get married. Then you must try to build his confidence, introduce him to people who will admire him, let him have a circle of friends his own age. Would you be jealous of him?"

"No, never. It would hurt, if he fell in love with another woman, a girl. But I would let him go. I know he thinks of me as a kind of mother. He would always come back. Wouldn't he?"

"I'm not sure. That's the chance you must take. If you make him whole, if you rebuild his ego, he might leave you. You love him enough to give him up if necessary, don't you?"

She nodded; I noticed the trembling had stopped. "But he doesn't want to see me any more. What happened?"

I shook my head. One aspect I didn't like was the simple old rule of three. It isn't superstition, at least in so far as suicide attempts. Invariably, if there are two attempts, there will be the third, and sometimes the third is successful. Any adverse combination of planetary positions could trigger a bad reaction. Nor did I like what I saw in the next few months in his chart.

"All I know is that he needs you. I'll see what I can do." The color had come back into her face; she sat there, smiling at me expectantly like a child waiting for a fairy godmother to produce miracles. And I didn't know what I was going to do, even as I promised.

Arthur N. had Saturn in almost the same degree of the zodiac as Peter. It is true that likes attract. But Arthur, even though he must have felt rejected by his father as a child, had a far tougher horoscope. He didn't need people desperately, he had the private world of the Scorpio to return to, and the realism and objective instinct of his cool Virgo moon. Although Peter had 29 degrees of Aries rising, his other signs subtracted from its potency. And he had to contend with the Taurus ascendant of his father. Both wanted to be boss, to rule, to lay down the law—only Arthur, by dint of age, position and the simple fact he was Peter's father, always won. And would continue to win, so long as Peter was under his control, financially or emotionally.

"Peter has to get away from his father," I said.

"Maybe he did."

"I doubt it. Not if he didn't have money. And if I know Arthur, he is in no mood to subsidize him. Right now, his Virgo moon is adversely aspected. He is going to be very conservative where money is concerned, and in short temper. Peter's Mars is right on his father's moon. Which means trouble."

"I wish I knew where to find Peter. I don't know what to do."

I stood up. "Let me talk to Arthur. It may not work, but it's worth a try. He came off the air at five o'clock. Unless he has changed a great deal, he is in his office right now, cooling off, letting people tell him what a great show it was. I'm going down there."

Mary had her car, a tiny Volkswagen. She hustled it through traffic. It was still not six o'clock when I reached the studio and the guard told me Arthur hadn't left yet, and should he announce me? I told him no, I was late—they were used to my being late—and hurried on. Riding up in the elevator, I hoped the guard had not warned Arthur I was on my way up. My main advantage, at this moment, was surprise. If Arthur had time to think, to wonder why Sandy disliked me, or what her reaction would be if she knew he had seen me, my job would be much tougher.

For an instant, I had the horrid thought Sandy might be there, waiting for her ex-boss, now husband. Then I remembered someone had told me Sandy had hand-picked her successor, and that she was an older and sourer version of the old fat Sandy. I would have to cope with her, but anyone was to be preferred to Sandy. A wife always has the whisper on the pillow going for her. In Sandy's case, I suspected it might be more like a tape-recorded diatribe.

Arthur was surrounded by the usual group of sycophants. Over the years, it had shrunk in numbers but there were still a few hardy souls who felt that, by association with the once great man, glamour rubbed off on them. I recognized all but one and she turned out to be a bite-sized child who looked as though she should still be playing with dolls but was a reporter from the *Tribune;* and, as I listened to her ask questions in a soft, hesitating voice, a very shrewd one. Hovering in the background was the secretary, such a carbon copy of the old fat Sandy that I placed her at once. She was on her way to stop me from coming in when Arthur gave me a big wave and a surprised hello. Thereby making Miss Carbon Copy a shade sourer and less like Sandy, whose façade had always at least been pleasant.

I went in and took the last chair, which meant that Miss Carbon

Copy had no place to park. She lifted a heavy shoulder, flounced a fat, unconfined breast, and left the room. After a few minutes, the reporter left too, with a deceptively mild kitten smile. Then the others drifted out. It was obviously quitting time for Arthur, he was due at the home nest. When I didn't take the hint, he said, "You look great, Katie."

I knew I didn't. I hadn't even stopped to check lipstick and my hair was on end. But I thanked him and returned the compliment. "Married life must agree with you."

He glanced at his watch. "Have you heard I'm going to be a daddy again? At my age, I'm afraid I'm not going to be very handy with the diapers."

"I don't imagine you ever were. And I know you want to leave. But I need to talk to you and I'm afraid I'm going to get out of line. You can throw me out but I wish you'd take five minutes and listen. It's terribly important."

He sat back. "Honey, delighted. You know I love to listen to you."

I took a deep breath. "Where's Peter?"

"Well." Arthur looked around uncomfortably, as though he hoped to find someone, preferably Sandy, who would answer the question for him. Finally he cleared his throat. "You see, it's this way. Frankly, having Peter with us in a not very big apartment didn't quite work out. A kid that age can be an awful nuisance. Of course, I wasn't there all day but Sandy said he used to lie around with the record player going full blast staring into space. It drove her crazy. Then he messed up the guest bathroom with a lot of smelly stuff and wouldn't clean up after himself. He said he had to have a darkroom to develop his pictures and whoever heard of a photographer with a darkroom which had to turn into a guest bathroom promptly at six o'clock? It didn't bother me, but Sandy's never had kids around."

"Did he bring in friends?"

"Well, no, not exactly. Once in a while that nurse he met in the hospital would come over and bring some of her records. Sandy didn't mind but she felt responsible and didn't like to leave them alone in the house because if anything happened—"

"So he moved out."

"Not exactly." Arthur looked around desperately. "There's no problem, Katie, and I don't know who is telling you there is, unless my ex-wife has been shooting off her mouth, getting all maternal at this late date. Peter and I are friends, better friends than ever. He and I talked it over man to man. The real problem was—frankly, I just couldn't manage sex with him around. It's crazy for a man of my experience to have a thing like this happen. But Sandy needs—she just hasn't had the experience to cope with distractions and I guess it got to me, too. Just knowing he was there in the next room was discouraging. The result was, we just didn't. You can't do that to a bride, pregnant or not. After she expected so much. Does that answer your question?"

"No. I wanted to know where he was." I decided to be very nice and not remind him that I had tried to persuade him to let Peter go and live by himself. Arthur, however, was no fool. He remembered and he knew I did, too. He looked at me with a small, embarrassed smile.

"I know. You told me so and I wouldn't listen. I thought I was so great I would manage fine. When I didn't—well, both Sandy and I got on edge. You know how it is or maybe you don't. I hope not. Anyway, I guess I said things which were meant to be funny and she thought were criticisms of her and—Peter got the message one night when Sandy and I had a row and got so loud he heard it even over the damned record player. He knew it had something to do with him. It was his idea to take a room down the block, in a kind of little hotel."

"And your sex life has improved?"

"I'd say it was none of your business, except it has. Although the poor kid is so pregnant now it isn't much fun for her. Anyway, you were right. It's really better for Peter to have his own privacy, too, no questions asked. He couldn't bring girls up to the apartment. Sandy acted like that cute little nurse was some kind of a prostitute."

"Are there any other girls besides the nurse?"

"How in hell should I know? One thing about me, I'm not going to interfere with my son's sex life. He's a damned attractive kid and at his age, in many civilizations, he'd be considered in the prime of life with all sorts of dames and kids running around."

"Arthur," I said, "I'm not worried about that. What does concern me is his chart. Has he ever talked to you about suicide?"

"Oh, Katie. He's at that age. All the kids run around wondering if they want to live in this horrible world, with their disgusting parents. I guess I did, myself. Did I ever tell you I ran away from home when I was fourteen and never went back? I've supported myself ever since."

"Your chart shows you didn't get along with one of your parents. I see precisely the same thing in Peter's. He ran away from his mother to you. I wish he had gone off alone. But he doesn't have your strength. It's apparent from a comparison of the charts of the two of you."

"Katie. Katie. Believe me, you are worrying about trouble which doesn't exist. Peter is OK. I've never seen him happier. He's on his own and he doesn't have a damned thing to worry about. I'm giving him money to pay for his room and meals and he can eat dinner with us any time in the week. If he needs more, he can go to work. He understands that."

"How is he getting along with Sandy?"

"Like a breeze. Now that she's big and uncomfortable, he and I get out together a lot, the way we used to. Movies. Football games."

"Is he going back to school?"

"No, and why should he? I got along all right without even a high school diploma. He's studying photography. I bought him a Roly and he can use the bathroom at the hotel for a darkroom without having Sandy fussing. Some of the stuff he's done shows a lot of talent. If you ever need any pictures, I'm sure he'd love to come over and take some. For practice. Shall I tell him to call you? I'll probably be seeing him tonight at dinner."

Miss Carbon Copy put her head in the door, directed a hostile look at me, and announced Mrs. N. was on the telephone. I stepped outside tactfully while Arthur talked to Sandy. Miss Carbon Copy flounced her other unfettered breast and allowed as how Mr. N. was *terribly* late starting home. On cue, Arthur appeared, wearing his coat.

"It's been good seeing you, Katie. We'll have to do it soon again. Can I give you a lift?"

I said I had to go back to the garage near my studio and get my own car. He was heading west and I had no intention of having him go out of his way and have to explain why at home. But on the way to the elevator, I said, "I'd really like to see Peter. I've done his chart and what I can tell him might be helpful. But maybe you don't mention that, right now. Just say I want some pictures and I'd be glad to pay him."

"Forget it, honey, that will be on me. Anyway, we'll be in touch."

"You have my number. Better still, let me call him. That would be more businesslike. Could I have his telephone number?"

"He doesn't have a private phone at the hotel, and the switchboard service is lousy. You can leave a message with Sandy."

"Arthur." I hurried, for the elevator was coming. "Arthur, please make sure Peter comes to see me. You aren't worried about him, but I am. There is a tricky period coming up in his horoscope. Pluto could trigger some adverse aspects. Besides, he can't spend the rest of his life half-living with you and Sandy. He needs his own friends."

"I'm not stopping him."

"You are, in a way. You're making it easy for him not to work, to do nothing. Yet you don't give him complete freedom. Subsidize him for a year in New York. Let him see what it's like. Shove him out of the nest. Away from your powerful presence he might just be able to fly on his own."

"He's all over the nonsense about being an artist. And it's just as well. He's too lazy. Besides, dammit, I'm not made of money. I still have Dick to support and Frances took a big chunk of my capital and with a wife and a new baby on the way—"

The elevator came. It was crowded, too crowded for anything except the most banal conversation between us. Besides, I felt discouraged. I was afraid Arthur would never tell Peter I wanted to see him and I knew Sandy would discourage it, if she were consulted.

Arthur and I walked out into the crisp early evening. Michigan Avenue looked glamorous in the dusk. Arthur said good night. I tried once more. "If you won't let him go, promise me one thing. Don't tease him—I know you think it's all in fun, but he responds badly—and make a point of saying you love him and want what is good for him. Scorpios have trouble expressing things they feel and Leos need to be told they are loved, over and over."

"Katie, you aren't making sense. First you tell me to let him go, then you say, moon over him, say you love him."

"Letting him go might be a way of showing him how much you love him. If he thinks you believe in him, he will believe more in himself. He needs friends. He might be able to make them if he has more confidence."

"It's not my fault the kid is a loner. Besides, what's wrong with that? I've spent a lot of my life alone."

"He's not alone by preference. He feels rejected by his mother, and clings to you, afraid you don't want him around, either. Without a feeling of being backed and loved at home, a Leo doesn't go out and make friends. He's too proud to beg and won't humiliate himself by making an advance he's afraid will be rejected."

"That is all—nonsense." Arthur's voice stung. "I don't know what you are driving at and I'm sure you don't know, either. Sandy said you are a troublemaker and I'm beginning to think she is right. You stay out of my life, and out of Peter's. Is that clear?"

I said goodbye, feeling sick at heart. I had said both too much and too little. On the way to the garage, I went into a Walgreen drugstore and called Mary Bates from a pay phone; the last thing she had done was scrawl her telephone number on an envelope and thrust it into my handbag. She sounded as depressed as I felt.

"I wish I knew the name of the hotel. I'd try to go there and talk to him. But maybe he wouldn't see me. I'll try writing him at the apartment. If he doesn't answer, shall I just be bold and call his stepmother and say he has some records of mine I want returned?"

"No. Don't let Sandy know what is going on. There can't be too many little hotels in the neighborhood. Ask at the desks until you locate him. He needs you, goddamn it."

I hadn't meant to swear at poor gentle Mary. But I felt so discouraged and depressed I had to take it out on somebody. I apologized but I went on feeling depressed. Ralph noticed and asked if I were coming down with something. I didn't tell him what had happened because, being Ralph, he might just take it into his head to go and see Arthur and tell him off for being rude to me. Which would do no good and might do more harm, if I hadn't messed everything up enough already.

The next day, before my first client, I studied Peter's chart again. As I'd told Mary, there was no reason why he should kill himself; the indications were there but it could be avoided. Always, in a chart which makes you think of self-destruction, the eighth house of death is linked adversely with either the first or twelfth house, and planets in those houses show great danger. I told Maggie, who had caught my malaise, "The thing which makes me sick is that somehow I flubbed it. I said the wrong things to Arthur. Or maybe I should have skipped him and seen the boy in person."

"Or maybe you should have stayed out of the whole thing."

Maggie whisked the folder off my desk, out of my hands. "Katie, you can't make people do what is right. You can try, and you certainly have. So don't blame yourself."

"I could have handled it better. I was in too much of a hurry. I should have picked a day which was better aspected for both him and me. And I don't like the next few months. Even Arthur has the progressed moon seven degrees in Cancer, opposing Mars in his chart. That means violence in the home."

"Sandy's going to have a baby. That will be hell for a man of his age."

I couldn't laugh, even feebly. "And in Peter's chart the progressed moon in Taurus is squaring Pluto. It's all tricky. He needs love and attention more than ever, and the smallest thing could seem like the end of the world."

Maggie tucked the folder under her arm. "You've tried, Katie. And Arthur isn't stupid. He'll think over what you've said. He might even follow your advice. Now forget it."

And, for a while, I did. On November 22, less than six weeks before an eclipse of the moon, President John F. Kennedy was assassinated. Most astrologers I know had feared this and many astrologers sent registered letters to the White House to warn him. Yet perhaps if he had postponed the fatal Dallas trip, death would have come some place else, in another way. For no matter what we do, we do attract the things which have to happen to us.

From time to time, I heard from Mary. She was on the night shift now, which she preferred, because, having had some bad nights herself, she understood what comfort she could give to patients in these lonely hours. Once in a while, when she was in my area, she would call me at noon and we would have a quick sandwich together. I grew fond of her and one day I rechecked her chart again, to see what encouragement I could give her, for Peter was drifting more and more out of her life, spending most of his evenings and all of his weekends with his father. They'd even taken a long weekend up in Canada, duck hunting. And when I'd asked how he seemed, she had tried to conceal her suffering.

"He's changed. If he's happier, which he pretends he is, I am glad for him. Usually I call him late at night, when I have my break for supper. He's always awake and seems to enjoy chatting a little. But he never mentions wanting to see me. Sandy goes to bed early and he and his dad sit up and watch TV. The late show, sometimes the late-late show. Then he comes home and sits up until morning, writing poetry. He sleeps all day."

She had managed to find him by going around the neighborhood, until she located him at a tiny run-down hotel. It hadn't been too difficult. What had been hard to take was his attitude toward her. At my suggestion, she asked him to marry her. He'd laughed at her, adding, "Go get yourself some nice fat young doctor and have lots of babies to mother." Then she had humiliated herself even more. She had offered to live with him, any place. He hadn't even bothered to say yes or no, just laughed again.

Many times I wanted to say, "You mustn't prolong the agony. Let him go."

But her chart showed me she wouldn't. She had been born March 20, 1939, and she had not only her sun but her moon in Pisces—her moon 28½ degrees. Often people born under these conditions are odd, talented but retiring, shy and a bit naïve. They lack self-confidence, except in their own specialized field. I had a client whose sun and moon were in this same position. He was a brilliant artist, a concert pianist, but a babe in the woods so far as the world and business were concerned. Luckily, he had a strong Scorpio wife who understood him and worked to support him until he made his big success.

Often Pisceans are very gifted. Mary's gift, of course, was healing, a fine field for people born under this sign. She was gentle, with intuition, sympathy and compassion. Although some people with both the sun and moon in Pisces seem out of step with the world, her choice of a profession had fulfilled one side of her nature.

However, up until she met Peter, she had never been in love. A virgin, I was sure; even her adoration of Peter seemed sexless. She was interested only in what she could do for him. Yet they needed each other, despite the difference between them. The attraction between opposites which I had already noted in Peter's chart—his Mars and Venus in Virgo opposite her sun and moon in Pisces—was accentuated by her Libra rising, a compliment to his Aries rising, also opposites in the chart. But the nodes of her moon were in Scorpio and Taurus, squaring his Pluto in the sign of Leo. This always means some problem between two people, no matter how much drawn together they are. Not infrequently, it is an indication of tragedy.

Christmas came, and she went home to Minneapolis and came

back looking thinner and even more subdued. It hadn't been a happy time. Her family had insisted she was working too hard and wanted her to come back and live with them on the family farm. On Christmas Eve she had called Peter long distance and heard him tell the operator that Peter N. was out of town and not expected back for several days.

"Shall I go over and try to see him?"

I told her no. I could not bear for her to suffer. And I saw something in her chart which made my heart ache for her even more. Her moon was squaring Uranus in the house of death—anything could happen. This had happened to me when my father died, when I was exactly her age. It nearly always indicates a sudden tragic event in a person's life, frequently the death of someone very much loved.

Around the middle of January, Sandy had her baby, a boy named Elmer Rolfe N., after her father. Arthur, to my surprise, called me the morning after. I was pleased he thought of me with enough warmth to include me in his good news. So I dared ask, "How is Peter?"

"Never better. He's moved in with me while Sandy is in the hospital. We're thinking of going farther out in the country and getting a big old house so Peter can have his own place, maybe an apartment over the garage. He wants to be a movie producer and I think he's on the right track at last. In fact, we're working on a script together."

Two days later, when I was with a client, Maggie interrupted us to say there was an important telephone call for me. I excused myself and took it in her office. It was Mary. She'd just heard on the radio that Peter had killed himself. He'd gone to the guest bathroom, put his father's shotgun in his mouth, and pulled the trigger.

She gave a hysterical giggle. "Now Sandy can really complain about his messing up the bathroom."

I found out she wasn't alone, that the supervisor of the club was fussing over her, pouring hot tea and sympathy. The older woman assured me that Mary was all right, but that she insisted on going to work that night, as usual. I said I thought it was the best thing she could do.

Later that day, when I felt steadier, I went over Peter's chart with Maggie. Aries, his ascendant, had moved to a position where it afflicted, or brought out the worst, in Pluto. The ascendant in any chart represents the vital forces, and in this case they were cut off by the adverse aspects related to Pluto. The rug had been pulled out from under Peter, in a degree of the zodiac which, according to Sabian symbols, indicates a "tendency to hysteria and to lean on transient excitement for self-realization."

In other words, Peter had chosen what to his mind was the easy way out. In the birth of his new stepbrother, he had encountered the ultimate rejection, he thought. Without confidence in himself, without the stability of a wife or friends of his own age to give him confidence, he had made his ultimate dramatic gesture and by his death tried to become for all time more important than the new baby.

No death is an absolute in itself. Its affect on the survivors is part of the unending pattern. This, of course, is always in the mind of the suicide. No matter how he pleads for forgiveness in a suicide note, or pours out his love for those he is leaving behind, there must be an intention to punish, even a little. So far as I know, Peter left no note. If Arthur found one, he destroyed it without telling the police. Or perhaps he hid it away, to torture himself.

I wrote him, and he answered. Not a letter dictated to his secretary but in longhand, in a cramped hand unused to doing that kind of laborious chore. In a last paragraph, he said, "After you talked to me, I tried to do everything I could to show Peter how much I cared for him. Perhaps you were right in saying it was too late, the early rejection had done the harm. I was busy with my career and I wonder now if Frances wasn't jealous of the boy. It seems strange to think any woman could possibly be jealous of her own baby, but Frances was a peculiar person. And I was to blame, too. From what I've learned through suffering over Peter's death, I know one thing. Sandy and I aren't going to make the same mistake with this new baby."

Love is the single most important gift you can give a child. But to an astrologer, the irony of Arthur's good intentions was all too apparent. After the tragedy, I had seen as much of Mary as I could manage. We worked together on the natal chart of the new baby, born under some of the same auspices which had triggered Peter's suicide. This is the kind of thing which no astrologer with any curiosity can resist, any more than you can put down a detective story without finding out who did the murder.

The baby had his sun in Capricorn, Taurus rising, his moon in Gemini. Of course he would have ambition. He will probably write. But as Arthur and Sandy draw apart, which is inevitable in both of their charts, the child will have the insecurity of knowing his parents are competing for him. Sandy with nothing more in her life (I did not see any indication of her having another baby) and increasing irritation with her husband, would spoil the boy. Arthur, in order to make up for what he did to Peter, would also overindulge him. Inevitably, with two people who are estranged and already a bit overage to raise a baby, the competition would become a battle.

The immediate victim would be the boy; like so many males with Taurus rising, he could become so ruined by adoration he would never grow up. And in the end, the person who would suffer most had to be Sandy. For the boy's moon in Gemini often produces a person who is really more of a split personality than those with the sun in Gemini. And as his moon hits directly on Mars in Sandy's chart, I can see a generation gap widening between mother and son which could bring her the kind of agony no woman deserves.

As I grow to know Mary Bates, I begin to suspect she will never marry. Her great love was Peter and it was just as well, for her, that she lost him when she did. Because he would have caused her only more agony. He enjoyed his power over her and he would have never let her go. Nor could she have resisted him.

The summer of 1966, on her vacation, she went to California. Her purpose, she later confessed to me, was to see a swami who might put her in touch with Peter. The swami, who sounds to me like a wonderfully gifted man, refused. He said to her, "The young man wanted his freedom. I can't try to reach him for you because it would mean keeping him here, tied to earthly obligations. Let him go. It is time for him to soar, to learn in the other world, so that when he returns, he will be a more stable person."

At the time, it seemed like small comfort. But Mary has grown up since Peter's death. It was a catalyst which thrust her from a small private world into real life. Her concern now is not so much with her own satisfactions as a nurse but what she can do to help the whole profession. To this end, she is training as a psychiatric nurse. She will never give up her first love, that of caring directly for people. But she hopes eventually to broaden her horizons by teaching others and trying to inject into young students her own compassion and understanding of human beings.

The last time I saw her, she told me, "I'm now able to look back on the few good months I had with Peter as a bright and happy part of his life, as well as mine. And I recognize how basically unsuited he was for living. In his way, he was even more childish than I."

I agree. For the difference between those who decide life isn't worth living, and those who do, is right there in the charts. People like Peter and Diana just didn't have the toughness and resilience to survive, particularly in this Aquarian age which demands so much of us all, particularly our youth.

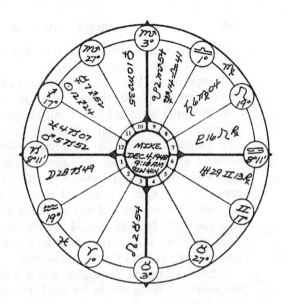

4
The
Pointless
Triangle

THE boy collapsed in the chair opposite me, looking utterly weary. Only his intense light blue eyes were alert. It was four days before Christmas. Always before, I had used the Christmas holidays as a respite, a delicious lull in my hectic schedule. But this year I'd had a rush of appointments which extended up until Christmas Eve. How I was going to shop, even for my husband, I hadn't a clue. The cards we'd ordered would probably go out sometime in January—with luck. I didn't even have any of my usual Christmas spirit; I had to restrain myself from asking my new young client crossly what his problem was, what reason he had to be so exhausted.

Then he roused himself to smile at me, and I melted. Quite frankly, I am for most of the kids of today, citizens of the dawning Aquarian Age. I find their challenging honesty a tonic and their genuine commitment to the world inspiring. But the area in which they seem to lack seasoning and judgment—in true Aquarian fashion—is in that of person-to-person relationships, contacts with family, close friends, sweethearts. Which is where I often come in.

I said, "You are Michael Foxx. Any relation to Ned Foxx?"
The smile slipped. "My father. Why?"

"It's an unusual spelling of your last name. And I've been introduced to your father, that's all."

"I suppose you know he's giving me this visit to you as a Christmas present. I explained that to your secretary."

As a matter of fact, I didn't. All Maggie had noted on the appointment sheet was: Michael Foxx—December 4, 1948, 9:18 A.M. Ottumwa, Iowa. The connection with Ned Foxx had just occurred to me. Ned was an automobile dealer, one of our Chicago men-about-town. I'd seen him with a variety of female companions of all ages, shapes, and types. Which, of course, didn't preclude his being married and the father of a son who was seventeen years old. Just the same, I was curious. No matter how tired I am, all I need is to start working on a chart and excitement grips me—as fresh as when I first started to study.

He had his sun in Sagittarius. But it was strongly balanced by the moon and rising sign in the solid earth sign of Capricorn. And a good thing, too. Because the boy had problems; or, rather, one big basic problem: Saturn was in his eighth house, turned retrograde when he was twelve or thirteen years old.

Saturn represents karma, fate, and a parent. When it turns retrograde, slowed down in its course in the regular pattern of the heavens, the spiritual significance of its position is emphasized—and it was in the eighth house of death. In other words, the backing up, the slowing down, means that whatever is indicated will have long-lasting effect.

"Did you lose your mother recently?" I asked.

Those remarkable eyes flashed; otherwise he did not change expression. "How could you know?"

"Your chart. And I also see that you've suffered deeply. The death of a parent always is hard. But in your case, you must be careful not to let it subconsciously affect your whole life, be a shadow always on your relations with women."

Silence. Sullen silence. I talked to him about the other aspects in his chart, wondering if, behind the blank face, he was taking anything in. Sagittarians are usually attractive, outgoing people. They are the ones who talk to cab drivers, exchange confidences with strangers in airports, come home from trips with their pockets full of addresses of new "friends." A Sagittarian woman may seem flirtatious—especially to her husband. Actually, she just likes people. (At least, in some cases, that's a good excuse.) She doesn't mind setting out on a trip unaccompanied, or spending a day alone in a strange city because she is never really alone, she is always picking up friends everywhere she goes. A Sagittarian male, on the other hand, can be cruel without at all meaning to be. He is an idealist in his love relationships, always looking for the girl of his dreams, thinking he has found her—and then being roughly disillusioned . . . So he is capable of walking out.

I said to Mike Foxx, by way of explanation, "You are not a typical Sagittarian because of your Capricorn ascendant and moon. You have a great need for family ties. Many Capricorn people have a feeling of both alone-ness and loneliness. Often, show business people who feel 'alone in a crowd' are Capricorns. And Capricorn people, oddly enough, often lose a parent early in life. I see it time and time again."

No comment. I went on. "Mike, you are attractive to girls. That is the plus side of being a Sagittarian. Yet I am glad about that Capricorn stability in your chart because Sagittarians can be very hard on women. I have one client who was divorced by his wife for unfaithfulness when their three children were small. He's an actor whose name you'd recognize. He has married several times—I've lost count—each time to a younger girl. Yet he still goes back to his first wife, a mother figure, if he is in trouble."

"He sounds like my father."

I'd been introduced to Ned Foxx by Burton Browne, client and friend. Ned hadn't struck me as a Sagittarian type, although, of course, when there are other strong influences in the chart you can't make an offhand judgment. But there was something about his compact neatness, the scrupulously tended fingernails, the meticulous precision—

I said impulsively, "I should have guessed your father had his sun in Virgo."

Mike straightened. I had the impression that, whatever test he had planned for me, I had passed. He now was ready to come to the purpose of his visit, the reason he had asked for the appointment. He slid a piece of paper across the desk. Worn and brittle, soiled in the creases, it had obviously been carried around in somebody's pocket for a long time. I looked at it hesitantly.

"Read it," he commanded.

The handwriting, fuzzed though it was by time, was still bold and firm, vital, that of a person in her middle years, probably greatly talented. I had half expected an adolescent love letter. Instead:

Michael, my darling, my baby, I'm writing this because I think I'm going to have to leave you, soon. Don't ask me why. I just know. But I want you to realize, as I've told you so many times, ever since you were a tiny baby, that we cannot ever be separated, really. I will watch over you from the other side. In you, I will accomplish the tasks I was meant to do but never managed.

Amount to something, Mike. Don't go in with your father in the agency. Write. Paint. Act. Whatever. The dollar must not be your God, as it is your father's. And Mike. When I go, if I go, please do one thing for me. I've always had a conviction I was born to die young, at least prematurely. Please go and ask an astrologer to do my horoscope and see if I am right. I wanted to do that myself, many times, but I was afraid. However, after the fact, it may give you the kind of extra support you will be needing without me. I was born on September 22, 1925, at 3:20 P.M. in Chicago, as you know. The same day as your father, which may have brought us together in the first place, but a different year, a different time. I guess this is good-bye. I love you.

There was no signature. But I didn't need Mike to tell me, "My mother wrote that. Her lawyer gave it to me the night she died."

"How long ago was that?"

"Three years. June 3, 1962. Three years and six months."

"Why didn't you come sooner?"

"I—I was afraid, too, I guess." For an instant, I had the impulse to take the huge young man in my arms. I have no children. My theory about myself, and other women with their suns or other significant planets in Cancer, is that Cancer, which governs the uterus, either gives us many children or denies them entirely. I was not able to conceive. But I suspect that childless Cancer women who are so instinctively maternal can be good with other women's children, giving them understanding and impartial, uninvolved affection.

I picked up a pencil and began to work on her chart. Meanwhile, I also talked, for I didn't want silence to grow between us now that we had established communication.

"Did your mother ever talk to you about astrology?" I asked.

"Not really. But she read a lot of books, books she kept in her desk. The night she died, Dad went in and threw them all out, along with all her papers. The next day he had a big bonfire in the back yard, the burning of the books, like Hitler."

"Mike, he was upset, too."

"Between us, we killed her."

"No, you didn't. It's there in her chart, as she suspected. She was meant to die young. I would say speed was connected with it, a sudden accident. Was it an automobile accident?"

"You can't see that. Someone told you. My father, probably. Didn't he?"

"Mike, look. You won't understand all this, but I want to explain exactly what is here in the chart I made for the moment of her birth. Uranus, ruler of Aquarius, is in 23 degrees of Pisces. This is a degree of sorrow, which we often see in charts of people who have tragedies in their personal lives. What kind of tragedy and its impact of course always depends on many other factors—never should one planetary indicator be taken out of context of the whole chart, set up for one specific person at the exact minute of birth.

"In her case, Uranus is opposite a cluster of planets, what we call a stellium, in her sun sign, Virgo. This clustering of Mars, Mercury, and her sun indicate fearlessness, frequently to the point of being foolish, rushing in, as we say, where angels fear to tread. Mars here means a love of speed which, in this position, could be carried to a point endangering life. Opposite unpredictable Uranus, Mars takes on an uncontrolled aspect—violence, something sudden and wild. Together with other astrological clues the picture is sudden death by accident."

He said, "Her car ran smack into a concrete pillar. The police said she died—instantly. We—I hope so. Because then it burst into flames. They had to check the license plate to find out who it was. Then they didn't know whether it was a man or woman, Dad or Mother or me."

I looked at him. Even his lips were white.

"If she had come to you for a horoscope, could you have told her?" he asked.

"I could have. But I wouldn't have dreamed of it. Mike, the value of a horoscope is to help us look ahead, to trace the stumbling blocks we may meet, so we can be prepared for them, in some cases avoid them. But I don't think it's the function of an astrologer to warn clients of approaching death unless it can be avoided. If we do see indications, of fatal illness, we can sometimes help the client to develop self-discipline and control, to cope with what seems to be inevitable. But astrology has its main function as a kind of preventive medicine, to keep us from falling into

bad behavior patterns. For example, in a chart, if I see the indications that a client might become an alcoholic or a drug addict,
as has happened recently with several of my "Aquarian Age"
young people, I can warn against developing a negative behavior
pattern before the fact. In your mother's case, however—"

"Could you have saved her?"

"I'm afraid not. There are so many trouble aspects in her chart.
She was a woman who was deeply disillusioned. If I had been
able to talk to her when she was younger, I might have been able
to point out how to avoid some of the rough spots in her path, instead of letting her go on and on until—"

"Did she kill herself?"

"Not in the literal sense. But her chart indicates she might have
been foolishly reckless. It was her nature, you know."

"Miss de Jersey." He was sitting up straight. "Mom was—something. She wasn't always fooling around the country club playing
golf, flirting with the bartenders, playing bridge, like a lot of other
women in Wilmette. She read books and listened to music. Sometimes we would go out and sit in the forest preserve and read
poetry. Once in a while she'd keep me out of school, send a note
next day saying I'd been sick, and we'd spend a whole day walking
through the woods with a picnic lunch, talking—"

"What about?"

"What it was like to be dead. What it means to be alive. Her
plans for me. She wanted me to do something which mattered,
help the world, not just grub away earning money for big cars
and washing machines. We were—so close. Until—"

"Until what?"

"Until she killed herself to punish me. I know it."

"Mike, let me tell you this. In her chart, I see that you—her
child—were the most important thing in her life, her reason for
being. You had nothing to do with the confusion which made her
unhappy. Take, for example, the conflict between her moon in
Scorpio and her Neptune in the seventh house of marriage.
Scorpio, a water sign, is highly emotional. And Neptune, ruler of
Pisces, another emotional water sign, was adversely aspected,
again in the seventh house of marriage. Let me spell this out to
you: your mother went into marriage full of dreams and fantasies
—we see this in her chart. A great part of this was her own confusion. If she had understood how she was torn by conflicting
emotions, it might have helped. But she, moon in Scorpio, tried

to hide her bruises. Perhaps poetry and music were her only outlets. And when she died, she was really escaping from her earthly
self."

"I don't—believe it."

"Saturn and Venus were side by side in Scorpio. She wanted to
love deeply, passionately, but she was afraid to give herself in a
love relation. She married your father expecting, almost demanding, utter bliss and communion yet also fearing deep down that
she would be hurt. That is the story of her relation with your
father. She wanted love yet not to be emotionally or physically
dependent on anyone else in a marriage. She couldn't tell him
what she needed, and at the same time, typically Scorpio, she resented him for not guessing."

"Dad. They were born on the same day, not the same year. I
remember his telling me it was love at first sight. He cut in on her
at some kind of a party and she asked, as a joke, what his birthday was, and she said, 'We're soul mates. We'll be married within
the year.' And they were. Yet by the time I was big enough to
know what was going on—he neglected her, Miss de Jersey. Honest to God. He was gone night after night on business. She finally
moved into her own room, across the hall from mine, because
he woke her up when he came home so late. And it was often—
terribly late. Once in a while I'd get up to go to the bathroom in
the middle of the night and she'd call to me. He wouldn't be home
yet and she was lonesome so she would make cocoa and we'd
sit there in her room and drink it and talk."

"Mike, what I am trying to tell you is that people like your
mother and father, although they both have their suns in the same
sign and were born on the same day and so shared certain other
aspects, can be very different. He wanted one thing; she another.
And because by her very nature she was unable to tell him, and
because there was no one else to tell him what was going wrong,
as an outsider, as I might have, things went from bad to worse."

"Then she did kill herself."

"I said I didn't think so. On the other hand, she didn't cherish
her life. She went into dangerous situations deliberately."

Maggie buzzed me on the telephone; I said we would be finished in a few minutes. I hated to end the interview with the extraordinary blue eyes looking at me so full of unshed tears. But
Mike stood up; he was a gentleman. Whatever his mother had
done for him, she had given him good manners.

I said, "What year was your father born?"

He shook his head.

"How old is he?"

"He was forty-four this year."

"And your mother would have been thirty-nine. His birth date is September 22, 1920. I'd like to know the time and place. It would help us. Could you call and give it to me?"

"Grandma Foxx might know. Dad gave me a hard time about wanting to consult an astrologer. I didn't tell him why, I just said all the kids at school were interested. He was the one who suggested you. Burton Browne, I guess, is a friend of yours?"

I nodded. "I wish I didn't have to leave. I'd like to compare your mother's chart with your father's. But we can do this over the telephone. Meanwhile, I've a speaking engagement in Evanston and I have to run."

"May I drive you? I've got my car downstairs. Even Dad says I'm a good driver."

Under ordinary circumstances, I would have refused. Driving my own car, being alone, gives me an opportunity to prepare myself, rehearse mentally. And relax. But I knew he had something more to tell me, something he had been holding back.

So I said, "That will be great. I'll get my things."

The drive started silently. Because I enjoy driving, I recognize that quality in someone else. So we were content. Then the car skidded—just a little. The roads were still icy after a recent snowstorm. Mike had not been watching. He made a quick, instinctive recovery but his glance at me was apologetic.

"I was thinking of something else. After the accident, the police called Dad at the office. He tried to call me at school to tell me Mom was dead. I was supposed to be at swim practice. I wasn't. I'd dropped off the team a couple of months back. I never told anybody."

I waited. After a long while he went on. "It was a girl. Mom said she was a tramp. Had round heels. She wasn't like that. She was lonesome. Her mother was divorced and had to work and Louise went home every afternoon and was all alone so she asked me to come and see her. And I got into the habit."

"Were you in love with her?"

He flushed. "She was a nice girl. My mom made fun of her clothes and things. It was just—nobody was ever nice to her at school. I liked her."

"And you were there the day of the accident? That is why you feel guilty?"

"Mom might have found out."

"Mike, she didn't destroy herself to punish you. You were the most important thing in her life. Perhaps the finest aspect in her chart was the favorable linking of Jupiter and Mercury—the bene-factor and the mind ruling the sector which represents you, her child. You were her reward—an unusual person with intelligence, strength, spiritual insight. And your mother, with her moon in Scorpio, understood why you were attracted to the girl."

"They tried to reach me, to tell me Mom was dead. The coach of the swimming team even sent one of the fellows out to try and find me. But they couldn't. When I went home, Dad was still at the morgue and our next door neighbor was supposed to be watch-ing for me but I came in the back door. I looked for Mom in her room. I went back to the kitchen and there was a cake on the table, a chocolate cake, my favorite. I supposed it was for dinner but I cut a piece and poured myself a glass of milk, when my Grandma Foxx came in the front door and told me. Mom had been fussing around the kitchen that morning when I went to school. She wanted to fix me breakfast but I was late. Usually she didn't get up. Dad and I took what was quick and easy, if we ate at all. I think she wanted to give me breakfast and when I wouldn't eat, she baked the cake. Like she gave that note to her lawyer just for me. I never told Dad about it. I was afraid he'd make me put it on the bonfire."

"May I say one thing, Mike? Don't let yourself turn bitter against your father. You need him now. It's very important for you, with your Capricorn moon to keep his family relationships intact."

"What about his wives? He married Carol when Mom hadn't been dead six months. Then they got divorced and along came Lorraine. We met her in Mexico. That divorce isn't final yet but he's got another chick in mind, not quite thirty. One of these days he'll be standing around senior high giving the girls the eye so he can bring one of them home to be my stepmother."

I tried to picture Ned Foxx and the various ladies I'd seen with him. Ned came through loud and clear—not too tall, stocky, deeply tanned. The word boyish flashed into my mind. And, Virgo-like, probably very aware of keeping in shape, eating a diet free of all those lovely rich foods we enjoy. But the girls, wives or dates, all seemed to me, in retrospect, to be the kind you never see by day. The ones who sleep until evening, then dress up to be worn on the arms of men like Ned Foxx. I couldn't imagine any one of them as Mike's stepmother.

He added, "And in between we have Grandma Foxx. Big deal. She treats Dad like he was my age and me like I was still in diapers."

"Mike, it is hard on a woman when her husband dies. But it is even rougher for a man. He can't cope alone and having his mother around, as you can see, isn't the solution. So he gets married."

"Until he runs out of dough. This one sounds expensive. Her name is Barbra. Like in Streisand. Barbra Bennington. She's a dancer. Flip, flip. He is mad for her. This time it's even worse than the others. When he's home, he's on the telephone talking to her. But most of the time he isn't even home."

"Do you like her?"

"Me? You don't understand. I don't count. He doesn't let me meet them until he carries them over the threshold. Or whatever. Except Lorraine. And that was only because we were all holed up at the same lousy hotel, Lorraine and her twins—she was a widow—and Dad and me. Just a big happy fivesome, we were. Even so, I never dreamed anything was going on until he looked sort of coy and said that he was having a special celebration on New Year's Eve and up turned this minister and they were married—"

"Mike, can you tell me about what time your mother's accident occurred? I might do a chart of that day. If it would help you to know exactly what went on."

"It was like noon. They said. Some guys in a restaurant heard the crash and ran out and tried to help."

"Would you ask your father? There must be a police record of the exact time, and I need it to do a chart. Also, eclipses—including many partial ones the public doesn't notice—have very strong influence on certain charts. There were two eclipses in the fall of 1961—which is very unusual—and also two in the spring of 1962. There could be a connection. I'll look it up. And don't forget to call me."

"I'll call. Only—"

"After Christmas. My secretary will tell you if it isn't convenient and set another time. And Mike—please don't feel guilty. That's the last thing your mother would have wanted. She didn't leave the note to make you feel guilty. You know that, don't you?"

"I guess so."

I still wanted more time with him, not to leave him with his guilt dangling, but we were in Evanston and he dropped me at the Orrington where my group was meeting. I was so late I didn't have time to thank him properly.

Later that night—much later—I put a hand in my coat pocket and found a piece of paper: the letter Mike's mother had written him. In the rush, I must have absent-mindedly tucked it away, as I often do with papers of my own I want to reread. Yet this gave me a chance to study it at leisure, which I did. Finally I asked my husband, "What do you know about Ned Foxx?"

"Practically nothing. We've had a drink once or twice at the Gaslight Club while I was waiting for you. Don't tell me he is a client of yours."

"Why not?"

"No reason, really. Except that—he's pretty critical of anything he considers out of his big-shot pattern. It would take a lot of courage for him to admit to himself he needed help. Especially from a lady."

"His son came to see me today and brought a letter his mother had written him before she died in an accident."

"Suicide?"

"He thinks so. And blames himself. I tried to point out to him that the pattern of unhappiness and frustration was in her natal chart. And her marriage provided extra tensions. Like many people, she married a man who answered her particular needs at that moment and they really weren't suited. I haven't done his chart but hers is brimming with unfulfillment."

Ralph put down his newspaper. "I'm no astrologer. But I can tell you one thing, from a male point of view. I wouldn't care to be doing business with Ned Foxx. He isn't dishonest. But if you are in a deal with him, you can be damned sure he isn't going to get cheated. His motto is, screw the other fellow before he screws you."

"He has his sun in Virgo but he sounds like Taurus rising. The insecure, hard-working, busy executive."

Ralph grinned. "You may be right."

"But I'm worried about the boy." Ralph's smile broadened.

He'd heard me talk like that so often about youngsters that he went back to his newspaper.

The generation born after World War II, of which Mike is a member, is what we think of as belonging to the Aquarian Age, although it technically has not begun yet. But events are moving so fast that these young people quite rightly have become its hope and its spokesmen. They are very different from the young people who were conceived during or slightly before World War II, who, unfortunately, fell under the astrological aspects that caused the war.

These Aquarians, just emerging now from their teens, are more flexible, more open, more articulate. Their interest in astrology, and their willingness to approach it, to give it a chance to help, is only one indication of their very real acceptance of things beyond the material. Because they do question and don't accept the old answers as gospel, I think they understand our generation far better than most of us understand them—in fact, perhaps better than we understand ourselves unless we have been able to acquire the same freedom to explore and cast off old strait-jacket prejudices.

This is why I have to say to parents, time and time again, that the generation gap today isn't the same kind which existed between us and our mothers and fathers. Many of our generation have no idea what is actually meant by the Aquarian Age. I heard one lawyer, an intelligent man but one who knew nothing about astrology, insist (he had seen the musical *Hair*) that it was the age of anything goes—wine, women, and song. Nothing could be more ridiculous.

Of course the young people have reacted against the phony concepts of morality which we took from our parents—the façade of righteousness, behind which anything could happen. I find young people today more moral than their parents in that they insist on being open about sexual behavior. The Aquarian attitude is idealistic, not material, dedicated to the idea of universal brotherhood, one religion, less accent on the family unit, more on the world in general and no separation between mind, body and spirit. Their concept is that every living thing responds to the pattern of the universe—plants, animals, as well as human beings. (Which is the basic theme of astrology, so it is not surprising they respond to it.) They are reacting against all the old sacred cows, against the Piscean Age out of which we are now emerging, and reexamining all the concepts which we've held up too long as absolutes.

Occasionally a father will say to me, as, I suppose, Ned Foxx might: "Look, the boy tells me how crazy I am to be so materialistic, to spend my life slaving away, yet he is perfectly willing to take the money which is the result of my hard work." That is true, because money in the minds of Aquarians is to be shared, spread out among all people.

There are other negative aspects to the Aquarian nature. Aquarians like to be surrounded by people yet they don't want the people to come too close; I think of Aquarian Franklin Delano Roosevelt and his smug aloofness all the while he was calling the citizens of the United States "my friends" in his radio fireside talks. Aquarians tend to depersonalize their emotions. They detach themselves and shun sentimentality rather than accept the burden of a love relationship with just one other person; they prefer to love the group, the commune.

If we understand the sign Aquarius, it isn't so difficult to know our Aquarian Age young people. As I drove into the office next morning, I was going from the general picture of the youth of Mike's generation to his particular aspects as I could see them in his natal chart.

Because of his moon and rising sign in Capricorn, Mike would be inclined to follow the Capricorn-male pattern of love—attracted to older women early in life, then to very young women as he reached fifty or sixty—a switch from mother image to daughter image. In addition, he would be influenced by the Sagittarian idealism, and in his case, because of the particular positioning of Saturn retrograde in the eighth house, he would hold the image of his mother in mind always when he was attracted to a woman. I could see problems ahead, soon. Unless I could be around to point out danger signals, he might make a disastrous early marriage.

I wanted to see him again. I said to Maggie, "Call Mike Foxx and tell him he left a letter here yesterday. Ask him to come in to see me when he calls for it."

"When?" Maggie's voice was impatient.

"Any time," I said firmly. "Put his folder on my desk. And get me a record of the eclipses in the fall of 1961 and the spring of 1962. I want to make some calculations."

Of course I was overoptimistic on two counts. I expected Mike

to come for his mother's letter promptly and I hoped to have some
leisure time to myself between Christmas and New Year's. But
Mike did not come and the pace continued into spring, when my
lecture-circuit engagements increased. One day Maggie quietly removed the Foxx chart from my desk and put it into the files. Occasionally, when I'd see a young boy on the street who looked
like Mike, I'd come back to the office fired with purpose to try
to reach him again. But something always happened to interfere
and, as I am of the school who believes nothing occurs by chance,
I had to accept the fact that, if I were to see Mike, the approach
would be from him.

And it was—eventually. One night in late summer, the telephone
rang as Ralph and I were finishing dinner. Burton Browne said,
"Katie, have I ever asked a favor of you?"

"If you haven't, I owe you one. Name it."

"I have a friend here who wants to take you to lunch tomorrow.
Will you go? Even if it means switching your appointments
around?"

I hesitated, thinking of Maggie. Then I made up my mind not
to worry, she would manage, as always. And she was as fond of
Burton as I am. When she knew it was a favor for him, she
wouldn't mind. "Tell me the time and place. And her name."

"It's a man. His name is Ned Foxx. The place is the garden of
the Art Institute and the time is 12:30."

I sat down abruptly. "What does he want, Burt? Is he there or
can you talk?" Burton and I, both with our suns in Cancer, seem
as unlike as two people could be. Yet we are on the same wave-
length in many ways, and I trust his instincts. Beneath the seemingly extrovert façade, which we both have, we are extremely
sensitive and even shy. The reason we both chose professions
which put us in the public eye is that limelight gives introverted,
sometimes insecure, Cancer people the security they need, once
they get used to the glare.

Burt said, "He wants to get married to a girl named Barbra
Bennington. A good kid, a dancer. But he is worried about his
son. The boy has been through a bad summer. Ned thinks his wife
—Mike's mother—killed herself and he's afraid the boy might do
the same. That is why he hasn't pushed the marriage. Now he
realizes that unless he marries Barbra soon, he will lose her and
he can't bear that. So the lunch date was set up tomorrow to introduce Mike to Barbra."

"And where do I come in?"

"Mike wants you to be there. He wants you to meet her and do Ned's chart. Before he marries again."

"And what does Ned say?"

"He would like you to come to lunch. That's all he cares about. He is sure that once Mike meets Barbra, he will realize how wonderful she is and there will be no trouble."

"Then I'm being used as a decoy."

"I told you it was a favor I was asking of you. All you need to do is produce the body. You can leave right after you eat."

"Why are you doing this for Ned? Is he that good a friend of yours?"

"Katie, the guy has had a lot of hard luck. His wife was no good. She was playing around and got into some kind of a mess and took the easy way out, suicide. Then he married a fashion dame around town who was only interested in his dough and she left him. And he got mixed up with a silly widow on the rebound. Now he is involved with a real dame. A wonderful person. He is really crazy about her. I think you'll like her, too. Shall I tell him you'll be there?"

"I feel like a sitting duck. But all right."

"And besides, old Ned could do with a bit of astrology. I told him I wouldn't make a move without you."

"Which isn't true. I can think of one occasion when I warned you that a would-be business associate was a phony and you went right ahead and—"

"Lost money and learned my lesson. No, Katie, what I'm trying to say is that Ned could benefit a lot from having you do a chart for him. I've told him that. But you can't push him into doing anything. He's stubborn as a—"

"Bull," I said. "Probably he has Taurus rising. But consider the favor done."

I was in the bedroom looking through my closet wondering what a sitting duck should wear to lunch, when Ralph came in. "Stop frowning. It can't be that bad."

I said, "I don't like being put on the spot like this."

"Katie, if it hadn't been for Burt, I would never have met you. So far as I'm concerned, I'll be eternally in his debt."

Ralph and Burton became friends when Ralph came to Chicago to work for the same company for which Burton was ad manager. When Burton formed his own ad agency soon afterward, Ralph had joined another electronics firm, and Burton obtained the account for his agency. Their professional and personal relationship became closer through the years while Ralph was becoming chief executive officer of his company, and Burton was achieving the position of top agency in electronics advertising.

On my part, I'd met Burt through a client. As his office was in the old Italian Court Building, too, we saw each other frequently. Then one evening in June 1951 he asked me to do his chart. I told him, "In two years, you are going to change your profession, go into something associated with restaurant or show business. And you're going to hit the jackpot."

Burton had laughed at me. "Katie, you couldn't be more wrong. In two years I am going to retire. I've been working since I was fifteen and I'm sick of it."

I said, "You have Mars in the second house of money. Your progressed ascendant will join Mars in your natal chart and make you rich. You'll be dealing with the public on a large scale and, with the moon in Sagittarius, in your third house, you will travel more than ever before. When Jupiter enters Cancer, your sun sign, you will begin a whole new life, much more exciting because Jupiter stands for venture and expansion."

A year later, Burt came to see me again. He had an idea—a key club for businessmen to entertain clients. He said, "Will I lose my shirt?" I showed him his chart, and reminded him of what I'd said the year before. On October 27, 1953—I selected the date by astrology—he opened the first of his chain of Gaslight Clubs in Chicago. He has been fabulously successful—the touch of Midas in his chart. And has continued as a good friend as well as a client.

All of which I told Ned Foxx, by way of explaining why I was playing truant and joining him for lunch, something I seldom have time to do. Mike was there, nine months older than when I had seen him last, already maturing, with fewer of the raw edges showing. And Barbra was, unexpectedly, lovely. She wore a soft gray cotton dress which only hinted at the strong young body underneath. Her blond hair was long and straight, probably "ironed" straight, the way the kids were doing it. Although she looked young, heartbreakingly young it seemed to me for a man the age of Ned Foxx, she was all woman. I could quite understand his infatuation. And I suspected Mike was not unimpressed, either.

She said to me directly, "I'm sorry about the Barbra. I mean, the way it is spelled. My name was Barbara and my agent thought it would be a cute idea to spell it like Barbra Streisand, somebody might get us mixed up. Not that they ever did."

"How could they? I mean, you are much prettier." The three of us turned when Mike spoke. He flushed red. On the way out, I took his arm and led him into the building. Ned, with Barbra beside him, was still paying the check.

I said, "Mike, you wanted me to come and I did. But it wasn't necessary. You like her and so do I. This is going to work out for you."

He nodded. I went on. "You've never come by for your mother's letter. And I want to talk to you a little more about your father's chart. Make it late some afternoon and I'll buy you a Coke."

Again he nodded. I thought that was all I was going to get out of him—Barbra had the only triumph with him that day, it seemed —until he burst out, "Miss de Jersey, I won't be around much longer. Dad is sending me East to prep school."

"Are you pleased?"

"I guess so. Anyway, they don't want me around."

"Mike, don't let this make a break between you and your father. Keep communications open. You need him and I think he needs you."

"I said I thought it would be a good idea if he had his horoscope done, that you'd told me a lot of things which made good sense. I said you had seen Mom's accident in the chart before I told you anything about it. He said you must have read about it in the newspapers. He thinks astrology is crazy."

"Then don't push him. You can't force anyone to do what they resist, especially someone with Taurus rising, as I think he has. Physically, he is much more a Taurus than a Virgo."

"I'm not going to push anything. I'm off now." He was poised for flight. Barbra and Ned Foxx were coming toward us. I said urgently, "Mike, come and see me before you go. Please."

In an instant, he was off, long legs flying. His father and Barbra and I left at a more sedate pace. When she went to get his Buick, which apparently she was using, Ned Foxx and I waited on the steps of the Art Institute. The sun was warm but already we could feel September in the air.

"Mike tells me he is going away to school," I said.

"I hope it works out. If not, he can come home. The thing is, Miss de Jersey, after my wife died, I couldn't stand living alone.

It was like being in jail. I made a couple of foolish marriages which didn't work out. I'm afraid Mike felt I was being unfaithful to his mother's memory. We've had a rather rough time."

"Mr. Foxx," I said, "the school idea may be fine. But don't let him go thinking he doesn't need you. He does, very much. Even if he seems to resist, you make the advances."

He glanced nervously down the avenue. The car was not in sight. "Miss de Jersey, Burton Browne thinks the world of you."

"And I of him."

"I mean, as an astrologer. Would it be possible for me to make an appointment with you? I want to talk about Mike. Or is that ethical? You did his horoscope last Christmas. I gave it to him as a present."

"I remember. No, it isn't unethical. Astrologers aren't like lawyers, who represent one interest or another. We simply want to tell people their potentials, their patterns, so they can live life to better advantage, help them understand themselves and those around them. I would be glad to compare your chart to Mike's and explain your reactions to each other. Do you know the hour you were born—and the exact minute, if possible?"

"I'll ask my mother. She and Mike kid around about astrology a lot. And—it would please Mike a lot if you could talk a little about Barbra and me. Not that it's necessary, for I know it's going to be great. This time, I'm really in love."

"She's a very attractive girl."

"Not really a girl. She's thirty. You don't think she is too young for me, do you?"

I couldn't help smiling. "Not if you don't. Look, find out her place of birth, and date, and the hour if possible. We'll talk about it when you come to see me. Call my secretary." Barbra was waiting for us. He sat in back and I got in beside her. She was poised, serene. Even her driving had great authority. I caught myself hoping she was as much in love with Ned Foxx as he was with her, because he obviously was completely enraptured.

Next morning Maggie greeted me with, "Ned Foxx called. He wanted an appointment first thing this morning with a rundown of his relations with Mike, Mike's mother, Barbra, and the other two wives, whose names I didn't bother to take down. I said you were tied up for three weeks and it would take more than a couple of hours, if he wanted group horoscopes. Like Bluebeard."

"And what did he say?"

"Actually, he was trying to be very nice. Butter wouldn't melt in the mouth of the son-of-a-bitch."

"Maggie!"

She grinned at me, gamine-like. "I had a blind date with him one night. Between wives two and three, I think. Actually, it was a dinner party but my hostess expected us to go shooting off into the sunset together, she'd been telling me how great he was. And the way she described me to him, it must have sounded like I was a pushover because he was going home by way of some motel. Which, I've gathered since, is notorious for suburbanites who bed down with each other's wives."

"Did he know who you were when he asked for the appointment?"

"Heavens, no. I was your secretary and to him all secretaries are slaves. No, dear heart, he didn't know me from Eve. But I took delight in giving him a hard time, the old rapist. I told him such a complicated assignment would be time-consuming and expensive, suggesting he might not be able to afford it. He insisted money was no object. So I took tactic number two, and hinted you might not be able to fit him in. By that time, he was on his knees, begging. I told him to send over the birth dates of himself and all the girls in advance and we can have the horoscope charts done when he gets here. Actually, I'll do it—my pleasure. And I made the appointment for a Wednesday night, three weeks from now. He'll come in at 5 P.M. That's the night Ralph has a dinner meeting so you won't have to hurry."

I went into my office. Then I put down the sheaf of messages and went back to Maggie. "Look, I have an idea. Call Ned Foxx and suggest he send Mike in with the various dates. Then find out when Mike is coming and set aside half an hour for him. I want to take him downstairs and talk to him."

"And charge the fee to Daddy, I hope."

"No fee. This one is on the house."

Maggie made a face. But, in her usual efficient way, she fixed it. A week later, at 3:30 in the afternoon, Mike arrived with the envelope from his father. I gave him his mother's letter and steered him downstairs to a quiet corner in the drugstore. We had lemon Cokes in front of us before I asked, "Mike, why didn't you come back a long time ago for your mother's letter?"

He shoved his drink aside. "I was busy. You know how it is in the summer."

"You left it last Christmas. Why didn't you want to see me? And why did you ask me to come to lunch with you and your father?"

"And Barbra," he prompted.

"And Barbra. Mike, what's wrong?"

"Miss de Jersey, you told me that you wouldn't have said anything to my mother if you had seen early death in her chart. It wouldn't be ethical, or whatever. So why should I expect you to tell me anything?"

"What are you talking about, Mike?"

He reached for his drink and finished it in one gulp. "I'm going to die early, too. You saw it, didn't you? This summer, I've thought about swimming out as far as possible in Lake Michigan and then just letting go. They say it's an easy death. I'm like Mom. She didn't want to suffer. But, on the other hand, a gun is quicker and more certain. You don't swim back from a shotgun, placed in the mouth. Take off your shoes and pull the trigger with your toe. Off goes your head. Messy but sure. Sure-fire, as they say."

I put my hands in my lap so he wouldn't see that they were shaking. From time to time, many clients talk about suicide. Sometimes it is only a way to get attention, an excuse to get someone out of bed after midnight. But you can't be cruel enough to reject someone so miserable, even if there is no suicide aspect in the chart. And sometimes the suicide possibility is there, but so vaguely indicated that it simply lurks in the background, to be triggered only by a set of extremely powerful adverse aspects. I had seen no dangerous indication of suicide in Mike's chart. In fact, the very strength of his being a double Capricorn was good insurance against it. But, to be absolutely certain, I wanted to check again.

"Mike, you aren't going to kill yourself. It wasn't in your chart or I would have remembered."

"You wouldn't tell me if it were. Would you?" His voice was hoarse.

"No, I wouldn't. But I would have warned your father. And—"

"Are you sure you didn't?"

"Yes, Mike. I hadn't seen your father for over a year until that lunch the other day."

"You could have sent a message through Mr. Browne."

"But I didn't. Mike, where did you dream this up?"

"And you've been trying to get me to come back. Without

charging me. You're a nice lady, Miss de Jersey, you don't like people to kill themselves. So you are keeping in touch, watching me. Well, I've decided one thing. I'm not going to do it at home. I'll wait until I get East." He was rattling the ice in his Coke glass so loudly I had to lean over to catch his words.

"Don't you think your father has been through enough without your threatening to kill yourself?"

"I'm not threatening. I'm going to. Dad has Barbra now. She'll take care of him. They won't miss me. She may even have a kid of her own. Or a couple of little kids."

"Mike, you are feeling terribly sorry for yourself right now. But you aren't making very good sense. I didn't warn your father because I didn't see suicide in your chart. Come upstairs with me right now and I'll prove it."

Maggie's eyes widened when she saw us back so soon. I said, "Get me two folders. Mike's and Ben Franklin's. And try to get in touch with my four o'clock appointment. I'm afraid I'm going to be running pretty late for him."

"Katie, you can't. It's Mr. Bunting. He's come all the way from Peoria to see you."

I looked at Mike. "What are your plans for the rest of the afternoon?"

He shrugged. "I was going to a movie, I guess. Then meeting Dad and Barbra for dinner."

"Go into my office and sit down. When Mr. Bunting arrives, you can sit outside and help Maggie file charts. Then we can go on. Because I am going to prove to you astrologically why some people who seem to have every reason for suicide never do it—and other people, without what seems like any cause at all, simply can't resist the urge."

And when Mike had obeyed, I took the charts from Maggie, saying, "I won't answer the telephone. Call Ralph and say I may be late getting home. Let me know when Mr. Bunting arrives. As for anybody else—I've vanished. I'm in Alaska. Or Hong Kong."

Maggie said softly, "I hope he appreciates this. But I know it doesn't matter. To you, I mean. So good luck and I love you."

Some afternoons you can forget. They blur into countless other days just like them. Others stamp themselves indelibly on your memory, and years later come back as freshly as yesterday. This was one of the indelible afternoons and I am glad it was as significant to Mike as it was to me, because, as he told me later, it was then he decided to study astrology seriously. Perhaps he will go into it professionally someday. Right now, it has become an important, significant tool to guide him and the remarkable part is that he appreciates the fact as much as I do.

At a convention of the International Platform Association I had met a young man with a remarkable story. Two years before, he had been paralyzed from the waist down in a mountain climbing accident. He was eighteen years old and had been climbing since he was nine; he'd had, in his own words, a "love affair with the mountains." Despite his youth, he had been one of the few climbers in the United States to have scaled Longs Peak, 14,225 feet, four times.

"Climbing was his exultation, summits were his world," I told Mike. "And in instants, it was all over. He slipped on a jagged rock ridge, his rope broke and he fell 150 feet, breaking his back in four places, his pelvis in two. Two operations were performed but his spinal cord had been too badly damaged for the doctors to help him. He was told he would never have the use of his legs and have to spend the rest of his life in a wheel chair. Under those circumstances, would you have thought of suicide?"

Mike's strong big hands were clasped on the desk between us; I couldn't help noticing, however, that they were a bit grubby, like a small boy's. He licked his lips. "You mean he's still around?"

"A great many psychologists have tried to find out why some people, who seem to have everything in the world to live for, kill themselves, while others, trapped in a disaster like Ben's, or dying of cancer, go on, cling to life. They haven't found any really satisfactory answers. But astrologers have. All you have to do is to look at Ben's chart and you will know why he had the courage to go on."

Ben had his sun in Scorpio, strongly aspected, his moon in Leo and Sagittarius was his rising sign. A strong chart, as I pointed out to Mike, with many favorable indications: he was highly creative, would probably write and engage in some form of public speaking. Good-looking—it was all there—he could be extremely attractive to women, perhaps be a little spoiled and selfish. The love of the out-of-doors was indicated by Sagittarius rising and the daredevil qualities by a strong Mars. Like Mike's mother, he seized the challenge of danger. That had been part of his love affair with the mountains.

"Study this chart," I told Mike, "and you can see what Ben might have become—attractive but a bit too sure of himself, more than a little conceited, so secure in his prowess with women that he would lose some of his genuine appeal. And there are other elements in the chart which show he had to learn a lesson. In a strange way, the horrible accident saved him, made him a much finer and more spiritual person.

"Anyone who has his sun in Scorpio, strongly aspected in a richly endowed chart like Ben's, is nearly always called on at some time in life to sacrifice or suffer. Scorpio is the sex sign, so the suffering and trauma may come as a result of being denied this outlet. Or, in other cases, a sun in Scorpio man may be struck down in his prime—to prepare him for his next life on earth, perhaps, if you believe in reincarnation, or he may suffer because someone close to him is killed in tragic circumstances."

I mentioned Robert Kennedy as an example of a sun in Scorpio who had already paid dearly in suffering through the assassination of his brother and emerged a more spiritual person; his own death was then in the future. I also added that—although this obviously wasn't the case with young Ben Franklin—occasionally someone with the sun in Scorpio who has lived a life of great indulgence and selfishness will pay for it with a crippling and destroying illness.

I had been introduced to Ben Franklin through his mother, when we met at breakfast the day after I addressed the convention. She was interested in astrology so I did what we call a progressed chart for the time of Ben's accident. The horoscope which is always done first for a client is the one we refer to as "natal," for the moment of birth. This is the pattern. If we wish to discover the aspects for a certain period in that individual's life, as related specifically to him, we do what is called "progressing" the chart. The planets are "progressed" from natal position one day for every year. Basically—although the process is much more complicated in actuality—what I do is this: If I am checking an event which occurred when a client was four, I "progress" his chart from his date of birth and compare the planetary aspects with his natal chart. You can do this for any year and any specific date, from the beginning to the end of life. This is a very ancient method of calculation devised by the old wise men and each time I use it I continue to find the answers revealing and accurate.

In Ben's case, I progressed his natal chart up to the moment of his accident, April 14, 1963, at 6:30 P.M. He had been climbing just outside Boulder with two companions, freshmen like himself at the University of Colorado. Ben's progressed moon was in 24 degrees in Aries, the same degree held by the sun in the heavens that day.

"Whenever we see this," I told Mike, "we know something important is going to happen, or has happened. Whether that event is good or bad depends on other influences. In Ben's chart, as you see, the sun on that day was unfavorably aspected to his north and south nodes of the moon in Cancer and Capricorn, and was in a degree which means the show-off, the prima donna. Since Aries means the pioneer, the explorer, I think that, whether Ben realized it or not, he was showing off, adventuring, and created his own downfall. But luckily the aspects also offered a chance to learn from experience.

"His progressed sun was sitting exactly on the same degree of Sagittarius, his rising sign, in his natal chart. This also means an event of significance. In this case, it changed his life completely, smashing it from the physical point of view, making it from the spiritual point of view.

"The chart showed an awakening on higher levels, mentally. The first weeks in the hospital must have been terrible. His mother told me he was consumed alternately by grief and rage. If I had been able to talk to him, I would have said that this was the turning point, the beginning of a career devoted to the service of mankind, the good rising above the bad aspects. For in September of 1963, he went back to college in a wheel chair. The next summer, against all expectations of doctors, he discarded his wheel chair and went to Europe on crutches. There is little chance of his ever recovering completely although you must never underestimate a Scorpio. He now has 50 percent use of his left leg, 25 percent of his right. His athletic interests are necessarily limited to spectator sports. But his grades are brilliant. So is his spirit. We are expecting great things of this young man, whom many would call unfortunate. I don't."

I leaned back in my chair. It had been a long speech.

"You make me feel ashamed," Mike said.

"No. That isn't why I went into detail. I wanted you to see what I mean when I talk about a strongly aspected chart. Let's examine your own natal chart. Two things are important if an astrologer is told that a client is thinking of suicide. You look first at the aspects in the eighth house, the house of death. If the ruler of this house is the planet Mercury, which represents the mind, and if it and the sun, which is the life force, are badly aspected to Saturn, any astrologer must be concerned. Negative aspects to Pluto, a tricky planet, must also alert us to possible danger.

"In your case, you have considered suicide because your sun and Mercury are not well aspected to Saturn. On the other hand, the sun, ruler of Leo, on the cusp of the eighth house, is well aspected to Pluto and Saturn and strengthened by Jupiter. This in itself indicates you have strong stability, you won't kill yourself, no matter how many times the thought occurs to you.

"In addition, your Capricorn moon is in the first house of your natal chart, showing a strong personality, independent, practical, self-reliant. Even when you see some indications which are not especially favorable in a progressed chart, it depends on the essential nature of the person how he reacts to those events. You will always fight, that is what your natal chart says to me. You will never give up. You can be counted on, no matter what."

"Then why am I so—depressed?"

"I told you what I saw in your chart about your mother. I wish I could say that gradually, as time goes on, you will forget your grief. But you will always be strongly influenced by losing her. I suspect it is going to affect your relationships with other women. However, if you recognize this, you will avoid the obvious traps."

"Such as?"

Mr. Bunting had arrived. I excused myself and went out to greet him. Maggie said, "I'll take Mike down and buy him a banana split and come back in a little while. You can't expect a boy of that age to subsist on Cokes. He must be starving."

"It isn't necessary. He won't run away now." But Maggie shook her head at me. And they disappeared.

Mr. Bunting had problems. Information had been leaking out of his office into that of a competitor. He had brought me a list of the employees who could have access to certain secrets, together with their birth dates and pictures. I went over it carefully; no clues. Then I rechecked and asked, "What about your secretary? You haven't included her."

Mr. Bunting—weighing around 250 and on the dark side of fifty—shook his head. "Oh, no, Celia wouldn't. Besides, she's in love with me."

The answer, when I worked it out, was all too obvious. Celia was in love with him but she had finally given up, after getting no response from her married employer. Celia also liked to drink, and her tongue had been loosened by long alcoholic dinners with an employee of the rival company. It was all very simple except . . . "Do I have to fire her?" he asked. "She's terribly efficient." I had to tell him that was his problem, if he could manage to placate her and gain back some of her old loyalty, all right. Otherwise . . .

We shook hands and I told Mike to come in and Maggie to go home. I opened his folder again.

"Mike, one thing you must realize. Your mother had the moon in Scorpio. I've told you about Ben Franklin and other people with Scorpio suns. These are individuals with depth of feeling so intense that they often mystify and disturb those they love best. Your mother had the moon in Scorpio and her sun in practical, factual Virgo. Add to this her rising signs—Capricorn, like yours, with Aquarius intercepted—and you have a person unable to form a close love relationship with a partner. So you have a complex, highly confused woman."

"Everybody loved her," he said stubbornly. "You should have been at the funeral. People in shops that Dad and I didn't know came. And sent flowers."

"In Aquarian fashion, she loved humanity in general but detached herself from those closest to her. Your father. When you were small, it was different. She took you out in the country and read poetry with you. But as you grew older, if she had lived, you would have felt shut out, too."

"The Japanese gardener made a special wreath for the grave. He wouldn't let Dad pay for it. He loved her."

"Mike, she had Mercury and Mars in the eighth house of death. These are well aspected to Jupiter in Capricorn in the twelfth house as you have. This indicates that your mother was a sensitive, as we say, someone who believes in survival on a higher plane after death. The twelfth house is secrets, something hidden; she undoubtedly saw things concealed from other people. So will you, as you mature. If she killed herself—and if the accident was deliberate—it was a wild impulse. But she was so much out of this world she really wanted to be on the other side."

He said slowly, "I used to love chocolate. She always made a chocolate cake for my birthday. And at Christmas. I can't eat chocolate any more. It makes me sick."

"Mike. On the day of the accident, the sun was badly aspected to both the sun and moon in your natal chart. It was a tragic day. But she had the moon in Scorpio on the midheaven of your chart. She lives in your memory. She will always illumine your life. She may even continue to guide and protect you. But remember she was human. Don't reject a woman your father marries because she isn't your mother. She can't be. She is another human being."

"In other words, be kind to Barbra."

"You like her as a person. Continue to think of her as a person when she comes into your home."

He shrugged. "I'll be away."

"Is that really how you want it? You'll be ready for college in another year. You could go East then. Think it over."

He stood up, thanking me for the Coke and the banana split. I watched him leave and then called Ralph to tell him I was on my way. He said I sounded tired. I was. I felt run-down, drained. I knew Mike wouldn't kill himself. But I still worried about him. Which doesn't help me or the client. The only thing I could do now was wait until Ned Foxx came for his appointment and see what came out of that session.

Of course Ned didn't recognize Maggie. He gave her what could only be described as a practiced come-on he would have bestowed on any attractive secretary. And Maggie, in her turn, was the original ice maiden. She gave no indication that she had any idea who he was—or that, for the past week, she had been working on his chart and those of his numerous ladies, wives, and wife-to-be.

He was wearing a blue tie which deliberately accented the eyes, a deeper blue than Mike's. He was beautifully turned out in best Virgo-sun fashion. I glanced at the chart Maggie had done. Moon in Aquarius, Taurus rising. Mars in Sagittarius squared Saturn in Virgo in the fourth house, parents, the beginning and end of life.

I said, "You've had a pretty rough childhood. Not everyone realizes how you had to struggle. They take it for granted you were born full-sized, adult. Your mother and I and you know different, don't we?"

He flushed under the tan. It had been a brilliant Indian summer and I'd heard he was an ardent golfer. But the tan must also have been part of his protective coloring. Most men who are strongly Taurus are compelled to maintain a façade of being in control, mature and responsible because underneath they so often are little more than frightened children.

I added: "You rebelled as a child, which brought on part of your difficulty. Street fights, right? You had to be the champion. Not because you really wanted to be the boss but because you were afraid, if you didn't hit first, you'd be persecuted."

His thick eyebrows lifted. If he was angry, he was keeping it under rigid control. "Mike has been talking. Believe me, when he is goofing off, I can't help wanting to sock him. He has it pretty darned easy, compared to what I went through."

"Mike hasn't been talking. I'm looking at your chart. You lost your father early in life?"

"The old man walked out on us. So what? Good riddance." Time and time again, under the protective bluster, I've found Taurus men sentimental and avid for affection. Yet, although they can take almost any amount of mothering and devotion, they seldom know how to ask for it. And when they are denied, they turn difficult and stubborn. The problems Ned faced were, like most of our problems, of his own creation. Yet it was easy to see why he would be an enigma to many women.

His chart showed a disinclination to marriage, yet several marriages. He was really not too interested in sex, due to his Virgo sun and his moon in Aquarius, both intellectual signs but with quite different impact. The Virgo mind is orderly, concerned with detail and technique—indeed often overconcerned. I have one Virgo client who is so conscientious about packing for a trip in advance that she usually puts in everything including what she had intended to wear; her husband calls her "Mrs. Overpack." Aquarius is broader, wider in scope, more of an administrator than a detail person. He is concerned with what is best for the world and only incidentally for the woman he is holding in his arms. And both of these signs tend to be uncomfortable, even terrified, by the emotional demands made by the so-called "water" signs: Cancer, Scorpio, Pisces.

The Virgo attitude toward sex, unless there is a fire or water sign ascendant (his dead wife, for example, had her moon in Scorpio), is cool. A Virgo cannot love anyone he does not first like or respect; primarily, the attraction must be of the mind. A Leo client complains to me that her Virgo lover, before taking her to bed, always starts a fervent—but hardly erotic—discussion of current events. Another client, a Virgo male, complained to me that his wife refused to give him a "healthy" amount of sex. It was astonishing to her, a highly subjective, sensitive Cancer, that he wasn't concerned with why she was holding out on him. He only thought about it in terms of his own well-being.

I said, "Would you like to talk first about Mike?"

"He said he had a session with you. You explained a lot of stuff, as he put it."

"We talked about suicide. And his mother's death. I think he is straight in his mind about both things now."

"Did—does anything here say whether she killed herself or not?" I could tell it took considerable effort to ask that question. He even added apologetically, "Burton says you have ways of figuring out things."

"I have. Would you be interested in some information I have gathered about the effect of a series of eclipses on what happened to your wife?"

"I don't remember any—"

"These are partial solar eclipses and lunar eclipses. They have remarkable impact. The influences start before the eclipse. For example, on September 5, 1961, there was a total eclipse of the moon in 13 degrees of Pisces. It was in a trouble aspect to your son's sun in Sagittarius and your Mars in Sagittarius. Mars in a trouble aspect to Saturn in your natal chart indicates the loss of a wife. Did you discuss divorce at that time?"

"No. I can't remember." His face was closed.

"Are you sure?"

"That's a long time ago. But—OK, Miss de Jersey, I've never told anybody the whole story before. The night after she was killed I locked myself in her room and went through her desk and collected all those damned letters she had kept plus a locked-up diary which filled me in on every detail of her love life. Of course she had a lover. A local real estate man. With a history of taking sex-frustrated local wives to bed at a motel outside town. Back in September, I didn't know what was going on, precisely. But—a girl I knew—told me his car had been parked outside our house in the afternoon and we sure as hell weren't buying any real estate."

"Did you talk to your wife about this?"

"Damnation. Of course I did. I told her I'd divorce her if I heard anything more about her and Jim Barnes. That was the bastard's name."

"You and your wife share many good aspects, because you were born on the same day, although the years are different. But your marriage fell apart on the sex issue, didn't it?"

He jumped to his feet. For an instant I thought he was going to take off. Then, just as abruptly, he sat down again. "If we're going to discuss sex, I'm going to put everything on the line. After being married fifteen years, you don't feel about your wife the way you did in the beginning. Janet was a very proper type. She wouldn't bed down before we were married and I went along with it because I was older, I'd been overseas in the Army and seen plenty and—well, I was crazy about her. But after a while—she used to gripe about my being too interested in business, in making money. Let me tell you this. She'd have been the first to complain if I hadn't brought home the bacon. And plenty of it. But she was above such vulgar stuff as cash. She just charged and charged. And insisted on having her own bedroom because I disturbed her when I came in late. Then she gave it away to a bastard with a reputation for laying wives. Like a chippie."

"On September 20, 1960, two days before your mutual birthday, there was a partial eclipse of the sun in 28 degrees of Virgo. This fell in the eighth house, death, in her natal chart, hitting the sun and the planet Mars. The conflict between these two planets and her natal Uranus was triggered by the eclipse. You had violent quarrels. You were overwrought and she was brooding about your relationship. Right?"

"Sorry for herself, for God's sake. I'd planned a big birthday party at the club. Invited a hundred guests to a sit-down dinner. She said I'd planned it so I could deduct the whole thing as a business expense. Hell, of course I'd invited a few clients. My friends are my business connections. I'd had enough from her. I finally lost my temper. I told her I'd beat her black and blue if she didn't show up. She showed."

"And in October, she went to bed with this Barnes man for the first time. Her progressed moon was in Pisces in a trouble aspect to the fifth house, romance, approaching an opposition to Mercury in her natal chart. Actually, she was both fascinated and repelled. She wanted him, she wanted to get even with you—and yet she didn't want to break up her marriage. She was confused and drinking pretty heavily."

He looked up at me. His eyes were wild. "I tried to keep it from Mike. A drunken dame is a hell of a thing—she always drank secretly. Not at parties. She'd say, just a small sherry. But she'd already had half a bottle while she was dressing."

I nodded. "She'd reached pretty near bottom—not as near as she did later in June—but close to it in September. Then, gradually, Saturn and Mercury became better positioned. Although her moon squared Venus in the progressed chart, indicating a few furtive meetings, she gave the man up. Not until February did they really become lovers."

"Yes. Christmas was OK. You know, it's a funny thing. You talk about her being close to bottom. I was living in such a hell, too, that nothing was real. I existed from day to day. Waiting for the goddam thing to give. When I finally got the call that she was dead, I was almost—well, glad it was over. Did she kill herself, Miss de Jersey?"

"I've already progressed her natal chart to the day of the accident. This indicates no deliberate, premeditated suicide. Whatever happened, it was a reckless gesture, an on-the-spot madness. But if you would like me to study the planetary aspects for the exact time she killed herself, my secretary could do a chart while we are talking. Do you know when it was?"

"To the minute. It was 12:45. Noon. She raced out of the damned motel going like a bat out of hell and down the highway away from town. She smacked into a concrete pillar and the car burst into flames. The men in the bar connected to the motel heard the crash and called the police. Barnes, of course, ran out when he heard what had happened. I could have made it pretty hot for him but—"

I asked Maggie to come in. With just a quick glance at her long-ago blind date, she took the slip of paper on which I'd written the date and time of the accident. Ned didn't even look up. When she'd closed the door, he went on talking.

"But what was the use of dragging Mike through all that mud? I will say, Barnes got out of town. He and his wife moved to California. What in hell did she see in him?"

"Ned." His first name slipped out and I didn't bother to correct it. For I could feel the spoiled small boy sitting opposite me. What had really been hurt was his pride. He had been rejected by her selection of another man, particularly one he felt was less success-ful than he. But deliberate suicide would have been the ultimate rejection. To a man like Ned, a spoiled, stubborn Taurus ascend-ant who had never really grown up, and was despite his sharp façade deeply affectionate, the idea that any woman chose death as a preferred alternative to living with him, was unbearable.

It was my turn to get up from the desk and walk over to the view—an indulgence I seldom allow myself. The role of an astrologer is often difficult. You have to walk a delicate tightrope between the brutal truth on one side and being too gentle, too kind, and not useful, on the other. The only way you can really reach the right results is to treat the client as a partner, exploring what is there to be seen together.

Finally I turned around. "I called you by your first name a few minutes ago. With your permission, I'm going to do it again, just in this room. Because what I'm going to say is very personal and private. You sent me the birth dates of your two divorced wives. Carol is a Taurus. You thought she was going to be everything Janet wasn't—soft, affectionate, dependent, faithful. And you found out how really immature she was, self-seeking. On the other hand, Lorraine, a Sagittarian, appealed to you because she was so open and friendly—and made you wildly jealous because she continued to be open and friendly with everyone else. Neither one was right for you. You married on the rebound both times and, although I could compare your charts in detail, I don't think it is worth the time."

"In that case—" Like a small boy, rebuffed, he started to get up.

"Wait. There is something I want to tell you, for future reference. I've compared your chart and Barbra's. She has the sun and three other planets in Scorpio, and you have Scorpio in your house of marriage. And she has Saturn in Aquarius on the mid-heaven of your chart opposed your Neptune but trine your Venus—one bad aspect, one good. This means problems but eventual happiness. This marriage, for you, is fated. This is the girl for you. The other two weren't supposed to be, you were simply looking for security."

"Security? Carol married me for my dough. So far as Lorraine was concerned, she had a little dough but she wouldn't ever tell me how much. They married me for security. Not the other way around."

"Financial security, yes. You were looking for emotional security. You had lost your wife. You felt rejected—don't object, Ned, this is a not uncommon reaction of widowers even when there had been no emotional tension between them and their wives. You were ambivalent toward her when you remarried. In one sense, you were replacing Janet. In another, you were getting even with her."

"I'm—I can't take this on an empty stomach. Come out and have a drink with me."

Maggie was hard at work on the chart of the accident and so absorbed she hardly noticed us getting our coats. She blinked twice, annoyed at any interruption, when I said, "Maggie, if we're not back by the time you've finished, leave the chart on my desk. Go home."

Her name must have finally clicked the right lever in Ned's memory. He looked at her in astonishment. "You must be the girl I met at a party and drove home a couple of years ago."

Maggie glanced up, abruptly. "And tried to rape," she said. "I hope your technique has improved." Then she was back with the chart.

Ned made it clear he was in no mood for conversation until he had that sustaining drink. I wanted to shake Maggie, yet at the same time I was secretly amused by his reaction, confirming everything I was trying, gently, to point out to him. Finally, he turned into a bar which he seemed to know, dark as a pit. I fumbled my way behind him to a table and ordered a Scotch mist. He wanted a double bourbon on the rocks, no water. I waited until he had swallowed half of it, in a gulp, before I said, "Ned, your pride has been badly hurt by events piling on top of each other. Barbra is going to make up for a great many past problems. She'll be loyal and strengthening in many ways and you'll be good for her, too. I'd like to talk to her some day soon and explain some of the things I've told you. Meanwhile, I want to say two important things. This marriage is vitally important to your peace of mind, your future. You mustn't take her too much for granted. She is fourteen years younger than you are. She has her sun in Scorpio, which means she will need you to be more demonstrative of your love than is your custom. Be free with her, tell her how much you need her. Don't frustrate her. And don't delay the marriage. She's waited long enough."

He finished his drink. "Right now, we're thinking about Christmas. Mike will be home from school. Barbra thinks we shouldn't give the impression we don't want him around."

"She's right. I'll do an election chart for the marriage date, when we go back. Meanwhile, my other comment is about Mike. Barbra's instincts are right. She has Capricorn rising and under-

stands the deep need he has for family ties. The loss of his mother
has left him even more bereft than most boys of his age would be,
although he fights not to show this. Your other marriages hurt
him, he felt left out. He tells me he is going away to school. If this
is really what he wants, fine. But make it clear that the decision is
his, not yours, that he is always needed at home, from your point
of view."

Nodding at my full glass, he said, "Want another?" When I refused, he motioned for the check. But it wasn't until we were out
on the street again that he complained, "I've thought of nobody
but Mike. I kept all the mess about his mother from him. If I had
my way right now, Barbra and I would be married. I wanted him
to accept it."

"He has. He likes her. The idea of your marrying again does
bother him, naturally. That is why I want you to go out of your
way to let him know it will never alter your feeling for him in any
way."

"In other words, he's gaining a mother, not losing a dad." His
tone was flippant and his mouth was not pleasant.

I said, "Precisely," sounding like my British father. We finished the walk in silence. Maggie had left for the day, but the chart
for the time of the accident was on my desk. First, however, I
checked the aspects for a December 25 wedding. They were excellent. His progressed moon formed a 60-degree angle to Jupiter
in her chart, a sextile. The sextile aspect always brings opportunity
and Jupiter stands for success. "Keep that wedding date, please.
This can be a very good marriage and I know from experience
how wise it is to start any marriage with all the best possible aspects going for you."

"You really believe this stuff, don't you?" Teasing. I didn't
bother to reply. Instead, I reached for the chart Maggie had done of
the aspects for the time of the accident.

I told him: "There is every indication of danger through im-
petuous action here, and an accident in a car. My conclusion from
comparing the various charts is in line with what I told Mike. Your
wife had been drinking, heavily, because of her moon and Neptune
aspect. When she left the motel, she felt overconfident of her
driving ability (the moon was just past Jupiter) and needed speed
to discharge her feelings. If she drove into the pillar, it was a split-
second decision. She did not plan to kill herself. She felt she was
losing you, she was feeling guilty for her lapse (Venus was in a

trouble aspect to Saturn as it crossed her natal ascendant) and yet, I fear, she was brooding, blaming you in typical Scorpio-moon fashion."

"I know. I read her diary."

"Ned, you have another Scorpio in Barbra. I repeat, don't shut yourself away from her. In her own way, she will find it hard to reach out to you."

"You really do believe all this, don't you?" This time his voice wasn't teasing. So I answered.

"I try to watch my aspects constantly, to avoid minor as well as major mishaps. I can't advise my clients to do that. For one thing, I can't have my time or theirs wasted by frivolous questions, like, 'Is this a good day to go to the beauty parlor?' When I study the aspects I can say yes or no—meaning that the answer depends on whether you feel happy with the results or not, whether the set will last or fall apart. So far as I'm concerned, if I have a speaking engagement, I do think of the aspects. If I just want clean hair, I go at any time.

"On the other hand, planetary positions are very important when you are selecting a date, say, for a wedding or an operation. Some years ago, when I had a painful eye infection, I consulted four different specialists on a Saturday morning. I was in such bad shape they all took me without an appointment, and humored me when I asked each one his birth time. I chose the one who was best suited to the problem by astrology—and I was right. And even when I was under treatment, and he was extremely skeptical of the outcome, I was able to assure him that I had done a progressed chart for my condition and knew it would end in six weeks. Which, of course, it did."

Ned Foxx stood up and walked to the corner of the room, then back. Pausing, Virgo-fashion, to pick up a thread on the floor. "It had been a long time since she and I met at breakfast. The day she died whatever the stars indicated, she changed her pattern. She got up and fixed breakfast for me. Chipped beef. I'd loved it as a kid and she used to make fun of my childish tastes. That morning, she fixed it. The old-fashioned way my mother taught her with milk and flour, not cream. I didn't want to eat."

He came over and stood by my desk. His face was in shadow—and, shadowed, looked worn, tired. "If you want the truth, I'd been out with Carol the night before. Carol was the one who first told me Janet was playing around. We'd had a lot to drink and my stomach was upset. Also, I guess I was comparing Carol and Janet. Carol was so fresh and pretty compared to Janet these days, and she was only three years younger. I picked at my plate and she made a sarcastic crack about maybe Carol's cooking was better than hers. I said maybe it was but I didn't know, that Carol didn't have round heels. Then I stopped, because Mike came downstairs."

"She felt she was losing you both, by her own hand. And, in a way, it was true. Remember that."

"She tried to get him to eat something. He was in a hurry and grabbed an orange from the table, saying something about he'd be late coming home, he had swimming practice that day. He was on the team, you know."

He seemed to expect an answer so I said, "He mentioned something about it."

"Only he didn't go to practice that day. I don't know why. We tried to reach him and couldn't. When he got home, he found that chocolate cake she'd been baking—I smelled the damned thing as I was going out the door, the last time I ever saw her, and I asked what the hell the occasion was, because she'd got to the point where she could hardly bring herself to broil a chop, and she started to cry. I went over and put my arms around her and she reeked of liquor. I pushed her away and went out and got in the car and drove to the office."

"She'd hit bottom, Ned. Remember that."

"Later the police found out she'd met the guy at the motel. He had a room there he used as an office—and for babes. Somewhere around noon, he called and ordered sandwiches and martinis to be sent out to the pool. The boy delivered the order but nobody showed up. Finally he checked and Barnes signed the tab and told the boy to throw the tray away. I guess she'd had a fight with him. I don't know. They remember her walking out and getting in her car and the next thing, there was this crash. Maybe she'd had a few more drinks at the motel. They seemed to think she was pretty high when she drove off."

In the next studio, a telephone was ringing, a lonely sound in the dusk. Ned heard it, too, and picked up his coat.

"I've kept you. And Barbra's waiting for me. I feel—maybe I've finally buried Janet. I'm—more appreciative than you will ever know."

I saw him to the elevators, grateful that he had Barbra, grateful that Ralph would be home soon. Then I wondered, briefly, about Mike. But just about that time the telephone rang and it was Ralph saying he could make dinner after all, so we arranged to meet at Jacques' in ten minutes. And that was that.

At Christmas, we received the announcement of Ned Foxx's marriage to Barbra. And shortly after New Year's, I had a telephone call from Mike. Things were going great, he reported; he had made the swimming team and his grades were so remarkable that his father was beside himself with pride.

"And Barbra?" I asked.

A pause, so brief that I wouldn't have noticed if I hadn't been watching for it. "She's OK. As a matter of fact, it's the best thing that ever happened to Dad. He's turning into a human being. And one of these days, when I decide to go off on my own, I'll be glad he has a nice person there looking after him."

"You are growing up," I said.

"That is my intention." We both laughed.

Then I reminded him, "When you find the girl, come to see me. I'll compare your charts."

Maggie, who was at my desk, said, "That will be the day. I'm retiring his chart to the permanent file. You'll never hear from the ungrateful little beast again." By which I could see that, in her own way, she had succumbed to Mike's appeal, too; probably over the banana split.

I didn't see Ned around his usual haunts, either. One night I asked Burton Browne, who told me Ned and Barbra had gone around the world on a honeymoon trip and, so far as he knew, were becoming happily domesticated. So, I gradually forgot them all. I acquired new clients and new problems. In the summer of 1969, when I moved into my present studio in the John Hancock Building, Maggie found Mike's file and it was touch and go whether I'd retire it permanently to the files I keep in the basement at home or include it in the move.

I checked it briefly. There is nothing psychic involved, or even ESP, but I do get a general feeling about what clients are going to do, just from years of being exposed to them. I didn't bother to progress Mike's chart, but I did have the quick reaction that he might be in touch. "He's twenty," I said, "about time for a romance."

So we moved his chart with us. And we had been there a few weeks, with the workmen still competing with us for elevators, when Mike Foxx called. Maggie was taking time off to have her hair done so I answered the telephone.

He said, "May I come in to see you?" And when I expressed my delight—with my curiosity showing through—he added, "I'm thinking of not going back to school. You see, Miss de Jersey, I'm considering an acting career. That's one of the things I'd like to check you out on."

"And the other is a girl?"

"I'll tell you when I see you."

The first date I could make for him was three weeks away, unless there was a cancellation. I took his number again—he was still at home in the old family house in Wilmette—and asked to be remembered to the newlyweds.

"Not so newly," Mike reminded me. "It's been nearly four years."

When Maggie came back from the beauty shop, I told her, "I suspect Mike Foxx has a girl."

"And I'll bet he's planning to move in and let Daddy support them."

"Maggie, don't be so cynical. He's thinking of quitting school and going to work. Or at least, going into acting. I'm not sure whether or not he knows that is work."

Maggie nodded her satisfaction. "And he'll let the girl slug away at some dull office job to buy groceries. This is the Aquarian Age, where girls have more than equal rights, especially when it comes to forking out cash and removing their lovers from exposure to jobs where they might get their hands soiled. And, of course, girls also have the premium on getting pregnant."

"Mike isn't like that. You know it."

Maggie, mother of two girls, shook her head. "They are all like that. And it's ours not to wonder why." But she was as curious as I was about Mike's girl. She even came back from lunch early so as not to miss any part of the action.

He was prompt. And he had achieved the good looks which had only been a promise in the gangling boy I'd first met. He had a man's body, now, lean and muscular. The interesting pale blue eyes, changeable like water, today seemed to have a highly green tinge.

He said, "I have to get a job. I want to get married."

"Why are you thinking of the theater?"

He hesitated. "I know a lot of actors are Sagittarians—Frank Sinatra, Noël Coward, Jane Fonda. I thought—"

"That isn't quite all it takes. But you know that. You want me to check it out, of course. First tell me about your girl."

"She's an actress. A dancer, rather. If you see things look pretty good for me, I thought I might try New York. You can live pretty cheap in one of those lofts. And New York is where the action is."

"When was she born?"

He pulled out a card. "November 9, 1934, at 10:30 A.M. In Chicago."

"But she's older than you—nearly fourteen years."

He looked at me oddly. Then the words came all in a rush, Sagittarius fashion. "She has her sun in Scorpio. My mother had her moon in Scorpio. She reminds me of her in so many ways. She isn't like the rest of the suburban wives who think of nothing except bridge and clothes. We read poetry together. We talk about the world. She—"

"Is she married?"

"Yes. But he's older than she is. He doesn't understand her."

"Famous last words." I drew a chart toward me. "Mike, just on the surface, knowing your chart well, I don't like this. I warned you that, throughout your life you would be looking for your mother in relations with women. I don't say this is necessarily bad, so long as you know what you are doing. But I do have the strong feeling you can find warmth and maternal instincts in a girl nearer your age. You don't have to select a married woman who is fourteen years older than you are."

"I didn't select her. It happened."

The girl—or, rather, woman—had her moon in Sagittarius and Capricorn rising, like Mike. I said, "I do see why it happened. The great wise men of Babylon and Rome, who were all astrologers, knew that when a woman's moon falls on a man's sun, they will find each other. Many modern astrologers have seen this, too. Lovers who were separated by crises—floods, famines, even concentration camps during World War II—were more often reunited when the woman had her moon on her man's sun sign. And it is the ideal relation between a man and woman, because the moon represents the female in his life, whereas the sun is his ego. When she has her moon on his sun, she reflects him and illumines his life."

"Miss de Jersey, that's exactly the way it is!" He sounded triumphant. "I knew you'd see we were meant for each other."

"Wait a minute, Mike." I went back to the charts. "Your moon in Capricorn is on her Capricorn ascendant. This is good, in one way. Your personality, which is your moon, corresponds with her attitude toward life. You are both basically serious, ambitious, determined to succeed and capable of the hard work needed to achieve your goals. But you are both conventional, too. You care what the world thinks about you. Are you sure she is ready to get a divorce and marry a man so much younger? Liberated as we are today, some people still take a dim view of divorce and more feel a marriage between a woman of thirty-four and a boy of twenty is pretty strange. They might even get the idea she was taking advantage of you, robbing the cradle."

"That's why we are going to New York. In New York, people don't care what you do."

"Is that why you want to become an actor? So you can get away from Chicago and escape into an unconventional life? That's not a very good reason. Besides, neither of you would really like it. And an acting career isn't really right for you. Success is too precarious in the theater and requires qualities I just don't see in your chart. You will be happier in a career which will give you definite rewards. You do need an outlet for self-expression but you would never be satisfied with mediocrity, which seems to me as far as you would get in the theater. You need to be on top, to run the show."

Mike moved from the sofa to a chair. He ran his big hands nervously through his hair. For some reason, I felt on edge, too. It might have been his unease which communicated itself to me but I didn't think so. I picked up the Foxx folder and hunted through it until I found Barbra's chart. The birth date, supplied to me by Ned before their marriage, was there: November 9, 1934, at 10:30 A.M. In Chicago, of course. I looked at Mike.

"Why didn't you tell me it was Barbra you want to run away with?"

"How did you guess?"

"The birth date and time rang a bell. I compared her chart with your father's before they were married, at your request, I believe. I do remember charts, you know. They're almost as individual as fingerprints."

"And we don't intend to run away. Barbra is going to get a divorce."

"Has she told your father?"

"Not yet. As a matter of fact, we haven't really discussed details. But you saw what happened to my mother. Dad broke her on his wheel. She couldn't take his cruelty, his coldness. He was too critical, too stubborn. I want to save Barbra before it's too late."

"Barbra's chart is very unlike your mother's, Mike. It isn't a bad marriage at all. Barbra, of course, has to make most of the adjustments. But she is strong enough to do it. She has Saturn in Aquarius on the mid-heaven on his chart. She is the stronger one of the two, yes, but her influence is good, propping him up in many ways. True, he has Saturn on her Mars in Virgo, which means he tends to chill her intense Scorpio emotions, not good. But he needs her for security—there is a danger of disillusionment and bitter old age in his chart and he fears age terribly. She also has the sun and three planets in Scorpio and he has his north node in Scorpio in the house of marriage. A Scorpio woman is right for him, he was meant to find one."

"What about her?"

"She's a lovely girl but up until right now she has been too self-centered, concentrating too much on her own gratification. She also tends to undermine his confidence because of her own strength, cut him down, make him feel uncertain. She doesn't know she is doing this and he can't articulate his hurts. But he is by no means the brute, nor is she the victim. And have you any idea how you would hurt him if you took Barbra from him? He would never get over it, never forgive you."

"I've thought of that. But—"

"Mike, you need him as much as he needs you. You think you're in love with Barbra. But you also, subconsciously, are trying to revenge your mother's death. That is ridiculous. Her death was in her chart from the day of her birth. Your father couldn't have prevented it, no matter how hard he tried."

"You're wrong. I love her."

"You met her in September 1965—September 14—a Tuesday, as I remember. Your progressed moon joined Saturn. A second mother-figure entered your life. It was a good contact. Your moon had progressed to sextile—a 60-degree angle, a fine aspect—to Jupiter in her progressed chart. This meeting was something good, something which should bring great happiness to you both. Don't ruin everything. She owes your father something and so do you."

He grunted.

"Mike, you have more maturity than your father. Although he gives the impression of being shrewd, a brilliant businessman, he's emotionally insecure. He has been lonely much of his life. Barbra may, at the beginning, have misunderstood that fixed, earth nature of Taurus, the practical-in-material-things side of him and didn't realize he was like a child reaching out to her."

"We tried not to fall in love." Mike's voice was harsh. "Honest. When I met Barbra that day at the Art Institute, I fell like a ton of bricks. I tried to keep away from her. I was glad he was sending me to prep school. I made up my mind I'd think of her only as Dad's wife. I went skiing over the Thanksgiving holiday with some of the boys in my dormitory. Then she insisted I be at their wedding. And I fell in love all over again."

"Is she in love with you?"

"How can you ask that?" He jumped to his feet. His eyes were wild.

"Because I see certain things in her chart. You have Mars and Jupiter right on Barbra's ascendant. There is an irresistible sex magnetism between you."

"It's not all sex!"

"No, of course not. Sit down, Mike. You have Venus in Scorpio —your ideal woman is a Scorpio. Barbra also has Venus in Scorpio. This means you have similar love natures, both on an intellectual and physical plane. And your father, more because of his basic nature than his age, is incapable of meeting the challenge of her strong sex needs. In a way, when she turns to you, she is revenging herself on him for being what he can't help—a little cold in sex relations, particularly to an intense Scorpio."

"Him not sexy? You're kidding. Any guy who is working on his fourth marriage—"

"He has his moon in Aquarius. People born in the highly emotional water signs—Cancer, Scorpio, Pisces—often feel rejected by Aquarians because they have a certain amount of detachment in their love affairs and intimate relations. Your mother felt like this, Mike—especially as the Virgo side of his nature made him so analytical and such a perfectionist in tiny things, so apt to think of sex as something therapeutic rather than romantic."

"I told you he didn't understand Barbra."

"Just as she doesn't understand him. I know how it must be— being highly subjective in Scorpio fashion, she must seem to him secretive, too independent, hard to know. You may wonder why she married your father, because she is so much her own woman, a stoic, standing on her own feet. Mike, I think it was because she realized he needed her."

"Hearts and flowers. Bring on the violins."

"There are worse things than being needed, Mike. Like not being needed. Remember your sun in Sagittarius. You are a wanderer, always seeking the ideal woman. At the moment, you think you have found her. But what about afterward? You have your moon in Capricorn, which is her rising sign. The Capricorn who married someone older than he—or she—often divorces and remarries someone younger later in life. This is a pattern which Barbra, without realizing it, is reaching out for right now. Do you see how pat it all is? Your father is fourteen years older than she is and she fourteen years older than you."

"That makes no difference."

"Maybe not now. But it might later. Her Saturn is strongly aspected so far as your chart is concerned but yours is stronger because it sits right on her Mars. The attraction between you was impossible to resist, in the beginning. You said you tried, and I am sure you did. I know that Barbra, in her typically loyal Scorpio fashion, also must have fought it."

Mike's voice dropped suddenly. "We hate hurting him. If there should be another scandal—"

"Mike, come out of your dream world. Of course there will be a scandal if you run away with your father's wife. And you won't like living with it, either. You and Barbra are both too conventional. But even more important, the Saturn aspects between your chart could bring conflict, bitterness, even hatred after marriage. It would be hard enough on you. But think of her. Could she survive the breakup of another marriage?"

He sat down on the couch. "I never thought of it that way."

"Keep thinking, too, of what might happen to your father. He has Mars in Sagittarius, afflicting the sun and Saturn in Virgo. This aspect, plus the moon in Aquarius, can be very dangerous. He isn't strongly sexed but with Barbra, his basically faithful Taurus nature will sustain him, keep him from wandering far afield, from changing partners frequently to try to find sexual excitement. Without her, he might lose all sense of proportion. Quite nasty things might happen. I don't need to spell that out. Nor the fact that you and Barbra would feel responsible, blame yourselves and each other."

He was silent. I turned around from my desk and watched the sailboats out on Lake Michigan making a pattern of crisp white against deep blue. I felt sorry for Mike but he was young. He would find another love. I felt sorrier for Barbra. But not so sorry as I would have been if she and Mike had gone ahead recklessly and eloped, without his consulting me.

Finally he said, "How do I tell her?"

"Don't worry too much about that. She'll manage. She may even be secretly relieved. Giving up each other isn't going to destroy either of you. On the contrary, through a mutual decision to do the right thing because it is right, you are both going to grow. Instead of feeling guilty and blaming the other one—as I am sure would have happened if you two had gone through with this—you and Barbra will actually learn a deeper and different kind of love. You will have deep and lasting rapport."

"You make it sound easy."

"Not easy right now, perhaps. But far better than making what would have been a tragic mistake."

"It might be a good idea for me to go away for a while. Join Vista. Or the Peace Corps."

"I agree. Your father will understand that. And it will give him and Barbra a chance to work out their problems. Ask her to come in and see me one of these days. I think I can help her."

The house telephone rang, announcing my next client. Maggie came in to answer it, and to say goodbye pointedly to Mike. After he left, she turned to me.

"He didn't seem to be riding on Cloud 89 exactly. What did you tell him?"

"That he shouldn't marry the woman."

"Woman?"

"Actually, he's fallen in love with Ned Foxx's wife, Barbra. His stepmother."

Maggie sat down. "That will serve the old bastard right."

"But I had to warn him it wouldn't work."

"And he agreed, just like that? He couldn't have been very much in love."

I shook my head. "On the contrary. But he also has learned a good solid respect for what astrology can give a person. He's intelligent. Right now he is still fumbling but I wouldn't be surprised if one of these days he might decide to become a serious student. It could be a wonderful thing for him because he is going to have to live with his mother problem all his life. He's never going to get over losing her, and he could mess himself up pretty well trying to find a replacement."

"Or a lot of replacements, like Daddy. If I remember correctly, our Mike is a wandering Sagittarius. In that case, I'd say Barbra is well out of it."

"I think she'll agree with you one of these days. Maybe even now Mike's decision will come as a relief. Basically, although she and Mike were very much attracted to each other—and rightly so, because of their charts—neither of them is temperamentally suited to thumbing their noses at the world, living unconventional lives."

The doorbell rang. Maggie stood up. "Score another home run for astrology."

I smiled. "Score a three bagger. For eliminating a pointless triangle."

5
Mars For
Sex

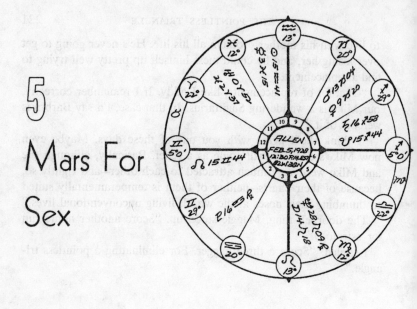

ON March 28, 1968, close to midnight, there was a potent partial eclipse of the sun, triggering an event which was to shake the nation a few days hence. On April 4, the great Negro leader, Dr. Martin Luther King, was assassinated in Memphis, Tennessee, fermenting riots, bloodshed and far-reaching antagonism between not only blacks and whites but blacks and blacks.

I was in Los Angeles that fateful month. My heart was heavy as the fog which shrouded the garden outside my hotel bungalow every morning and crept in with the chill each night. For such an eclipse hits widely varied targets . . . in this case, not only the leader of the black people but an attractive black couple who were supposed, according to the fan magazines, to have the kind of marriage "made in heaven."

The night Eve Cowles came into my life, I hadn't gotten in until nearly midnight. I was standing in front of the open fire in the lobby before collecting my room key. I was standing there in a half-dream of fatigue, thawing out the chill, when the night manager drifted over to me and whispered, "There's a lady waiting for you. She's been here a couple of hours. If you don't want to bother with her, here's your key. Slip out the back door and I'll get rid of her."

I took the key and glanced at the clock. Nearly midnight. I had an appointment call coming in from Chicago at 8 A.M. and my plane was leaving at 2 P.M. I'd look forward to being on my own at last, watching the late-late show tonight, perhaps sneaking a swim in the pool in the morning. I'd said goodbye to everyone. Yet . . .

"Did she tell you what the problem was?"

"Not that one. She's pretty upset, I could tell. But a dish. Quite a dish. Whoever is buying her clothes, he's being set back plenty."

It was the usual Hollywood attitude. If a girl wasn't a known celebrity and if she were young and pretty, the assumption was that some man was paying the freight, picking up the tab for her clothes. I was mildly curious but not very. I said, "Maybe I will skip out. Tell her I had a long day and am leaving tomorrow."

"I first thought she might be one of those Egyptian actresses. But then I decided she was just colored. If she was an actress, I'd at least have seen something about her in *Film Daily*. But she must be something in the hay." He winked at me. Up until then, I'd had no intention of taking on a new client. But his assumption annoyed me.

"What name did she give?" I asked casually.

"I guess I didn't ask. I didn't think you'd want to be bothered with a—but she sure is wound up about something. I bet she's smoked a pack of cigarettes since she came in."

I thought, damn. I was going home tomorrow. My appointment book would be jammed. I couldn't take on a situation my last night, much less one which might be complicated. And yet his attitude rankled. I don't like to see people kicked around because of the color of their skin.

"How long did you say she's been here?"

"Well, I came on at ten. She was here then, I guess. She had Frank, the bellhop who's on duty, bring her a cup of coffee a while ago. She gave him a dollar tip. Whoever she is, she must be loaded. Maybe she's one of those fancy ladies kept by the Mafia. She's sure pretty. Every time I look at her, she gets whiter." He winked again.

I was so tired I ached. But I also was too wound up to go to bed and sleep. I'd counted on the late-late show to relax me. I dropped my room key in my pocket and asked, "Where is she?"

He pointed to a corner of the lobby which was hidden by the usual screen of potted palms. I thanked him and went over to her. Except for an elderly man in an Aloha shirt planted smack opposite the entrance, so he wouldn't miss anything, we had the lobby to ourselves. It was a quiet night, Monday. I skirted the palms and dropped into an armchair opposite a young woman who was buried deep in a creamy cashmere coat. "I'm Katherine de Jersey."

She straightened. She was more than pretty. She was copper-colored and luscious, with straight small features and a cap of close-cropped straight dark hair. Her shoes and dress were lime-colored and her jade and pearl necklace was so discreet and underplayed it had to be real. She was a lady, obviously. Her voice confirmed it.

"I know. I saw you on television today. I shouldn't have come here to bother you. But it was a compulsion. I have to talk to someone and suddenly the idea hit me of consulting you."

"I'm sorry. I'm not out in California to work with clients. I haven't had time to contact even my regulars who live here. But I would be glad to give you the names of several local people who could help you."

"No!" I was startled by her intensity. I think she was a little embarrassed, too. She was obviously not the type who lost her cool very often. Nor was she the kind of woman who went around confiding her troubles freely.

"Scorpio?" I asked. She had the intense black eyes—the burning eagle eyes—we often associate with that sign. But she shook her head.

"Gemini. A duel personality, I've heard. I was born May 29."

"You're close to the Taurus cusp, which gives stability. I wouldn't cast you as a split personality. I also suspect you have Scorpio rising. But all this is beside the point. I know Los Angeles well enough to know what a tight little world it is, full of gossip. Whatever is bothering you is private, of course, and you are afraid that if you go to someone local, he might talk. I can assure you that the ones I would send you to wouldn't. Ever."

"It isn't that—entirely."

"What is it, then?"

"I want to talk to you. I feel you'd understand. It's a story I would dislike admitting to most people. I haven't told his sister much about it. I'm supposed to be meeting her at the airport tonight. God knows what he will think when I'm not home by midnight. If he's home by then himself."

"Who is he?"

"My husband."

I leaned back, thinking wistfully of the late movie. I'd checked that morning. It was Bogart and Mary Astor in *The Maltese Falcon,* which I've watched a dozen times from various beds in various hotel rooms and will probably watch a dozen more. "Look, my dear, I don't know who you are or what is wrong. But I have to leave tomorrow afternoon, early. If you are in trouble, can't you talk to his sister?"

"Val? No, he loathes her. Rather, it's a love-hate thing. He adores her and he hates her for what she does. In other words, she's a very high-class call girl. She no longer needs the money. She does it for kicks. It amuses her—she's no youngster, either— to be seen with important executives. She is flying in with one of her clients tonight. That's why Allen wouldn't meet the plane."

"Are you afraid of your husband?"

She shook her head. "No. He wouldn't harm me physically. At least, I don't think so. But he is a big, powerful man and he's been terribly out of control recently, when he's been drinking. I don't like the way he talks to the children. The other day he asked our eleven-year-old son if he had slept with a girl yet. Only he didn't put it that nicely. He used a gutter word."

"Is there anyone else you could consult? Your mother? Or his?" Again, an intense reaction. And again, a giant effort for control. "My mother's dead. And his—I don't know where she is. Miss de Jersey, I wish I could tell you, a white woman, how desperate the plight of the black woman is today. Once it was the black woman who kept the family together, who could always get some kind of work to feed the children. She was important. Today, our black men are taking revenge on us. We have no control over them. They hate us for all the things black women did, had to do, in the past, to survive. Allen thinks all black women are bitches—his mother, his sister and me, his wife. We are trying to tell our children black is beautiful. Don't you believe it. Black men don't want us any more. They want the white woman, the ones they see on television. And the frightening thing is that they can have them. White women think it is very with-it to go to bed with black men."

I looked at her. So pretty, so chic, so bitter. So underplayed one moment, so close to violence the next. This is characteristic of the Gemini—up in the clouds, then dropping down with a thud. Highly strung—often more than they realize themselves—and so alert to the ever-changing vibrations of the rest of us that they often catch negative reactions and thoughts in others before we are aware of them ourselves. To be married to someone with his or her sun in Gemini is a challenge; I know it well. But it is seldom dull.

I said impulsively, "I should think it would be very hard for any man to resist you."

That quick flush of pleasure. The quicksilver smile. Then the frown. The depression. "Think back to all the stories you've ever heard. Even twenty years ago, a black man could be lynched for touching a white woman, let alone trying to make sexual advances to her. It was not permitted by the very white men who exercised their right of ownership or their whims over black women. We weren't even whores. We were used, casually, and tossed aside. Like animals. You would think that our men would feel some sympathy for us, for what we went through. But it isn't that way. Now Blacks have won some small position in this society, the black man who amounts to anything doesn't want a black woman. He wants one with white skin and blond hair. A status symbol."

"Does your husband like white women?" It was only recently that I'd learned to say "black" instead of Negro. And it was also recently that I'd encountered clients who were considering interracial marriages. It occurred to me that this girl was pointing out something which we Caucasians tend to be slow in noticing.

The beautiful woman sitting opposite me smiled as though I'd asked a foolish question. "What do you think I'm talking about? Of course."

"How deeply involved is he?"

She hesitated. "There have been two that I know of. The one right now—Allen says she is to blame, that she won't let him alone. I suppose that could be true. But I remind him he could say no. Then he says, 'She is desperate. What if she should kill herself? Do you want me to be responsible again?' "

"Again?"

"The first one killed herself. She was a neurotic."

I stared at her. "How can I help you?"

"Allen lies to me. I know it. He told me this one is so rich and powerful it would ruin his career if he rejected her. Then in the next breath he says she is a young girl. Sometimes he weeps and begs me to help him get released from the hold she has over him. The next night he stays out, all night. With her. I am so mixed up. I don't know what to believe."

"My dear, I would like to help you. But in order to do that, I would have to do your chart, and his, and compare them. I'm going home tomorrow. You should have someone here in California."

"You can't understand what it does to me, Miss de Jersey. I love my people. I want to help them. But for Allen, having a white woman on his arm makes him feel important. He never knew his father, and his mother had to work as a domestic. She never got home until late at night. All he knew of white people he learned from watching them on television, using deodorant, driving in big cars. If the white women could only understand that he doesn't really want them; it's what they stand for. And they are sleeping with a black man, to show how liberal they are."

I touched her gloved hand. Mine was bare. I had been raised as a small girl always to wear gloves, no matter what the weather, preferably white kid gloves. Of recent years, I've been liberated from this tyranny of convention. Whereas the black woman opposite me, dressed far more expensively than I was, wore them as her symbol of breeding, of having risen in the world. "I wish I could help you. I really do. But this isn't a simple problem nor is it something which can be resolved in a few minutes. You need someone nearby, with whom you can talk frequently."

"I don't want to go to another astrologer."

"How about your doctor? Or a minister?"

"Allen says it is nobody's business but his own. He has changed so dreadfully. He isn't the man I married. Liquor never used to interest him. Now he drinks to keep functioning, he tells me. And he takes pills to sleep. Last Saturday they called me from a bar to come and get him, he was too drunk to drive. When I got down there, he was gone. It was a miracle he got home for he was weaving all over the road. One of these days, he may kill himself. I told him that after he'd sobered up and he said he didn't care. He begged me to go away and take the children, he said I was too good for him."

"I think this is a problem for your doctor. He must give him the sleeping pills."

"He did. But Allen can be so convincing. He insists to the doctor that I'm the one who imagines things. I don't know what kind of stories he tells but the last time I saw the doctor he suggested I might be benefited from therapy. I'm not going crazy, Miss de Jersey. It's Allen. But he is such a clever actor he can fool anybody into thinking anything he wants."

"Including his sister?"

"No, Val isn't fooled. But he won't listen to her. He calls her a whore. Maybe she hasn't lived the kind of life you and I have, Miss de Jersey, but there were extenuating circumstances. During the depression they didn't have enough to eat. Allen's mother was accused of stealing when she brought food home for them. When Val was eight years old, she was with a man for the first time. He gave her candy and she took half home for Allen."

I shivered. This time she touched my hand. "I never knew anything like that. We didn't have much money but by comparison with Allen we were rich. I should think Allen would sympathize with Val, would understand why she is the way she is. Instead—he is beginning to think of all black women in terms of his mother and Val. Including me. In the beginning, I stood for a great many things he never had known. He'd been raised on the streets. He wanted a home, security. I wonder sometimes if he doesn't hate me for helping him have those things."

"What is your name?"

"Eve Cowles."

"Should I know your husband?"

"If you watch television, you probably have seen him. He's on the *Jeopardy* show on Friday nights."

"Allen Cowles." It was a name which was being mentioned with increasing frequency in television circles. But I couldn't recall a face to go with it. And then I remembered one Friday night, when I was working and my husband was watching television. He'd called to me to come and see something. It was a marvelously attractive young man literally dancing on the rooftops. It was almost ballet. He was life and joy personified, whether the camera concentrated on his body or on the lean, charming face. I said again, "Allen Cowles. Yes."

"I thought you'd remember him. He's quite a favorite with white women. He has an all-white fan club. They had them on television a few months back, chasing him down the corridors in the studio, grabbing his clothes. It was—disgusting."

"But harmless enough."

"I disagree. I called him at the studio afterward and told him he should have his head examined for allowing anything like that to appear. What kind of dignity can our people have when they expose themselves to such stupidity? That night he didn't come home. He stayed out all night. With one of his fan club, I presume." Her upper lip curled.

"I heard you had a cup of coffee while you were waiting for me. Did you eat dinner?"

"I can't remember. I fed the boys before the sitter arrived. I think I ate something, too."

"I never eat before I lecture. I'm hungry. Why don't you come over to my bungalow and I'll order club sandwiches and tea?"

"I'm not hungry. And I don't want to be a nuisance."

I put my arm through hers and guided her out the back door. I took a certain satisfaction in smiling sweetly at the night manager. Then I was sorry. We all of us are the product of experiences and those mysterious electromagnetic fields which, like computers, stamp out our patterns at the moment of birth. We can't help what we are. But what we do about it, is something else again.

Eve did eat a little, birdlike, as she wandered around the room, light and rhythmic in true Gemini fashion, touching, feeling—Geminis have great tactile appreciation—and still smoking. Chain smoking. While I got out charts and pencils, she explained how she had discovered me.

"Gene, our youngest boy, was restless. I suppose I've been short-tempered with him but Allen has been so—difficult. I sat Gene down in front of the TV set, something I never do except for certain children's programs, and just turned it on and let it run." She turned to me in one graceful swoop. "Then you came on. And I knew I could talk to you. Don't ask me why. It was like a message. And here I am."

"I almost slipped out the back door without talking to you tonight."

"I know. I was watching. That little fellow in the flowered shirt promised to follow and see what room you were in. Then I planned to come and knock on the door. Do you hate me now?"

"When was your husband born?"

"February 5, 1928. In Charleston, West Virginia. At high noon, or shortly afterward. Val stayed home from school to help the midwife. She was six years old. He's forty years old and she's forty-six. Neither one of them look it. That's why he's beginning to lie but it doesn't do any good. After all, he did play football at UCLA in 1948. He can hardly pretend he was ten years old when he was that great open field running back."

"And you?"

"I don't want to talk about myself."

"May 29, you said. What year, what time and where?"

"Athens, Alabama. May 29, 1933. Around 4 P.M. But it is Allen who matters. You say you don't have much time. Explain Allen to me."

I ate while I did the charts, realizing for the first time that I was starving. His horoscope had "star quality" all over it. He could have succeeded as an athlete but acting was spelled out, too. And he was a full moon baby.

Full moon people are nearly always highly talented, yet also stirred by conflicting emotions, at war with themselves. I said, "One thing you must recognize about your husband. With the sun in Aquarius in the tenth house of fame and career and the moon in Leo in the fourth house, which stands for parents and the beginning and end of life, he is driven by a need to succeed. He is terribly ambitious, but he is mixed up about how to achieve that ambition. And I think when he says one thing to you, and then contradicts himself, he is genuinely confused, mixed up about his motives."

"I wish . . . He doesn't try to make sense any more."

"He has the sun on the mid-heaven, a position which promises fame but not necessarily happiness. Everything in his chart indicates how much he suffered as a child and how scarred he has been by those events. Yet instead of holding him back, the horrors he remembers have driven him to prove himself. The deep-seated psychological tension which always comes with having been born under a full moon has also driven him. He needs to impress himself on people because he was ashamed of his mother, and never had a father. He has to prove himself as not only as good as, but better than most. This is the secret of his success. And his failure as a husband. He can't see anything except that one goal."

"I wish he'd chosen anything except acting."

"He could have been an athlete. But I think the acting was inevitable."

"I think I could have managed better if he had been an athlete. I don't like actors or acting."

"Why not? Because you think you could do it yourself—and didn't have the chance?"

"Of course not!" Her answer had come too fast.

"It shows in your chart. You do have talent."

"We met when I was working part time in the Theater Arts Department at UCLA. He'd graduated the year before and came back to play a special role. I'd heard about him, of course. He'd been a great football player. He came to UCLA on a football scholarship and then switched to acting. One of the sportswriters used to say he ran like the wind, he was poetry in motion."

Like a flash, I had a picture of Allen Cowles dancing on the roofs. "His ascendant in six degrees in Gemini which makes him a bit vain and self-centered, yet easily influenced."

"We used to love to dance together. We made love together well, too. They say it goes together." She picked up a piece of toast and nibbled. "Such a long, lost time ago."

"Have you ever thought of having a career of your own?"

"Never. I quit school to marry him. I didn't want to be like those other black mothers, leaving their kids to grow up by themselves. I stayed home with my boys. I gave them everything. I even make up for the father who is never there. Besides, I'm too old to try to act now. I'll be thirty-five in May."

"There are other things besides acting. Even in Southern California."

"I suppose so. But when we were married, I promised I would make being his wife a full-time job. He needed me, then. That's why I find this—affair—so confusing. He says he still loves me. He begs me to be patient. Sometimes I believe him. I do love him terribly. He is the core of my life. Without him, there is nothing. And yet there have been times when I felt I didn't exist for him. I was just one of the crowd out there watching him on television.

"He started in movies. Back in those days, there weren't many parts for a black actor. He did everything from bits as jazz musicians to waiters—God, how he hated being a waiter. Then he got a big break. Do you remember an actress named Priscilla Ross? He played the part of a black detective in a movie where she was a dance hall girl. It made him."

I don't get to that many movies; time doesn't permit. Nor did the name Priscilla Ross ring any bells. "In his progressed chart, there is a romance early in 1966," I said. "His sun was in 23 degrees of Pisces which often means a tragic ending. It was a strange romance, unrealistic, more like an illusion."

"She killed herself before the movie was released." Eve settled lightly on the arm of a low chair. "She was older than he was, although he was no child. But she was pretty and blond and pink and white. As I look back on it now, I suppose she represented all those little white girls on the streets of Charleston that he could look at but wasn't supposed to touch."

"Eve, the success and gratification he wanted were slow in coming. They arrived at the same time he met her. Do you see the connection?"

"It was his first starring role. In the movie, he fell in love with her. And I think she really did fall in love with him. In a way, it was her last chance. She was drinking heavily and her looks had suffered. She kept saying she needed him to keep her sanity. I think for a while he believed her. Then he began to see her for what she was."

"He gave her up at a time when the aspects in his charts show he made a wise decision."

"She kept threatening to kill herself. Then she'd turn around and plant items in the gossip columns about their being together at various places. It wasn't true, of course. At least, so far as I knew."

I poured myself tea and offered her some. She refused but came over and took a black olive in one hand and a piece of bacon in the other, nibbling like a little girl. It was hard for me to be severe with her but she had asked for help.

"Eve, there is one thing which is all-important in your husband's chart. Your standards are so different it may be hard to understand his tenacity. His ambition is the underlying force in his life. The pattern is so strong no one can change it. He is going to go higher, get more acclaim but at the end of his life, there will be disappointment and tragedy. He will need support then, all you can give. And you are a strong and loving woman."

She looked troubled. "I don't mind anything except the love affairs. With white women."

"You have your moon in Leo. So has he. Two people with strong pride have some things in common, but you can short-change each other in appreciation. And he has one significant aspect in his chart, Mars is in the same sign as Venus. Mars is for sex, Venus is for love. He is a highly sexed man, as you probably know. Even more important, these planets are in Capricorn, the sign of ambition, of success. Do you realize what this means?"

"I'm not sure."

"He uses his sex appeal to advance himself. We can't criticize him too harshly for this. It's the way he is. Don't you realize that he looked up to you, too, when he married you? He was attracted, yes—who could blame him? But you also represented a stability, standards, a refinement of living he had never known."

She dropped the olive pit in an ashtray. After a minute, she lighted another cigarette. "He made me go and talk to Priscilla. At least I knew about her. I don't even know this girl's name. Or who she is."

"There could come a time when he wanted to be rescued from her, too. I see an ending, a definite end, preceded by several breakups."

"Oh, God." She closed her eyes. "Priscilla promised me she would give him up. Then she would start drinking and call him, saying she'd kill herself if she didn't see him once more. At first, he would get dressed—the calls always came in the middle of the night—and go over. Then one night she called and he said to tell her he wasn't home. I did. They found her the next morning. Sleeping pills on top of the liquor."

"Did he blame himself then?"

"No." She looked at me oddly. "I called the police and told them about her trying to get in touch with Allen. I said it wasn't the first time. They understood what I was talking about. There are lots of women out here who go the same route. And they were very good about not implicating Allen or his family. One of the detectives really took to little Gene, who was a baby at that time. And of course they saw I was standing by my husband."

"You Geminis have a knack in emergencies. It's as though all the information and bits of accumulated experience you've picked up over the years suddenly emerge. You are good people to have around when things go wrong, quick to act."

"But what can I do if he won't let me help?" She went over to the fireplace where one log was smouldering. "I never thought he felt guilty about Priscilla's death. But now he tells me he doesn't dare give up this new girl for fear she will do the same thing. He says he won't have the death of two women on his hands."

"Isn't he dramatizing himself a little?"

Again the odd look. "You're a bit uncanny, you know."

"No. A Leo always dramatizes his role in life. I suspect you do, too."

She ignored that. "He began having nightmares in February. No, January. He began talking about Priscilla in his sleep, saying he'd killed her."

"Are you sure he was talking in his sleep? He is an actor, you know."

"Oh, God. At first, I tried to comfort him when he wakened. It was all such nonsense. One night we got into an argument. In the middle of it, we made love. It was the first time he'd wanted me spontaneously in a long time, for nearly a year it had been the same old Saturday night routine. Then after it was over, I got mad all over again. He walked out for the second time that night and never came home. Now it's happening so often I've lost track."

"But he doesn't try to hide the fact he is with the girl."

"No. It's strange but I never thought of it that way before. With Priscilla, he lied. Once when he was down in Acapulco on location, there was a note in a gossip column about their being together at a night club. He denied it, saying she had simply planted it in a column, he wasn't there at all. Of course he was lying. But he seems to want me to know he is with this woman. Whoever she is."

"There is a powerful sex attraction indicated. I'd like to do her chart and compare it with his."

She shook her head. "He won't even tell me her name. He pretends I'd recognize it."

"Is that part of the dramatization?"

She collapsed—sagged—back into the chair again. She was like a doll from whom the stuffing had leaked. "I don't know. It is so strange. He borrows my car and I find things she's left in it—once, a yellow scarf. Another time, a pair of driving gloves. I think I am even beginning to recognize the perfume she uses.

"Then just last week he borrowed my car and asked me to take his to the service station and have it washed and the oil changed. That isn't his way. Usually he doesn't like me to drive the Cadillac. When I opened the glove compartment to give them the credit card, I found a hotel bill, stamped paid, for two nights in a Los Angeles hotel. All sorts of room service on it. Those were nights he disappeared without explanation. When I handed it to him, he said yes, he was with her. He couldn't help himself."

"Does he tell you he loves her?"

"No. He says it is sex. Pure sex. And that she is the one who insists on seeing him. He says he tries to escape her. One Saturday night he called me at hourly intervals from ten until nearly five in the morning, saying he was on his way home. He finally turned up at six. He dressed and took the children to Sunday school. Then he came back and tried to make love to me. He says he can't

help himself. He begs me to help him. But how can I help him
if I don't know her name?"

"Do you believe he really wants you to stop him?"

"I don't know. He says I have to save him, that all he has is me
and the boys. Then he turns around and tells me I am too good
for him, I should leave him and take the children. I don't know
what to believe. That is why I want you to help me." She started
to get up, and sank back in the chair, adding, "Then, when I won't
let him make love to me, he tells me how wonderful she is in bed.
How generous. The other night he accused me of using sex like
a whore, of not going to bed with him until we were married. It's
true I wouldn't but those were my principles. I was a virgin when
I married him. He insists the white girl went to bed with him the
first day they met. When I asked if she was a virgin, he laughed
at me."

"It is part of the new freedom, the Aquarian Age."

"These white career and college girls have less morals today
than the ghetto prostitutes. At least, the prostitutes need money
and they have no other way of earning it. These girls do it the
way you take a cup of tea. Like it meant nothing. And when they
see a man they want, black or white, they go after him. I asked
him how he met her. He said, 'I just looked around and there she
was.' "

My tea was cold but I didn't have the energy to call room service
and ask for more hot water. Fatigue had at last won out. My eyes
stung so I could hardly see Eve Cowles across the room.

"I'm going to send you home. You can come back tomorrow
around noon and we can finish, because I'm just not making sense.
I'll walk out with you and make sure Frank is around so he can
get your car. I don't want you wandering around the parking lot
this late at night."

"What if he leaves me, Miss de Jersey? I've seen too many
black women alone, raising their children. I know I sound like a
broken record. But what am I going to do if he leaves me?"

"Allen has his sun in Aquarius and the moon in Leo. This is a
potent, attractive combination of Leo pride and Aquarian beauty
and magnetism. Aquarians are humanitarians and often have such
magnetism that they are very hard to resist. But they cannot be
possessed by one woman and any wife who attempts to keep her
Aquarian husband on a short leash is making a mistake. If you

let an Aquarian have his public, bask in its adoration, he will always return to base, his home, his wife."

"I'm not sure I can bear that."

"You have your Leo-moon pride, too, and your Scorpio ascendant possessiveness. If you understand why you react the way you do, it may be easier. I don't mean that unfaithfulness is ever pleasant. But women who don't try to control their Aquarian husbands, who let them have their small flirtations, knowing they will come back, often feel more secure. Twice I've had as clients musicians with the sun in Aquarius. Both times I've been well aware that their wives, if they hadn't been astrologically oriented to the almost inexhaustible needs their husbands had for applause and flattery, would have broken up the marriages. As it is, both marriages are considered idyllic from the point of view of the public."

"I'm not concerned with the public."

"He is. He doesn't want divorce."

"I'm not trained for anything. I didn't even graduate from college. He swept me off my feet. We were married secretly in May and then again in June, when we went back to Athens to have him meet my family."

"Eve, you will always manage." I stood up, putting out my hands. I could see her as a remarkably pretty young girl at UCLA, winning her professors because she worked so hard and competently and yet was always a lady. She had her sun in Gemini, making her quick and facile, able to grasp almost any kind of task with amazing speed. Yet Scorpio rising kept her from being too glib, too facile, although it would have been hard for Allen or anyone else without astrological knowledge to detect the strength and intensity beneath the charm of her bright surface.

When she had come close to me, I told her, "But you aren't quite as uncomplicated as you seem. Any Gemini can change from an angel to a devil in one instant, from a laughing boy to a sullen individualist. Sometimes a Gemini, without realizing what he is doing, withdraws when he or she is needed most. You don't see this in yourself because you are too intensely caught up in your own mood, but you sense it in other Geminis. Allen has Gemini rising. You've been aware of times when he seems to have failed you, haven't you?"

She withdrew. "He wasn't happy when I found I was pregnant with Gene. The first one, little Allen, was enough. He had his son. I was sick a lot. One morning he woke up when I came back from the bathroom feeling horribly rocky and asked, 'What in hell is wrong with you?' "

"And you in your turn keep things hidden from him. The Gemini is sometimes accused of being shallow, changeable, fickle. But you have hidden depths and hidden devils, deep below the surface."

"I've never told him I would have liked to have been an actress. If that's what you mean. When I was working in the Theater Arts Department, I used to slip in and watch rehearsals and imagine what it would be like to be up there on the stage, acting Ophelia or Candida. Then one afternoon Allen Cowles came back to school to play a role in a production of *Our Town*. Just a small part. Afterward I talked to him about the problems of being black in the theater—that was back in 1951 and there were very few places for us, even fewer than there are today. He called me the next week and took me out to the Pasadena Playhouse. It wasn't a big thing at first, we were just good friends. We knew each other well before I even let him kiss me."

"The marriage was an impulse kind of thing on his part. It shows in his chart."

She nodded. "He came to pick me up. I was living with one of the women administrators in the Theater Arts Department, a nice Mexican lady whose daughter had taken a semester off to travel abroad. She liked Allen. That night he said to her, 'What if Eve and I get married secretly? Would you let me come and spend weekends here? I haven't much money but I'll help you with the car and the yard work.' And he did. He cleaned out the garage, which had been loaded up with all sorts of junk since the lady's husband died. He helped paint the house. I sometimes wonder if he was in love with her, too."

"Eve. Eve, my dear, don't look for trouble. You are getting things twisted. Your Scorpio ascendant makes you brood too much and sometimes probe more deeply than you should."

"I've given up my life for him."

"Let's try to be realistic. You have gained out of the marriage. You like being Allen Cowles' wife. You like beautiful clothes. You have good taste and you enjoy being surrounded with nice things. Allen gives them to you. But you must make concessions, too. That's what marriage is about. Have you, for example, really ever forgiven him for taking up with Priscilla?"

She turned away from me. "Why should I?"

"He did give her up."

"For himself. For his own reputation. People were beginning to talk and he was afraid."

"You and Allen both have Leo pride. You also have the good qualities associated with Leo, the style, the flair. You were attracted to each other because you both are generous and loyal and outgoing. But you both have the same Leo negatives. And, just as you don't understand some of the Gemini problems you share, you don't realize when you are failing to fulfill the Leo needs of each other.

"Leo is the king of the jungle—or the queen. If you hurt a Leo's pride, he will react, sometimes savagely. He may forgive you but he will never forget and he will bring it up at inopportune moments. At the moment, Allen is center stage. When you met him, you were star struck. You really hoped to attain your goals through him. So you gave up your career. But you still blame him for your sacrifice, although it wasn't his idea."

"I've been a good wife. I've never looked at another man. Doesn't he owe me loyalty, too?"

"He is loyal, in his way. He admires you. He wants you to save him. Those calls he makes to you when he's with her. That bill he left for you to find. They are cries for help."

"Why should he try to get me to help him when he is being unfaithful? Do I owe him anything?"

"Yes," I said and watched her turn back to me, reacting to the first real jar I had been forced to give her. She didn't like it. For a moment, I could feel her disliking me.

"You have been using sex as a weapon against him, you know."

"In bed he tells me about other women who have admired him. I think he does it to get excited. Sometimes I feel I am nothing except the receptacle."

"And sometimes you use Gemini tricks on him in sex. A Gemini will use a quarrel, an argument, to excite his partner. With most people, once the quarrel is resolved by making love, it is forgotten. A Gemini is capable of bringing it up again, quite as though there hadn't been a sexual interval."

"Perhaps. But he makes me so angry."

"And, in his way, he loves and admires you. He needs your strength. You are important to him and mysterious: Saturn is in his seventh house of marriage. You are a rock to him, a great strengthening influence. The only danger of this astrological position is that, if you aren't very wise, the rock could become a millstone around his neck."

"I came here for help. You are blaming me for the terrible thing he is doing."

"I'm only trying to explain the problem between you and pointing out ways you can live with him, make things less painful."

"How can I make him get rid of—that woman?"

"It won't last between them. That is all I can tell you. If I knew her birthdate, I could be more specific. Meanwhile—come along. I'll walk over to the lobby with you."

"You want me to make all the adjustments."

"He won't. So you must. You came to me with a problem. I would spell out certain things to him, if he had come. But as it is—do get your lovely coat, my dear. You are so beautiful and are so genuinely clever you could be hard on others, expect too much. Remember Allen was born during the depression. He was born under some of the bad aspects which caused the depression. You were born when it lifted. And to a different kind of parents."

"My mother brought me up to do things right. We weren't rich, not by a long shot. My dad was a postman and my mother worked as a caterer. They both worked hard. But they taught me never to lean on other people, to stand on my own feet."

I picked up my own coat. "It's late. You may come tomorrow, if you like. But I don't think there is much more to say, really."

The cold air struck us like a blow, after the too-warm room. We didn't talk until we reached the lobby, where a sleepy Frank went to collect her car.

The car came and I slipped my arm through hers. "I would be able to help you with more details if I could find out when she was born."

She pulled her coat collar tight around her. "It's a curious thing. He might not even know. Do you care about when a girl was born if you are bedding down with her?" Then, without saying goodbye, she ran for the car, moving like a dancer. I walked slowly back to my room and put away the Cowles charts. In bed, I fell asleep almost instantly.

Next morning, after Ralph and I had talked on the telephone, I ordered breakfast. The room service waiter named Red delivered it. In California, especially Southern California, all room service waiters tend to be characters—who knows, won't somebody discover them one of these days?—and Red was no exception. It seemed part of his act that the breakfast invariably arrived with one important omission which meant Red had to go back to the kitchen and so had an opening for additional conversation when he returned. It had pleased him mightily to be told he had his sun in Leo, like Leo Durocher and Lucille Ball.

This morning I cut his usual comic introduction short by asking, "What do you know about Allen Cowles?"

"Him? Oh, real hot stuff. He sure has the body. He was a football player at UCLA before he decided to become an actor. He had a rough time at first but you should see the ratings on *Jeopardy*. He won an Emmy last year, too. Of course, there are those who call him an Uncle Tom. The white dames sure go for him. You should have seen the show when his fan club chased him right into the men's room at the studio. It was a riot."

"I heard about it."

"He's married, too, I think." He was setting my table with fastidious care. I checked and found out this morning it was the coffee pot which was missing. After I pointed this out, he reacted with his usual amazement. "Those people in the kitchen don't have their heads screwed on right until the sun is over the yardarm. I'll get it right away. Anything else?"

"Ask the people in the kitchen if there is any celebrity, probably white, whose name has been linked with Allen Cowles."

"What's up, Miss de-Jay?"

The nickname wasn't original with him. Lots of my friends call me that. But, Leo-like, he acted as though he had coined it out of thin air. "Nothing much. Somebody mentioned him to me and I was curious."

"Okay, Miss de-Jay, I'll try it on for size." With that, Red was gone about fifteen minutes. When he returned, he did have the coffee, but it wasn't very hot. He also reported, "Allen Cowles, aged forty, sun in Aquarius. Two kids, male, aged four and eleven. A black wife, kitchen sink type. He gets photographed at a lot of parties with white dames. One named Priscilla Ross killed herself because she couldn't get to first base. But there are others."

"Who?"

"Starlets," Red said sternly. "On the make. Dumb little dodos. They do anything to get their names in the paper. Tell me, is it true what they say about black boys being so sexy?"

I told him I didn't know, which disappointed him so much I overtipped him. Then I finished packing, put on my bathing suit and went out to catch a little sun. Although the pool was heated, the cold wind discouraged me from trying to swim. I dropped down on a lounge. I hoped to at least have a pink face so my clients wouldn't think I'd been hiding under a rock in California.

To anyone raised, as I was, on Lake Michigan, there is nothing as soothing as the combination of sun and water. I fell asleep, and came awake with a start at the sound of Katherine de Jersey being paged on the loudspeaker. I was afraid I'd overslept, but it was only twelve-thirty. Half-annoyed at being interrupted in the midst of a delicious cat nap, I went to answer the pool telephone. A resonant male voice said: "I'm Allen Cowles, Miss de Jersey. My wife said you kept her up half the night. I decided it might be a good idea for me to come and see anyone so fascinating and find out what she could tell me. Could you have lunch?"

"I've just finished breakfast and I must leave for the airport in half an hour. I'm afraid I can't. Sorry."

"Why don't you let me drive you to the airport? I'm at loose ends and I'd really like to see you. My wife took our younger boy, Gene, to the doctor this morning. If it's mumps, I'm going to move out as I've never had them. I can be over there in half an hour. OK?"

I said OK. Then I couldn't resist adding, "If it's mumps, you've already been exposed. What's the point of moving out?"

"Eve has been talking. As usual."

"She has some reason, hasn't she?"

A pause. "I hope you're not going to be one of these militant feminists. Eve thinks I'm being horribly unfair to her. She may be right. But it isn't that simple. I'll be waiting outside for you at one o'clock. Tell the boy to put your luggage in the trunk of the white Cadillac."

Of course I was curious; I'm human. I took another fifteen minutes in the sun, by which time it was warm enough to swim and I didn't have the time. Then I went in and changed. When I mentioned a white Cadillac to the bellhop, he nodded vigorously, "Allen Cowles. He's some hunk of man, Miss de Jersey. He's forty but not an ounce of fat on him. Most athletes go to blubber. I remember when he played football at UCLA. Nobody could tackle him. He had that trick of shifting hips when anybody tried to move in close."

"Gemini grace."

"What say? I don't think there's a lady with him."

"Does he run around with women?"

"How should I know? Just the same, I've heard stories—"

"Mentioning who?"

"The daughter of some network big shot. I think these girls are out of their minds."

I decided to try the direct approach. Straightening my shoulders, I went out to meet Allen Cowles.

I expected he would be attractive; he was an actor, wasn't he? I anticipated his magnetism and good looks; he was an Aquarian. But I was totally unprepared for his size, his total impact, the appeal of his flagrant virility. I felt like a schoolgirl beside him. "How tall are you?"

"A bit over six feet two. Television makes you look shorter. And with movies you never can tell. If a man is short, they stand him on an orange crate before he makes love to the heroine. Did you ever hear the story about Katharine Hepburn and Spencer Tracy? When she complained about how short he was, he said, 'I'll cut you down to my size.' "

"I'm curious about why you decided to come and see me."

"Well. Eve was in a bit of a state when she got home. She had told me she was going to meet my sister Val at the airport. Apparently she lied. She didn't want to confess she was off hunting up an astrologer."

"And why not?"

"Calm down, Miss de Jersey. I don't know why not. But Eve gets funny ideas. She's far too fancy for the likes of me. I wouldn't be where I am right now if it hadn't been for blind luck. They scouted me in West Virginia, just a poor Southern nigger boy, and offered me a football scholarship to UCLA. I was so dumb I almost didn't take it. Then, because of my size, some crazy dame in the Theater Arts Department thought I'd make an Othello who would scare the hell out of white females. I thought, why not? That was what did it. I decided acting was a hell of a lot easier than getting your brains and your teeth knocked out in pro football. There are times, though, when I suspect there was a peg loose in my brain for trying to make it in show business. It was pretty much hand to mouth, all the way, until I hit *Jeopardy*. And I'm forty years old, Miss de Jersey. I haven't got that much time left."

"What do you want to do?"

"Not play a fat-assed black Robin Hood the rest of my life.

Even if it did get Eve a sable coat last Christmas. I want to ask you one question, Miss de Jersey. Why does anyone in Southern California need a sable coat? It's only snowed once here in like fifty years."

"How long has *Jeopardy* been running?"

"Two years. If you ask me, another year and I've had it. And here I go again, standing in line with a hell of a lot of black actors, most of them younger than me, for the few roles available. It's hell. I wonder why I keep knocking myself out. There must be better ways to make a living."

"None as well suited to you."

"What gave you that idea?"

"I've done your horoscope. Last night."

"Well, I probably will end up back in Charleston, West Virginia, knocking my knees together on the cotton platform. Or on relief."

"I doubt that. In fact, your big break is just around the corner. In two years, you will be bigger and better known in show business. You'll have success, fame."

"Did you tell my wife that?"

"I don't remember. Why?"

"Because." We stopped at the light on Hollywood Boulevard. I've ridden in cars with celebrities before, but never had I been with one who attracted so much attention. He was noticed, and obviously liked it, but pretended he didn't see a thing. It was rather endearing. "Because I'm afraid Eve isn't interested in me any more. She's sticking along with me for the ride. The day I fall on my face, Eve will be the first one to get off the ship."

"That isn't true."

"Acting isn't my bag, anyway."

"You have your sun in Aquarius. It's surprising how many actors and other show business people are Aquarians. And, although you haven't had a real opportunity to display what you can do in the field, it's on its way. You are going to hit the top in another five to seven years."

"I'll be fifty by then. Too late."

"No. Aquarians have a need to identify with the world in general. I think they respond to acting because it puts them on display in that world. Applause is a necessary part of your life. And being noticed. You found it first in athletics and later, more solidly, in show business. But the artistic success, the recognition you really want, is still to come."

"You make me feel better. Sometimes—Eve married me expecting a lot. It hasn't been all that easy. Once in a while, I'd make a big hunk of change but then there was a long time between jobs. And Eve, cute as she is, hasn't been exactly the little woman sitting there patting me on the back. She wants a hell of a lot."

"So do you. It's all over your chart. And you are going to win fame, I promise you. But not necessarily happiness."

"Happiness. What the hell is that? Have you ever gone to bed hungry, Miss de Jersey? I'm not feeling sorry for myself. I'm just saying it won't happen again, not to me. I'll kill myself first. Eve doesn't understand that. She is black middle-class, God help her. More refined than refined. Compared to my folks, hers were rolling in dough. When we went back to get married—or remarried it was because she wouldn't shack up until it was legal—it had to be a long white satin traditional gown. Traditional, so help me God. She doesn't have the slightest idea what I am talking about when I say I will never go hungry again. I'll see everybody in hell first."

"You both want recognition. Success is all tied up with proving yourself, showing you are better than your parents."

"I never knew my dad. And my mother ran away with some fellow when I was in high school. For all I know, she's dead. For all I care. The black bitch."

"You've had a rough deal. How do you know it wasn't a lot rougher for your mother?"

"Dames have their own way of taking care. Eve, for example. She's not made any different from any other black female. They all have the same equipment. But she puts on airs. I can tell you, when I first met her, I thought she was something pretty special. I'd never seen anything quite like that cute little coffee-colored rabbit. She was pretty. And clean. And bright—or, at least, so I thought. I thought there was nothing she wasn't going to be able to do. She was living with a Mexican lady just like she was her daughter. She had a bedroom and a bath all her own. She'd go out and pick flowers. There was always a rose on her desk, just one rose. It was like the movies." He smiled, remembering. "It's still like the movies. But I'm the prize cat who brings home the dough so she can have that rose on her dressing table, and the sable coat and all the rest. She's bright enough to make me go through my little act for her. But there are limits. She's not so bright she can keep kicking me when I'm down and make me like it."

I said, "I talked to her last night about your charts and compared them. I think she does care about where she has been going wrong. And I can see you belong together because of many similarities. Even when you first met, your progressed moon was opposite Saturn in the house of marriage in your natal chart."

"Which adds up to?"

"Fate. You needed her. You still do, in many ways."

"And I'm behaving like a skunk. Or worse. I suppose she told you all that."

"She told me. I'd like to know the birth date of the girl you're involved with. And compare her chart with yours. And Eve's. It is often surprising how often the chart of the other woman hits that of the wife. You see, the same man is a link between them, whether they like it or not."

"You have no idea how different they are. Deb—my girl's real. She's honest and kind and open. She doesn't put on airs. Do you know Eve once nearly cut off my sister's head because she brought a milk carton and put it on the dining room table? My God, how fancy can you get?"

"Your girl, whoever she is, must be very secure. She doesn't need to be fancy. She can put a milk carton on the table and to hell with it. Eve hasn't had her advantages."

He turned his dazzling, disarming smile on me. "One thing which bugs me, Eve is always picking at me. A man may be a louse. But he sticks around home a lot more if he feels he rates there."

"Oh, dear. You have your moon in Leo and so does she. You both need to have your egos built up and don't do it to each other."

"Come again."

"You married her because she fulfilled a great many of your needs. Her planets are grouped in certain signs and yours in others —you complement each other. In other words, we say in astrology that she supplies the half of the apple which you are missing. But you must tell her you appreciate her. You must compliment her. She'll be easier to live with and you'll benefit."

He said, "I earn the money she has to spend. She never had it so good. All I ask is that she takes care of me and the kids. Half the time she isn't even there when I call up. She's running around and a sitter is there watching TV and the kids are running wild. Last night when I got home little Gene had a temperature of 102. I had to call the doctor. She hadn't even noticed."

"She had other things to worry about."

"I'm a little tired of her going around complaining about me to everyone who will listen!" He stepped on the gas.

"Please don't punish the car for what your wife has done. Besides, the reason she came to me was that she didn't want to see an astrologer locally. She was afraid your privacy wouldn't be protected."

"Why in hell does she have to see anyone?"

"She's a human being. She's not a thing. Do you expect her to sit there and wait for you to come home happily when she knows you are out with another woman?"

"Miss de Jersey. Considering how long we've been married, I think I've behaved pretty well. I've only had two affairs and I haven't lied to her about either one. I've been honest with her."

"It's not the kind of man-to-man honesty you can expect a wife to appreciate."

"What is a man supposed to do when he gets bored being ignored at home and wants a little fun?"

"You don't seem to be having much fun with this girl, at least from the way you're reacting at home. And I understand the other one killed herself. Is it significant that you chose white women both times?"

"It just happened that way. Besides, if I may sound immodest, I didn't chase them. They picked me."

"You could have said no."

He cut in front of another car impatiently. The driver honked at him furiously and then yelled "nigger bastard." After a minute, he slowed down and smiled at me. "Thank you for not saying I didn't need to do that. I deserved being yelled at. So far as Priscilla was concerned, that was a mistake all around. But she killed herself because I gave her up."

"And for a lot of other reasons. There must have been a weakness in her chart."

"All right. As for this new girl, she's beautiful and she's talented and her father is loaded. She wants to marry me. And believe me, after listening to Eve bitching, the idea has its attractions."

"You aren't going to marry her, I can see that. There is a strong element of destiny between your chart and Eve's, if only you don't go too far and hurt each other too much. And you have the boys."

"The boys. Yes. The kids are great. They have all the things I never had—our own swimming pool, clean clothes always ready to put on, vitamins, tennis lessons, private schools. Out of my pocket. I don't resent that. I don't resent Eve spending a fortune on clothes. Hell, I flash money around, too, now. I get a kick out of being able to pick up checks and give expensive presents to the kids on the show at Christmas. Remember I was a charity case, only the charity was few and far between. We lived on what Mom could 'tote' home and when she got fired for taking too much, we went hungry, Val and me!"

"I know. And the compulsion to succeed, the need for recognition by the world shows all over your chart. You were a full moon baby, talented, ambitious, but full of confusions and complexities. You do know this about yourself, don't you?"

"What I resent about Eve is that she loves the dough I bring home, she spends it as fast as I can make it, but she is always complaining that I don't do enough for my people. She likes being the wife of a TV star, she is always tossing it around who she is. Yet she calls me an Uncle Tom. Because I work when and where I can. Because I played the part of a white doctor on a radio soap opera, she says I'm not proud of being black. Well, maybe I'm not. And what in hell did my people ever do for me? Personally, singlehanded, I dragged myself out of that lousy shack with the dirt floor in Charleston, West Virginia. Let the rest of them do the same. They don't have to sit there eating pig swill. They can get out and work, the way I did."

"Let me try to explain why Eve has the concern for her people. She has Saturn, the planet of Destiny, in the fourth sector of the chart, representing home and parents. She may seem superficial and extravagant to you many times but she is a deeply dedicated person spiritually. She had emotional security in her childhood and she wants to help those of her people who didn't."

"What about me?"

"She married you, Allen. She was determined to dedicate her life to you. The aspects were very strong and loving for both of your marriages, the secret one and the later public one."

"I was crazy about her, too. It was a kick to see her, so cute and tiny, zipping all over the Theater Arts Department a mile a minute. Boy, I thought she was the brightest little chick in the world. I went for her, I really did. But she no, not until she had the ring on her finger."

"So one night, on impulse, you said, 'Come on, let's do it.' And you did. Even the second marriage still carried an element of impulse. I saw it in your chart. But there is a problem I didn't mention to your wife. Because of the planetary positions at the time of both your marriages, there is an element of risk. Your marriage could end as abruptly as it began."

"Are you using psychology on me, star lady?"

"I'm only telling you what the chart shows so you can be warned before the fact and avoid danger. This marriage is important to you, even more important than it is to Eve. It is your stability, and there will come a time when you will need what she can give you more than you realize now. She hasn't been entirely intelligent in her attitudes, either. But she did come to me for help and I tried to explain to her where she had been going wrong."

"Right now, we have an armed camp at home. She puts it on the basis I've deserted my people and all that crap. Listen, I do care what goes on in the world. I do."

"I know you do. You have your sun in Aquarius."

"That's why I think all this nutty business about black rights and black schools and teaching black history is crazy. Our one salvation is not to be separate, to be absorbed, integrated. What is so awful about my bedding down with a white chick? For all I know, I've got a lot of white blood running around in me from my pappy and I'm sure as hell Val has. Eve, too, although she pretends that coffee color is pure nigger black blood. Have you ever been to Honolulu? The most beautiful people in the world are out there and most of them are such a mixture you couldn't figure out what if you tried. This is the way we should solve the black-white problem and to hell with the Black Panthers and Eve and all the rest of them."

"Won't you tell me when Deb was born?"

"Who in hell are you talking about?"

"Your girl. Isn't that her name?"

"I'm not going to tell you her name or anything about her." He clamped his jaw shut and concentrated on the road. I closed my eyes behind dark glasses and thought about his chart. He needed acclaim and prestige so much that everything else was subordinated. His passion for women with white skin was part of the status picture, but his chart (Jupiter squaring Mars and Venus) showed that money as well as the white skin meant a great deal to him. In the beginning, Eve had been a step up. However, her Saturn was on his sun, which can tie two people together but with a knot that snarls.

"Would you tell me when she was born? That wouldn't mean giving away any secrets. I could rough out a natal chart for you."

"I'm not going to answer any questions about her."

I thought of the planet Pluto opposing the Mars-Venus combination in his chart. "Yet, in a way, you want to be rescued from her. There is an indication in your chart that some woman could, whether she wants to or not, bring you harm, exert a subtly undermining influence on your life. You say you're in love with the girl, yet you're afraid of her. Wouldn't you be interested in knowing if she really will hurt you, one way or another? Or finding out why she was attracted to you?"

"That's easy. It was chemistry."

"What does she look like?"

"Red hair. Dark blue eyes. In glorious living color. And that beautiful redhead complexion. All over. A honey."

"Taurus, maybe. Or Libra. Young?"

"She is a Taurus, and she'll be twenty-one this year. And that is all I'm going to tell you. I didn't know she was alive and she had been in love with me for two years. She saw me at a benefit where I was on the dais. It was love at first sight. She went around hunting up old films I'd made, some in which I'd only had bits. She got the movie studios to screen them for her. Her daddy's a big shot, so she has connections."

"And she goes mad when you kiss her throat."

He whirled on me. "Who in hell told you that?"

"Watch the road, Allen. You've done very well so far, and I've provoked you. I am teasing. Taurus women love to be kissed on the throat. It's a trigger area, a very erogenous zone for them."

"It was funny," he said, turning back to the road. "The first time we kissed it was on camera. She leaned over and hugged me and it happened. Then when the show was over, I grabbed her again. It didn't mean a damned thing, just the way you feel when you've finished a job. Up. Euphoric. It landed on her throat. She whispered something about her car being downstairs, a red Austin. When I went down, she was waiting. That's how it all started."

"She is young and she is beautiful and rich and she loves to be kissed on the throat. But she's poisoning your marriage. You're going to give her up eventually. Why wait until it is too late?"

No answer. I tried again. "Allen, you are the man in Eve's life. You'll always have a strong influence over her, she can't escape. She has Saturn in Aquarius—You are and always will be a catalyst, an influence. But she could leave you if you push her too far."

No answer still. We were near the airport. Once more I made an effort to get through to him. "Allen, she talked to me about the problems of black women today. You are being unfair to her, she thinks, because you are blaming black women for all the troubles which really were the fault of us whites."

"That's not true."

"Then why do you keep repeating that all black women are bitches?"

"Because they are. Look at my mother. One day she ran off with a guy and left Val and me. Once in a while we'd get a letter from her with some money in it. I don't know whether she is alive or dead."

"Don't you think it is pretty wonderful of her, if she is alive, not to have tried to contact you now that you are well known and making money?"

"She wouldn't dare. She knows what I'd do to her."

"Does she? She is your mother. Mothers are funny about loving their children, they tell me."

"I would throw her out in the street if she came up to me this minute. Black women are all tramps. They get their fun and their little side benefits, cash sneaked under the pillow, from white men. Look at Val. I loved her. I loved her like hell. She wasn't much older than me but she brought me up, her baby brother. She even took me to school with her so I wouldn't be left alone. That's why I could have killed her when I found out she was as bad as Mom. Worse. Because Mom was a fool and she didn't know any better, she believed anything they'd tell her. But Val was smart and quick. And she did it for money. She was a prostitute. A whore. When I finally found out, I cried and begged her to stop and she said, 'Oh, honey, it's nothing. I've been doing this since I was a little kid. Where did you think all those candy bars I brought you came from? Black kids don't dare steal, they're too scared. Men gave them to me, and I always asked for more, because I wanted to take something home to my little brother. They thought it was cute. How in hell did you think I got that football you wanted? I told a white man my little brother was going to be a great halfback. So he gave me the money for the ball. It was a kind of bonus.' "

He drew up in front of United and tossed the keys at a black porter, so he could get my bags out of the trunk of the car. The porter recognized him, of course. I said, "Don't get out. And thank you for the ride."

I had one foot out of the car when he leaned over toward me. "Black bitches, every one of them."

"You're only hurting yourself, Allen."

"How do you know?" But he wasn't angry any longer. A little group was forming on the sidewalk. He tipped the porter—too much, I was sure—and went around and made a big show of helping me check my bags. He signed autographs for two little white boys and one white grandmother type. He wrote his name on the band of a hat belonging to a teenage black girl. I was included in his smile, his warmth. When he finally handed over the small bag I was going to carry on the plane, I thought he might even kiss me. But he didn't.

Instead he said, "When Eve was pregnant with Gene, she thought she was going to lose him. Frankly, I was so broke at the time I would have been glad. She went and got an appointment with some big-shot doctor and he put her in a private room at the Cedars of Lebanon Hospital and she stayed there for two weeks. Two weeks. I borrowed money from Val to bail her out. I could have killed her. In cold blood."

"But you have Gene. You might not, otherwise. Allen, you have so much. Don't hate Eve or Val or your mother. It's such a stupid waste of time, hating people."

"Right on. Did it ever occur to you that it's easy for you to talk?"

He walked away from me. Lightly, ready to take off. He might have been dancing. A woman standing next to me said, "Wasn't that Allen Cowles? He's even better looking in person. I think he must have white blood in him, don't you?"

I said I didn't know and boarded the plane, feeling sad. On the way back, I decided I wouldn't tell anybody, even Ralph, about my consultation with Eve Cowles. I put the charts away in a desk drawer at home where odds and ends collect until I throw them out, and I didn't send her a bill. Then, to my amazement, one day Maggie came in and put a check on my desk, signed by Allen Cowles.

"What have you been up to?"

"His wife consulted me the last night I was in California."

"He must be very grateful, from the size of the check. What did you tell her?"

"I told him he was going to be famous. Even more than he is now."

That satisfied Maggie—almost. Suddenly she asked, "And where are the charts? Home, I bet, tucked in that old rattrap desk of yours. Do I have to call Ralph and have him remind you to get them out and bring them in?"

"I'll remember," I promised. And I did, and watched Maggie make out a proper folder marked *Allen Cowles*. That night I even duly reported to Ralph that I'd been consulted by Allen Cowles' wife and that he'd driven me to the airport. Gemini-like, Ralph sensed a little mystery. "Why are you telling me at this late date?"

"I forgot. Until I got a check from him today."

"I'll bet you weren't going to charge him, Katie. Why? He certainly isn't starving to death, from what I hear."

"He was, once. He hasn't had an easy life."

Ralph put his arm around me. "You sound like all the fan magazines. Well, I'm glad he was decent enough to remember to pay you. Not all actors would."

From time to time I did think of Allen Cowles, but all of us in astrology were primarily concerned with the effect of planetary conditions on our nation. A little over two months after the March 28 solar eclipse, which had triggered the King assassination and its aftermath, Robert Kennedy was murdered under another ominous full moon in June. We do know that the same full moon which brings disaster down on the head of a national figure also has its effect on lesser human beings. In March, Allen Cowles had his progressed sun in 23 degrees of Pisces, and that was hit by the full moon on the same night King was killed. In June, the moon which was responsible for the culmination of frustrations which ended in the Kennedy assassination, also had its effect on Allen Cowles.

He made a movie, which I didn't see, although it had fair reviews. His *Jeopardy* show still had high ratings and once in a while Ralph and I watched parts of it. It seemed to me—or was I imagining it?—that some of the magnetism was gone. Then one morning, Maggie put a clipping on my desk with an item marked in red. It said: *There are rumors that the Allen Cowles are splitting; is he getting too big for his beautiful tight-fitting britches?*

I thought of calling Eve. I took her chart home with me. And, as often happens with clients when I tune in on them, before I could dial her number, she called me. "You saw it? Well, it isn't true. In fact, it's the other way around. He and the girl have had a row. She went over to Rome to do a TV special with some Italian director and Allen kicked up a fuss and she told him goodbye forever. Now he wants me to go to Paris with him. He's doing two *Jeopardy* shows on the Riviera and he thinks we should have a week in Paris alone. A second honeymoon. Should I go?"

I didn't like the aspects. Her chart had been badly affected by the solar eclipse in the spring and a lunar eclipse which was in the near future was badly aspected to Mars in Allen's chart. Quarrels and sex were in the offing, not exactly the prescription for an idyllic second honeymoon. "I'm afraid it will be a disappointment if you do."

"But I don't like to think of him in Paris with Debbie in Rome."

"You know who she is?"

"He's confessed and insists it's all over. She is Debbie Lawrence, a Los Angeles socialite who has some little TV show in the afternoons. The girl reporter. But she is rich and her father is an executive at the network."

"Eve, are you sure the affair is over?"

"He's promised. I'll try to explain to him why I shouldn't go. But I'm not sure he'll understand. I'll write you."

She went because he insisted. And the trip, as I had feared, was a fiasco. I had a letter from Paris: *It's raining and I've been sitting in the room at the George V wishing I were any place but here. Paris is beautiful and I hate it. The French are mad for Allen and mob him everywhere he goes. Sometimes I get pushed aside and he doesn't even miss me. Last night I took a walk on the Pont Neuf and a man took me for a whore. Allen explained later I shouldn't have gone out alone at dusk but how was I to know? Anyway, we snapped at each other and I got mad and he got worse and tomorrow he goes off to the Riviera—and Rome, I suppose—and I fly back to California. Why did I come? I don't know. Perhaps because I am a fool. Val also encouraged me. She is staying with the children while we are gone. She has bought into a travel agency in Beverly Hills, mainly, I think, because she is worried about Allen. He is so strange, so morose. And the show's ratings have been slipping. That is why they are moving it around, trying to inject a foreign flavor. But if you ask me, the person they need to inject something into, is Allen . . .*

Christmas came, and January. *Jeopardy* was switched to an earlier time slot and I never got a chance to see the Riviera episodes. Then one April morning, Maggie gave me the day's schedule, adding, "We have a new client, a TV girl from Los Angeles. She does a girl reporter thing out there."

"Debbie? Debbie Lawrence?"

"Right. Do you know her or are you getting clairvoyant?"

"I know—of her. When was she born?"

"May 13, 1947, at 2:50 A.M. in Los Angeles."

"Taurus." I nodded. Maggie looked at me oddly.

"Of course it's Taurus. And she wants to discuss some man, as usual. What's gotten into you, Katie? You look so odd. Spring fever?"

Spring was bursting out all over in Chicago but it wasn't spring fever which nagged at me. It isn't unusual for me to have several members of a family as clients, even a family which is split into enemy factions. No matter how much I have heard about an individual from other people, once we meet over a horoscope there are always surprises, dark areas which can be illumined. Yet I was so involved with Eve I was unable to think of Debbie as anything except a troublemaker. And that isn't right, when you are taking on a new client. Several times during the morning, I considered asking Maggie to try to reach Debbie and suggest she consult another astrologer. Each time, I realized I wasn't being fair. She'd made the appointment from California. And well in advance.

Then she walked in. Redheaded, with deep, huge dark blue eyes in that thick-cream redhead skin. Slim, lithe, yet with just a hint of voluptuousness which is characteristic of the Taurus beauty. And, like so many Taurus women, obviously pampered. Her suit, simple as it was, could only have been cut by a master designer. It did all the right things for her—including accent her long lean legs and slim hips. Her hair shone with California care—expensive beauty salons—and equally expensive sunshine and beautiful food. She was simple, forthright, too—with the simplicity which comes from utter confidence.

She said, "Should I say Allen sent me? Or is that too corny?"

I took out a blank chart and penciled in her statistics. "I know who you are. I wasn't sure it was fair to take you on as a client.

I've already told him your association is not going to be permanent."

"Why don't you call it an affair, Miss de Jersey? And I suppose you're shocked because he is black."

I excused myself for a moment and asked Maggie for the Allen Cowles folder. She whispered, "Don't tell me that Debbie Lawrence is the white chick in the gossip column? Golly."

When I returned, I said to Debbie, "I've already done Allen's chart. If you agree, I will do your natal horoscope and compare them. And if there are any special periods involved, I will have time to progress both your charts."

"Whatever is the usual." She sounded indifferent. I worked for a few minutes while she glanced around the studio. Finally she said, "You have a rather nice view."

"I love it." But I didn't look up from my calculations. She studied her nails. She walked over to the window, then she came back and sat down. Finally she said, "I'm not sure why I'm here. I guess maybe it's because I don't know what else to do. I'm plain goddamn miserable. Which I suppose you think is pretty funny."

"Why should I think unhappiness is funny?" I still did not look up.

"Why shouldn't you? I'm the other woman, the fly in the ointment. I am trying to mess up Allen's life. I went after him, it was all my fault. And I'm young enough to be his daughter. Or so my father tells me. It isn't quite true. Daddy isn't so ancient he doesn't remember what a sex life is but I'm afraid in his day, nice ladies didn't go off the deep end. The way I have. Are you shocked?"

"I'm not even surprised. It is all here in your chart, and Allen's. You both have Venus conjunct Mars. People with this combination are highly sexed. And when one person with this combination meets another, it's dynamite. You couldn't fight the attraction. And you are two of a kind—you have the moon in Aquarius on his sun."

"Well." Suddenly she seemed younger, less poised. "I'm not a child. I had my first affair at seventeen and I've slept with a number of men. Some of them very experienced. But with Allen, I was overwhelmed just seeing him at a distance. I was mad for him two full years before he as much as touched my little finger. I dreamed about him. I made Daddy pester the studios until they filmed his lousy pictures for me. I'm no dope. I'm a sophisticated Hollywood brat. I teethed on movies shown in our own projection room. I knew his pictures were terrible and I still swooned. It makes no sense."

"Perhaps not to you. To an astrologer, it is clear and simple. Your chart shows everything, including the fact you're in television and your father is a show business executive. You have inherited money and in late 1965 or early 1966 something electric came into your life."

"Allen told you about that. He thinks he is very astute about keeping secrets. Actually, he blabs everything. But I love him anyway."

"Your chart shows infatuation at a distance, strong physical attraction for an older man, from a totally different world, and you decide to go after him. No holds barred."

"You make me sound like a tigress." She tried to laugh. "Actually, I'm a sweet simple little girl, gently raised, who has been victimized by an ambitious ruthless black man. Ask Daddy. I think the term was black bastard, actually."

"You have your sun and Mercury in Taurus. But your ascendant is Aries and you also have your Venus-Mars combination in Aries. You are determined, self-willed. You'll always go after what you want. When you saw Allen Cowles, you decided you wanted him. You were barely nineteen. You carried a torch for two years before you met him. And when you did meet him, it was through your own efforts."

She hesitated. "I'm not the faithful, long-suffering type, either. It's been a family joke. If a boy didn't go for me right away, it was on to the next one."

"Aries influenced women aren't patient, as a rule."

"How do you account for the way I feel about Allen? I still do, you know. I decide I am through with him—and then he touches me and—I dissolve."

"Mars is sex and Venus is love. When you find these planets together in the natal charts of two people of different sexes, the love strengthens the sex—and vice versa. And, of course, with your Aries ascendant you had to be the aggressor. You enjoy that role and probably always will—which is why you should have a man who is equally aggressive and potent, to hold you. Allen isn't strong enough."

"I warn you, that's not the way to turn me off Allen. Daddy has tried that technique and it doesn't work. In fact, he put all his big guns on me from the beginning. It was a benefit, one of those ghastly command performances for Daddy. Mummy couldn't make it, or maybe wouldn't, and I was elected. Allen was sitting on the dais. Maybe he spoke, I can't remember. If he did, it was nothing. What got me was his smile. It reached out and grabbed me, really grabbed me. God, I saw it all day and dreamed about it at night. You know the Cheshire Cat in *Alice in Wonderland?* The smile was the first thing to appear when it materialized and the last to go when it vanished. I was out of my mind about the guy. I switched from psychology to Theater Arts at UCLA because I found out that was where he got his start."

"And met his wife," I said. "Besides, you have the planet Uranus in the third house of communication. You were meant to go into television."

"I begged Daddy to introduce us. Daddy isn't square. He's pretty liberal about skin color and all that jazz, as liberal as the older generation can be, I guess. I think he would have taken his little daughter up and had her meet a black star. Sure. But the point was, Allen was involved just then with a funny old creature called Priscilla Ross, really a pathetic old thing. Don't ask me why he got involved. I haven't a clue. Maybe I should ask you."

"I don't know her sign but I can explain a little about the attraction from Allen's chart. He has this Mars-Venus combination in Capricorn, the sign of ambition, success. I am going to tell you something about Allen you may not want to hear, yet I'm sure you must have suspected it. Allen is driven by ambition. Whether he realizes it or not—and I doubt if he does right now at this point in his life—he is naturally attracted to women who can advance him, either socially or in his career."

"I don't believe it."

"I suspect you do, as I've said. You've sensed something wrong about Allen, haven't you? Of course it's a flaw, but we all have flaws in our life patterns. The answer is to learn to live with them, not to be trapped into bad situations."

"Priscilla was certainly a bad egg." Debbie jumped to her feet. "If he hadn't come to his senses, she could have ruined his career, like that. As it was, it created a pretty grim stink when she knocked herself off. I watched the way Allen handled it and I fell in love with him all over again. But I knew it was no use meeting him through Daddy. I had to do it on my own."

"You will always be aggressive in sex, but so self-sufficient that if you hadn't found Allen immediately responsive, you would have dropped him and gone on to someone else. You really aren't realistic in your attitude toward love and you're quite capable of pretending idealism in order to get what you want. Even the patience in waiting for him was part of the game. For you enjoy shocking people. Allen had all the ingredients for a sensational romance. He is black, attractive, and he'd been involved in a messy affair with a white actress. He seems everything a nice girl would shy away from. Actually, you try to be so subtle you become obvious. Even Priscilla—your capturing Allen was a triumph over the dead woman."

"Priscilla was a poor silly little jerk. Believe me, she didn't kill herself for love. She killed herself for the reason all the silly jerks do in Hollywood. She'd reached the end of the road and she didn't know what else to do."

"You're young and intolerant. To Allen, Priscilla wasn't a silly old actress, long over the hill. She represented glamour. She was white. He'd probably watched her on television. Certainly, he had heard of her. She may have chased him. But he didn't run away very hard. He let her fall in love with him because he was flattered."

"You make me cringe."

"Later, of course, he was disillusioned. He gave her up. There were a number of reasons, some of them well motivated."

She moved deliberately around my studio. It's always interesting to watch clients do that, during an interview. The Leos pace and the Crab-Cancers weave. Debbie was not wandering aimlessly. She was curious, inquisitive, taking in the total scene. She even looked in on Maggie. Then she came back to stand in front of me.

"I have my little show, called *Debbie on the Move.* I go out with a TV cameraman and a mobile unit and catch little feature stories. Sometimes if they are hot enough, they run them on the evening news. But it's up to me to get the idea and carry it through. One day I took an Allen Cowles fan club to the studio to meet him. You've heard about his fan club?"

"It's all white, isn't it?"

"Yes, and terribly straight middle-class. Square. Little middle-aged ladies in gloves and hats. Well, I took his little bunch of squares over to the studio to watch a few minutes of filming and afterward invited them back to his dressing room. Well, it was a blast. They swarmed all over him. It ended with them chasing Allen down the corridor. He ducked into a staircase and I followed him. Allen and the cameraman and I all landed in the men's room with the dames pounding on the door outside. I told them they couldn't come in, it wasn't proper, and he kissed me. On camera. End of show . . . with the camera moving on to the indignant ladies. Even Daddy howled when he saw it."

"How did the ladies feel?"

"That was what made it so great. They didn't mind, the poor old half-wits. They were on television. And Allen—well, he grabbed me and kissed me again when it was all over. It was just a natural response, the way you feel after you've finished a job and know it is right and good. It landed on my throat, by accident. And all those things I'd always heard about happened. The earth trembled and rockets flared and the volcanoes went up. I told him to meet me down in my car. It was January and raining like hell. We drove out to the family beach house and spent the night. Alone. We drank gin and I fixed tomato soup and we made love on a blanket in front of the open fire. It was—heaven. No matter what else could happen, we had that."

"That was a night which had to be, astrologically. Mars was on your moon, meaning sex fulfillment. His chart shows you coming to him . . . a 'lady of prestige.' In your chart, we see a serious romance with an older man. But your Venus and Mars were hit by the lunar eclipse on April 13. And your Neptune was affected by the solar eclipse in March. You were wildly in love at times, yet you found yourself infuriated by him just as frequently. By June, the full moon in 20 degrees Gemini hit Uranus in your chart. Soon afterward, there was a violent change in your relationship with him. Always the quarrels, the frustrations had been subordinate to the sex, you could clear everything up by going to bed. But by July, although the sex was still good, the glamour of the affair was subsiding. And in October, you made a definite break."

She traced a design on my desk with a long lacquered fingernail. "I had a chance to go to Rome to do a TV special with a big Italian producer. A wolf type but marvelous. Allen already was scheduled to film a couple of episodes for *Jeopardy* on the Riviera and I'd fixed my schedule so I could fly over and have a week in Paris with him before he started. When the TV show came up, we had a brawl. He didn't want me to go, which would have made me more determined even if I hadn't been mad to work with Monelli, the producer. So I went."

"And he took his wife to Paris for a second honeymoon."

She shrugged. "It didn't work. He called me nearly every day. We flew home together. For a while, it was heaven again. Then the holidays came. I lived through Thanksgiving. But on Christmas, I flipped. What in hell was the good of being wild about a man and knowing he was gathered around the tree with his black wife and black little ones on Christmas? I would have taken the kids, you know. I would have gone anywhere with him and them."

"But there was Eve. Have you ever seen her?"

She crossed her arms and hugged herself fiercely. "Once. At the Academy Awards. Again, I went with Daddy. She looked OK. But unsure—as though she knew she didn't belong there."

"She hasn't had your advantages."

"Well, there's such a thing as knowing your place, isn't there? Oh, God, forgive me. I'm acting like a snob. Anyway, on New Year's the family went down to Palm Springs, where we have a house. I called Allen and asked him to join us. He came. At midnight, I kissed Allen and told Daddy we were going to get married."

"And Allen was terrified."

"How do you know?"

"You aren't really suited to each other and you both realized that in your honest moments. Of course, for a while you filled his secret needs, answered his long-suppressed yearnings. You were the rich white girl he had seen on television. But deep down underneath he knew well that he didn't belong in your world, so you actually underscored his frustrations. And he is drawn to Eve, too. In many ways, through her love, she has a stronger hold over him than you could ever have. I doubt if he could ever leave her, divorce her, for you."

She sat down. "Daddy noticed it. The next day, we drove Allen to the airport. Then Daddy and I tried to play golf. I finally gave up and cried all through nine holes and Daddy piled up a score which looked like the national debt. I insisted he was prejudiced because Allen was black. Daddy said he just didn't want me to ruin my life. That night, I drove back to Los Angeles alone. I called Allen and told him I had left my family. He came and stayed with me for a week. And then he said he had to move back home, he didn't want a scandal."

"And it's over now, isn't it, Debbie? That is why you came to me."

"I don't know why I came to you. Except that you had talked to

Allen and he seemed impressed. I don't know what to do. I love him but he has no guts."

"Debbie, you can afford to be independent. You were a silver spoon baby with inherited money—it's all there in your chart. He came up the hard way and has had to work fiercely for everything you take as your due. You don't know Allen as he really is. That's why you say he has no guts. You dream of a knight in shining armor on a white horse carrying you off. Debbie, what I have to warn you about is this—always behind the visor there is a man, a human being with foibles."

"Money means nothing to me."

"Debbie, money is all over your natal chart. You have Jupiter in the eighth house, inherited money. You have success, a rich father. The material doesn't interest you because you have always had every luxury you wanted. Taurus is one of the so-called money signs. Taurus people don't value money for itself, but for what it supplies. Luxuries are so much a part of your daily life that it never occurs to you what it might be like if you had to go without manicures and wash your own hair and buy your clothes in the bargain basements. Like so many Taurus people, you are adorable —but spoiled."

For the first time, she faltered. I watched her unbutton her jacket and then, realizing she was naked underneath it, rebutton it quickly. She said, a bit apologetically, "It's warm in here." When I offered to turn up the air conditioning, she shook her head. So I went on.

"You are a real silver spoon baby. Of course, you are part of this new age and want to be involved with human suffering and help the minorities. But you are so emotionally insecure you have no tolerance of people like Eve. Or Allen, really. His white Cadillac means nothing to you except something to ride in; you even feel it is a little ostentatious. His swimming pool is to you something everybody in California has. To him, the Cadillac and swimming pool are important as symbols. He has to have money and success because he was born with nothing. He is still hungry. To him, you are a living, breathing symbol of success, product of an old, rich family. And yet he still wasn't quite able to toss over those other success symbols, his wife and his children, for you. He doesn't love you. Enough."

"He adores me."

"Sexually. And your money. Money is his secret passion. It is a problem between you, isn't it?"

She lit a cigarette. "I try to tell him, money doesn't matter."

"And I'm afraid he isn't articulate enough to explain that it does and always will, to him. You were never meant to have much more than wonderful sexual rapport together and there is always a point where this fails if there aren't stronger reasons to hold you together. Ironically, there were more powerful planetary aspects pulling you together when you first saw him, long before you met him, than when you two really did meet. Only your moon on his sun in Aquarius has held you together this long. Your love affair was over before it began. Face that, my dear."

"It's not easy. I've never felt like this about anybody else."

"You're not quite twenty-two. And you're going to be married this year. Before Christmas, I would say. I am sure it will be a man with his sun in Aries. It won't be a conventional kind of marriage, but he isn't a conventional man. You will quarrel and argue and fight like hell, but you won't bore each other. I think you already know him but haven't considered him from the point of view of a husband, because of Allen."

She put out the cigarette. From her shoulder bag she produced a cable. "I get one of these every week or so. He wants me to fly over and help him make a documentary in India. Of course I can't. It would mean giving up my show. And he is a notorious wolf. He has a mistress for every day in the week."

"He is the man you worked with last October? Why don't you go with him? He sounds like a man well worth fighting for. And with."

"He's an Aries."

"Well matched. You need someone strong. And challenging."

She hesitated. "That is what Daddy says. He promised to get someone to help out with my show if I decide to go. Of course I haven't the right clothes. God knows what I would need for India."

"You can buy them there."

She tucked the cable back in her purse. "The one damned thing, I feel so guilty about Allen. He counts on me. If I just walk out on him, what will it do to his ego?"

"Debbie, maybe one of these days before too long, when the raw edges of this era of intense racial consciousness have been softened, when Allen's sons are growing up in a world where others besides the whites have swimming pools and Cadillacs, a girl like you and a man like Allen can live happily ever after. But it wasn't in your life patterns. You tried to fight against what was there but it wasn't supposed to work. Go to India and have fun. You might fall in love again. If not, it will help to be on the other side of the globe from Allen."

When she left, a little of the glow went out of the room. Maggie came to stretch her legs and collect the charts. "That is a formidable female. Is she going to marry Allen Cowles?"

"No. She's on her way to join another man in Rome."

"Did you talk her into that? Don't answer, Katie. You might incriminate yourself. Just tell me what poor Allen does now."

"Poor Allen is going to make a lot of money and have a lot of success. For a while. He'll forget Debbie. He'll move on to other problems and other women."

"In a way, I'm sorry for him." Maggie went to open the door to our next client.

As 1969 progressed, we added to the Allen Cowles folder. He was busy, and getting more publicity than ever, but the tone of it had changed. The young people were pulling away from him, he was appealing more and more to the clubwomen, the Pasadena matron types. I wasn't surprised to have Maggie bring me a clipping from *Variety* in which it said his TV show was, characteristically, in jeopardy. By September, it was canceled. The next word I got was a publicity release. Allen Cowles was to star in a Broadway musical. It never opened but one night in December Ralph and I turned on a talk show and there was Allen as the host, graceful and effusive and—let's face it—sexy as hell.

The next day, the reviews were raves. For a little over two months, his name and face were everywhere. Covers of magazines. A lead piece in *The New York Times*. Then, catching him one night on TV in one of those strange hotel rooms after a lecture, I knew he was bored. He went through the motions but his heart wasn't in it and the attitude was contagious to his guests and, speaking for myself, his audience. The next day, I rechecked his chart; a new career would begin for him in a few months. I asked Maggie to try to locate Eve, for I felt this was a time they would both need encouragement. It turned out I was right. Two days later, Eve called me from New York.

"Allen is pretty much in the dumps. The show is being canceled and he doesn't know whether to go back to California or stay here."

"The chart indicates he should not make any drastic moves right now. By March 1970, something is going to turn up. He must stay where he is and explore new angles. His next venture will be different from anything he has ever done and it won't be in television."

"There's another complication. I'm pregnant."

I checked her chart. There was not going to be a baby. "Was it intentional?"

"Not really. I think Allen was pleased when we found out. He felt it was a way of keeping me. You see, Debbie got married a couple of weeks ago. To an Italian producer, a pretty fascinating wild man. Allen tried to kid himself it was on the rebound but he knows it wasn't. He lost her months ago and never was able to face up to the situation. The baby at first seemed a way of making sure I wouldn't leave him, too. But recently, I have the feeling he doesn't care. I've never seen him so low."

"Give him my message about the career."

"I will. And Merry Christmas."

That was December 23, 1969. I had a Christmas card from Debbie in Rome—her name was now Monelli—announcing that happiness was a new way of life. And in early January there was an interview in one of the newspaper entertainment sections with Allen Cowles about the place of the black actor. He said, "I was one of the pioneers for which I get little credit from the establishment or my own people. I went through a lot of hell and cut quite a few corners. Once I played a white man in a radio soap opera; the young blacks today call me an Uncle Tom for having knuckled under to pressure. The brass in the industry think there is something peculiar about me because I am a professional in my attitude toward work. I don't make the rest of the cast stand around waiting for me because I am black. I don't turn up in my air-conditioned Cadillac and ride on to the set in the desert where the white cast is baking it out. I don't demand champagne in my dressing room and I don't lay all the actresses on the set.

"Which, in a way, puts me down as a has-been. I'm old hat. I conform. I don't use vulgar words on television and I don't tell newspaper reporters off. I suppose I am a victim of progress. I was the bridge, or part of it. And we haven't come far from the days when blacks were performed by white men in black face and were strictly for comic relief. Frankly, I don't feel very funny these days. Unlike the new kids coming up, I don't want to be treated as a black man first and then an actor. I'm a human being. And I am waiting for the day when I'll be offered a role in Shakespeare other than the first one I ever played, Othello."

Maggie, reading over my shoulder, commented, "Sad. I like the man. And he makes sense to me."

"That's because we're part of that bridge he was talking about, white liberals. We're out of date, too."

"I wonder what's going to happen to him."

"A big break in the spring of 1970. Wait and see."

Spring was cold and rainy and busy, for me, I had to postpone a trip to Hawaii because of commitments, so it happened I was unexpectedly free when Eve Cowles telephoned from New York and asked if she could see me the next day, on the way to California.

She had changed. She was even more beautiful but the fragility had vanished. And the elegance. She was wearing an Afro hair-do and a new midi raincoat, a serviceable tan with military collar and pockets. Underneath was a knitted dress so tight and brief I didn't have to ask if she had lost the baby. But she caught me looking at her and got the message—both messages.

"Miscarriage. We were both delighted, although I went through that usual week of trauma. At least, the doctors told me it was usual. Allen admitted he had deliberately tried to get me pregnant as a sort of revenge. On me and Debbie. At least he is being honest with me now. His latest plot is for me to live in California with the children while he maintains a bachelor pad in New York."

"I've never mentioned the word divorce to you before. But it is indicated here in both of your charts. This is the end of the road."

She smiled at me. "That is what I told him last night. It was strange. I was packing. I've always been a very fussy packer, layers of tissue paper and special cases for different things. Last night I was throwing clothes and shoes on top of each other. He came in and asked what the hell was wrong with me. And I said, out of the top of my head, 'I've changed. Every Gemini has another side and from now on, this one is going to be showing. And so far as you are concerned, I suppose it's time for a change, too. I'm leaving you.'"

"Eve, I once told him that he had married you on impulse and that the marriage might break up just as suddenly under the same aspects."

"I don't know why I said it. Now I'm a little frightened. For myself, not for him. That big break you mentioned for him—it's happened. A very rich woman in New York has established a repertory theater. Very far-out and experimental. She got the idea from reading the piece by Allen when he talked about never being given the chance to play anything except Othello."

"Is he pleased?"

"Terribly. It gives him a chance to be serious and pretentious and talk about art with a capital A. I'm sorry, Miss de Jersey, I don't mean to be bitchy. It's just that I knew him when he ate fried potatoes with catsup for breakfast."

"There is a new woman in his life, too. The rich one?"

She nodded. "Older than him. I think one reason he wanted to hang on to me was to have an excuse for not marrying her. But it's time he took on the whole package deal. So long as she is footing the bills, it is right for him to step into her world, to be what he is instead of pretending he's just a nice family man with a little black wife and two bright-eyed black sons."

"You are bitter."

She shrugged. "I suppose so. It's been a long time and Christmas was pretty awful. Val came East and brought the boys with her. We all went up to Vermont and *Show* magazine photographed us having a white Christmas. Just as soon as the magazine people left, he went, too. His sponsor was having some kind of a house party in Palm Beach and he was expected. To give the party color, Val told him.

"Val and I got to know each other awfully well, the rest of that holiday. We sat and talked while the boys skied. Allen has always resented her because of what she did to get money, even though she was doing it for him. But we figured out that in a way, he has done exactly the same thing, only he wouldn't admit it to himself. She used white men to get money. He's getting ahead through white women. Poor Priscilla was a mistake; he thought she was more important than she was. But he was right on target with Debbie. He used her, and I think it might still be going on if she hadn't consulted you."

"That was Allen's idea."

"No. It was mine. I planted it and he produced it as his own. You told me that relationship was going to break up and I wanted her to hear it, too."

"You are quite a woman, Eve Cowles."

"I'm beginning to be, thanks to a lot of things, starting with you. You said much that first night I didn't like, until I started to think. I've always lived too much on the surface, trying to act out my image of myself. I told myself I could have been as good an actor as Allen, but I sacrificed my career for him. That isn't true. I would have made a mediocre actress. I really only am suited to one thing, teaching. I'm going back and finish college and get a degree and a teacher's certificate. It's about time I did something, instead of sitting there in my sable coat complaining about Allen being an Uncle Tom."

"Eve, this is a beginning. I'm proud of you."

"Don't. I've wasted most of my life being noble, hating Allen for doing what he couldn't help, while I was taking everything he gave me and criticizing him for not being ashamed of the way he earned it. I wasn't even as honest as Val. I didn't need the swimming pool, the boys didn't need their fancy private boys' school. They would have survived and been stronger if I had sent them to public school. It was my pride which needed all the icing on the cake. So I accepted—no, I demanded—them all from Allen. And told myself I was better than he was. I wasn't. I was worse."

"Did you tell him this?"

"I tried to. He didn't understand."

"I'm afraid he's going on, making the same mistakes. This relationship isn't going to last, either. Whether he marries her or not, he is going to make the same mistake over and over, using women for his own purposes. Eventually, they catch on."

"I'm not going back to him, whatever happens. I'll let him see the boys and perhaps as they grow older, they will be closer to him."

"Eve, you're going to marry again."

"No. I've had enough of marriage. I'm ready to be my own woman."

"You will find a man who will appreciate that. Nearly every Gemini's life is divided in half. You're beginning the second chapter. You will change your way of living. And you will find a different kind of husband to fit into it. A man who will share your life. Another teacher, perhaps. A dedicated man."

"We'll see." She reached for her coat.

"I sent Debbie back over to Rome to meet the man she married," I said. "One of these days I may do the same for you."

She put out a slim hand and I reached for it. Then, suddenly, she darted down and planted a kiss on my chin and went flying off down the corridor, like a Gemini.

6

The Girl
Who Ran
Away

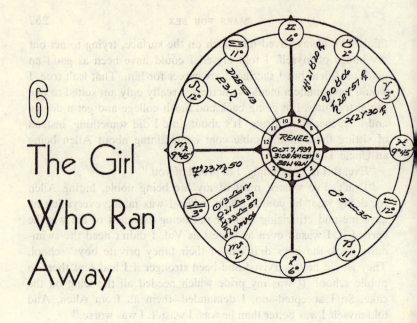

"KATIE, please wake up. It's Julie Lord. Renee has run away."

I turned on the bed lamp. Astrologers, like doctors, get middle-of-the-night emergency calls, which isn't easy on the person who shares your bed. However, Ralph was groaning good-naturedly. He's used to all the side-effects of being married to an astrologer.

I said, "Let me get on a robe, collect my wits, and call you back, Julie."

Julie Lord had come to me years before because she had fallen in love with a married man. He was a Libra of enormous charm and sophistication, an older man who professed to love Julie very much but couldn't—or wouldn't—divorce his wife; being a Libra, he simply couldn't make up his mind to take a step as drastic as divorce. I steered her through the long affair, knowing it wouldn't have a happy ending. And when it was finally over, I watched her pick up the pieces and build a new career as a television interviewer. She was a beautiful girl, a sun-in-Cancer, with glowing auburn hair and deep blue eyes. She looked marvelous on color TV and, Cancer-like, enjoyed having an audience, being in show business.

But, in a curious way, she had turned against me for a while because I'd been right about her Libra lover. So I hadn't seen her for about a year when I ran into her at a Christmas party given by a mutual friend. I was there doing mini-horoscopes as door prizes. Eric Van Sand was one of the winners. Afterward he said dryly, in typical Gemini fashion, "I think astrology is for the birds but it's been interesting to see you work." Then when he opened the door of the little office which I was using, I saw Julie Lord waiting outside. She told me, in a voice as dry as his had been, "Eric is my blind date for tonight, but don't get any ideas. We can't stand each other."

I replied, only half-teasing, "Don't be too sure. From what I see in his chart, you're meant for each other."

Eric told me, during the few minutes I'd described his chart, that he'd been recently divorced. He was understandably bitter, because he'd had to give up everything he owned, and his ex-wife was also awarded the custody of their eleven-year-old daughter Renee, whom he adored. Now, as I fumbled in the dark for my robe—Ralph had slipped back into sleep as soon as I'd turned out the light—I remembered vividly how tenderly he had talked about his little daughter.

During their stormy courtship, Julie had returned to me as a client. She insisted neither of them wanted to get married. But their charts said differently. He had Venus directly on her sun and she had Neptune on his Venus. In chart comparison, this meant he was to be the love of her life and for him she represented bewitchment, enchantment, an allure he could not resist. They both had Libra rising, interesting because Julie's former lover had his sun in Libra and many of the things which fascinated her in a Libra—his taste, his gracious way of living, his love of music and beautiful things—she also found in Eric.

In both of their charts, Mars opposed Uranus, which makes for temper, rebellion, impatience. In Julie's case, this gave her the fire and courage, despite her shy Cancer nature, to fight back and resist the Libra lover who had tried to be a Svengali to her. In Eric's it was the negative side of the dynamic personality. I've heard it said that it takes one Mars-opposing-Uranus person to understand another, realize why the other person explodes. Certainly, they both exploded often enough but always ended in each other's arms.

She used to complain to me during their early courtship that he came on too strong, he insisted on pushing her around, telling her what to do. I'd remind her that this was because he had his moon in Aries. But Aries also made him the ardent, delightfully impulsive lover she could not resist; Aries men in sex are the most daring, the most experimental of all the signs of the zodiac. She and Eric also made an attractive-looking couple; people turned to watch them, whether they were in the midst of one of their squabbles or were walking dreamily down Michigan Avenue, arms around each other, oblivious to the world. In a good mood, he had the completely winning Libra smile. Although he had the long nose characteristic of many men with Aries strongly in their charts (when you see that nose, look for a man who gets the job done, follows through) he gave the total impression of being handsome. Astrologically, this is because Venus, ruler of his ascendant Libra, is on the midheaven of his chart; people with Venus in this position always manage to outshine those with more classic features because they have an "aura" of good looks.

Now, as I padded barefoot out to the little room in the back of our apartment which I use as a study when I'm at home, I remembered how much Eric and I liked each other, despite his opinion of astrology. No one except Julie and Eric had been happier than I when they finally decided to get married. But, despite all the good aspects between their charts, there was one indication in Julie's which worried me: Uranus, ruler of the fifth house of children, was in a trouble aspect to Mars in the seventh house of marriage. One of these days she was going to have trouble with a rebellious stepchild.

I thought of this, as I dialed Julie's number in Evanston. Shortly after the marriage, I had warned her tentatively that Renee might someday be a problem. I wondered if Julie remembered our conversation.

She answered the phone on the first ring. "Katie, thank God. I was afraid you might not be home."

"Tell me what happened."

"Renee has run away from a hospital in Urbana, Illinois, near her college. We're terribly afraid she may try to kill herself. Ten days ago, without telling her mother or Eric, she committed herself because she was suicidal. This afternoon, after a session in her doctor's office, she walked out of the front door of the hospital instead of returning to the psychiatric ward. She's disappeared. She isn't at her sorority house; they haven't heard from her. We're beside ourselves with worry. Eric's ex-wife blames him and I'm afraid he blames himself."

"Julie," I said, "three years ago, just before you and Eric were married, I warned you that you might expect trouble from her. Are you sure she's really suicidal? She could be using this whole thing as a device to get Eric's attention."

"I don't know, Katie. Eric thinks she is quite reconciled to his marrying me. He keeps telling me how sweet and loving and darling she is."

"You haven't met her yet?"

"Not yet." She sounded a shade defensive. "You don't understand, Katie. It's not that Eric didn't want Renee to get to know me, he understands how fond I am of children. It's just that he saw so little of her before she went away to college. When she was younger, her mother wouldn't let her come to Chicago alone to visit her father and whenever he went out to the place where she and her mother were living—her mother's old home town—Paula made such scenes that everyone was miserable. So now he wants to get reacquainted, to have his darling little girl back, to make it up to her for all the years they were separated."

I knew from Eric's chart how paternal he was, but just the same . . .

"Julie," I said, "do you know her birthday?"

"She'll be twenty-one next October. She's a Libra, simply an angel, Eric says, so sweet and dear to everyone. His marriage brought him a lot of heartache but Renee made up for almost everything. Even when she was a baby, she was always trying to make her mother stop nagging at Eric. And when Eric would feel sad or depressed, she would crawl up in his lap and tell him how much she loved him."

I thought, oh, dear. Danger ahead. "Do you know whether she has ever had any kind of psychiatric problem before?"

"It's strange you should ask that. Eric's ex-wife, Paula, told him tonight that Renee had some sessions with a psychologist attached to the medical school down at the University of Illinois. Of course, she is very aware of that angle. When she graduates, she plans to become a nurse and work with retarded children."

Libra children are so darling, so sweet and courteous and tactful, that parents often aren't aware that they can use their charm deliberately, to get what they want. Ruled by Venus, they love beauty and harmony, are disturbed by anything inharmonious or ugly. But there is a negative side to Libra. Sometimes they are so eager to step away from quarrels, for peace-at-any-price, so disinclined to offend, that no one knows what goes on deep down in their hearts.

Least of all the Libra himself or herself, who doesn't want to face anything unpleasant.

I said, "You'd better let me talk to Eric. He knows you have called me, doesn't he?"

"Yes. Katie, he's desperate. He's tried everything. He doesn't know which way to turn."

And when Eric came to the telephone, he confirmed that. He said bluntly, "You know what I've always said about astrology. Right now, I have no idea whether your charts and planets can help. But you've made a little basic sense in the past, particularly when you insisted Julie and I would and should marry, so I'm willing to give it a whirl, if you are. Do you think you can find my daughter?"

I said, "I am willing to try. I know how much you love her. First, I need some information. When and where was Renee born?"

"October 7, 1939. Oak Park, Illinois. At 3:08 A.M." I couldn't help smiling. He might not go along with astrology but, Gemini-like, he had watched me and knew what I needed in order to do a natal chart.

"What time did she leave the hospital?"

"June 15, 1960, at 6:30 P.M. That's as close as I can come. She committed herself on June 6. After the session with the doctor last night, she told the nurse she was going to make a telephone call from the lobby before she went upstairs, because the pay phones in the ward were always busy. That explained why she turned toward the door, not the elevators, when she left the office. Nobody has seen her since. Unfortunately, she wasn't missed until the nurse came to give her some sedation around nine o'clock. Her dinner tray was still there, untouched. They called her mother. Who called me. The time was exactly 9:55."

He might be in a state—I was sure he was—but in true Gemini fashion, he rose to the occasion. Partly it was his moon in Aries, the man who gets things done. But, being married to a Gemini, I am always impressed how these mercurial, dual personalities, people who are either all the way up or in the depths, rise to a crisis. It's as though all the bits and pieces of information they have collected in their dilettante butterfly way suddenly come together and make sense.

"Have you checked out the college?"

"Right after I talked to my ex-wife. Paula is a bitch, you might as well know. She's done all she could to turn Renee against me.

Dear Renee, bless her heart, is wonderfully loyal. But she was damaged by the divorce. However, I knew that it would have been even worse on her if we had tried to continue the marriage. There were times when I could imagine myself killing Paula. In cold blood."

"Julie said Renee had some earlier therapy before she committed herself this time."

"The doctor who has been treating her this time told me that she'd been seeing one of the Ph.D.'s in psychology. I didn't know it, neither did Renee's mother. The problem, he said, was that Renee thought I was rejecting her. First the divorce, then the remarriage. I suspect Paula planted that idea but I thought by this time Renee understood how much I loved her. I just didn't see as much of her while she was finishing grammar school and when she was in high school because I couldn't face going back and getting into brawls with Paula."

Geminis are dual personalities. They frequently marry twice. On rare occasions, when a man has Gemini as his rising sign, it can mean—other aspects being in the same direction—that he is a homosexual. And a Gemini can have two true loves. Which is hard on both females involved, especially if one is a beloved daughter and the other is an adored—and adoring—second wife.

I said, "Isn't Renee a little jealous of Julie?"

"They've never met. When they do, I know it will be all right. Right now, Renee is worried for fear I love Julie more than I do her. I tried to explain that it's an entirely different kind of love. She will always be my little girl."

"Why haven't you taken Julie down to meet her? You've been married three years."

"I'm having Renee up here next summer, for the whole summer."

"Why didn't you ask her for this year?"

"She said she wanted to go abroad with some girls from the sorority. Now my ex-wife insists Renee wanted to wait before she met Julie. She didn't want to meet her while—well, while 'the honeymoon was on,' was the way Paula put it."

I said, "I'll call you back. Will you be awake or shall I make it in the morning? It's nearly 2 A.M."

"Call tonight, if you don't mind. I've talked to the doctor, I've talked to the police in Urbana, I've talked to the housemother at her sorority. I couldn't possibly sleep."

"Try to lie down and rest. If I have news, there may be a busy time ahead."

He didn't agree to try anything. I hung up and went to work.

Renee's chart came first. She was Libra, a beautiful balanced sign. She should have been a happy child, with her sun, Venus, and Mercury in Libra. But they were squared by a Cancer moon. When the moon is badly aspected, as it was in her chart, it brings out the negative characteristics of a sign: in Cancer, a person who is over-sensitive, quick to take offense, who broods over every imagined slight or wrong. The negative Cancer is doubly unfortunate in that while he or she longs desperately to be loved, he does everything to make himself not lovable by demanding more than anyone, parent or lover, can possibly give. I know one Cancer woman who, despite her brains and good looks, can never hold a man because she is constantly trying to enclose him, asking impossible things and turning into a frenzied witch when he finally drops her.

Renee was undoubtedly pretty (Venus in Libra) and prettily vain about it. Libra people adore flattery, even when they recognize it as merely flattery, but that is part of their charm, of which they have plenty. Renee also had a good mind, with Virgo rising. It wasn't surprising she had chosen to work with retarded children, for Virgo people frequently lean toward medicine, make good nurses as well as doctors and research workers. Nor that she sought psychiatric aid on her own, for Virgos are independent.

But she was in trouble, her progressed chart showed clearly. On June 6, when she went to the hospital, asking to be committed, Mars, ruler of the eighth house, death, was in a bad aspect to Venus. Her progressed moon had just joined the south node, a trouble aspect, squaring still another trouble aspect, tricky Pluto in her natal chart. Everything in her life was approaching a point of climax. She was depressed, disorganized. She probably had thoughts of suicide. But I could not see any aspect, in her progressed or in her natal chart, which indicated she would kill herself. Instead, as I had suggested earlier to Julie, these suicide thoughts, even threats, were actually a pathetic way of asking for love and attention, her negative Cancer moon crying out for more and more—and then more.

About an hour after Renee left the hospital, the moon was in Pisces, 23 degrees. This is a degree of instability and sadness and its position in Pisces accentuates the effect. In other words,

Renee was confused, unstable, reacting badly, negative. But I was sure she was alive.

I reached for the telephone. It was nearly four o'clock. If the prospects had been grim, I would have waited until later, hoping Eric might be sleeping. But good news is worth waking up for.

Julie answered. No, Eric wasn't asleep, but he was in the bedroom, resting. "He blames himself so terribly. I think he is even sorry he married me now. This business of Renee is breaking his heart. If she should be dead now—"

"Let me talk to him."

Eric came promptly. But his voice was tired, dead. "Have you any ideas? Paula called a little while ago. She has the idea Renee might be on her way up here."

"I don't think so, not according to the charts I've done. Eric, this is very complicated, doing charts for specific moments and then comparing them to Renee's natal and progressed charts, too complicated even for many astrology students to grasp. So I will only tell you specifically what I see in them. Renee has left Urbana and gone in a southwesterly direction. Can you think of anyplace southwest of Urbana where she has lived briefly, where she might know her way around a little?"

"I can't remember." Suddenly, his voice quickened. "For a while, a short while, before she decided to become a nurse and wanted a broader scholastic background, she went to a school in Little Rock. It was more a finishing school for young ladies. But that was the first time I was able to visit her alone after the divorce, the first time she'd been away from her mother. Let me get an Atlas."

He returned quickly to say, "Little Rock it must be. There isn't any other place in a southwesterly direction she had any reason to know. I spent two, three days with her down there. It was spring, a little earlier than it is now, and everything was in bloom. She wandered around the town. I was happy and I thought she was. Why would she pick a place like that to—kill herself?"

"She isn't going to kill herself. She is too stable, essentially. She is a Libra, supported by Virgo. She is depressed right now, even disoriented and perhaps a little violent, but when a certain astrological condition is over, she will slowly come back to herself. That will happen on Friday, sometime in the afternoon, late. But not until then."

"I'll call the police in Little Rock. They can find her."

"Wait. First let me do a chart of the city and compare it with Renee's. We have to be sure."

"A chart of a city?" He sounded doubtful.

"We use the exact time of incorporation of a city as a natal date. I can find that tomorrow. Or could you do it for me?" It would, I thought, at least keep him occupied.

"I will. I don't know how, but I will." He sounded grim again. "I could go down there tonight."

"Wait until I am sure she is there. And there is no hurry. All over these charts, I see an element of karma, destiny. Everything which is happening right now in the heavens, the movements of the planets in their relation to Renee's chart for this time, show that her running away isn't the result of a sudden impulse, it is the harvest and culmination of many influences."

"But she will be found?"

"On Friday, in the afternoon."

"Alive?" His voice broke.

"Alive. Mars up in the heavens is joining Saturn in Renee's progressed chart. Mars creates violence, upheaval, and Saturn stands for trouble, disappointment, challenges. When Mars approaches Saturn, it has a chilling effect on that hot planet, making everything worse, tormenting frustration. Yesterday afternoon, in Renee's chart, Mars and Saturn came together: sudden violence, an explosion. But on Friday, sometime in the afternoon, Mars will pass by, leave her Saturn. Everything will be over. She will be alive, and needing you."

"You sound so sure."

"There is no mystery. Everything is here, in the charts. I'll be in my studio tomorrow morning, shortly after nine. Call me whenever you get the information about Little Rock. And try to get some sleep now. We have a few hours left."

Ralph woke up when I got into bed. I said, "Sweetie, this was urgent. Julie's marriage is in danger, although I'm not going to make too much of a point of that with her. Eric's daughter has run away and he blames himself for remarrying. I think she's in Little Rock. By tomorrow I'll be sure. Meanwhile, I believe he should take Julie down there with him and, if he asks me, I want to go, too."

Ralph drew me close to him. "Why do all the girls I love have cold feet?"

I started to push him away and we both laughed. He said, "OK, go away. But come back quick. I'll miss those cold feet."

The next morning, I packed a small overnight bag and put it in the trunk of my car. I was glad I had, for when I did the chart of Little Rock and compared it to Renee's, the certainty she was there would have shouted at anybody who knew their astrological ABC's. I told Eric that, adding, "Why don't you take Julie with you? She doesn't need to see Renee but it will help you to have her. There's going to be a period of waiting, which is never easy."

He said, "That's a good idea. And how about you? Would you come along? I'm not sure why you've got me believing in this but you have. I want you there, in case we need you. The plane leaves at four. I'll pick you up on the way to the airport."

"Do you really want me to come with you?"

"Didn't you think I would?"

"As an astrologer, yes. As a matter of fact, I packed a small bag and brought it with me this morning."

I caught Ralph before he went out to lunch and broke the news that I would be away until Friday night. My husband never inserts himself into my business but, loving me, he does worry a little. Sometimes. His last words were, "Honey, you've stuck your neck out a mile. I hope you haven't misread any signals. Remember, Eric doesn't believe in the stars."

I was sure of what I had seen in all those charts I'd made. Yet I took them along, and put in Eric's and Julie's for good measure. I spent the flight checking and rechecking. Everything was there, just as I'd seen last night. Renee was confused, hostile, feeling the approach of the collision of Mars and Saturn in her chart when she went in to confer with her doctor. Whatever went on that day in his office, her planets were too much in turmoil for the conference to have helped her. If she had been my client and come to consult me on Wednesday, I would have realized what a state she was in, no matter how skillfully—being a Libra—she had tried to hide it. I would have done my best to stop her running away. Whether I would have succeeded is, of course, another question. Sometimes the karma is spelled out so distinctly that no matter how hard you try, you cannot change the course of events.

I could imagine the little Libra, so used to concealing her motives and desperation behind pretty manners and a charming smile, practicing her deception on the doctor, pretending cooperation when all the time she was making plans to escape. When she walked out of his office, destiny was involved.

During Thursday and much of Friday, until Mars passed Saturn in Renee's chart, she would not be able to think clearly or behave rationally. It was possible she might be violent. Yet I had to offer Eric the comfort that this was inevitable. Renee's Saturn was in 29 degrees of Aries, a degree of danger and trouble. This was something which, disagreeable as it was, had to run its course.

On the plane trip, Eric was expansive, hopeful. He dropped us at the hotel and went directly to the police station. They were extremely helpful. Not only did they check out the possibility of accidents, they suggested he appear on the ten o'clock news on television, displaying Renee's picture and asking anyone who had seen her to get in touch with the police or the TV station. Eric was very persuasive. Julie and I watched him from the hotel. But when it was over, she was in tears.

"I'm afraid, Katie. He has his hopes so high. The charts could be wrong."

"They aren't," I insisted, thinking of Ralph's final warning to me. I didn't sleep much that night. I kept checking and rechecking charts. On Friday morning, I reassured Julie and Eric over the telephone, leaving them to breakfast alone, and looked up astrologers in the Yellow Pages. There was only one in Little Rock, a woman named Caryl Holmes. Needing the comfort of a kindred spirit, I called and explained what I was doing. She was gracious enough to cancel her appointments and we had what, in the world of medicine, would have amounted to a consultation in the coffee shop of the hotel. After she left, I felt infinitely relieved.

But then I had to cope with Eric. His early optimism had given way to despair, depression, in true Gemini fashion. He did not say he blamed me for having brought him to Little Rock, he merely stared at me and talked about our being off on a "wild goose chase." When he left to make another check of hotels and hospitals and go to the police station, Julie and I stared at each other. There were deep circles under her eyes and I knew she hadn't slept, either.

The day seemed endless. We had sandwiches and iced tea sent up to the room and tried to eat. Whenever the telephone rang, we jumped for it hopefully—but it was always Eric, reporting no progress.

A crucial time passed, 3:30 P.M., when Renee should have been emerging from her depression. No word. I ordered a Scotch from room service. It was nearly six in the evening when Eric called and asked to speak to me. His voice sounded dead. "Katie, just as a matter of touching all bases, I am making one last appeal on the afternoon news. Then I've had it. The police have been great and so have the TV people but they believe she isn't here and so do I. Somebody would have seen her and reported it. There have been a lot of silly crank calls but that's all. I've caused them a lot of nuisance checking them out and I'm not going to sit around here when I've already worn out my welcome. You did your best but I shouldn't have expected miracles. I'm all for getting out as fast as we can."

All I could say was, "Eric, the evening isn't over. I know she'll be found tonight."

"Katie, I've talked to Paula. She thinks Renee is dead and so do I. I don't blame you for trying, I just blame myself for being idiot enough to hope. Tell Julie I'll be back right after the broadcast. We'll go out to the airport and take the first plane out of town." It wasn't like him, I thought. Geminis never give up. It was merely the mood of the moment. Yet, under its influence, he was capable of acting on ill-advised impulse.

I told Julie what he'd said, adding, "I understand his feelings. Just the same, you mustn't leave. I know she will be found."

She shook her head. "If anyone is to blame, I'm it. I shouldn't have dragged you into this." Then she turned on television. At 6:25 Eric made his plea and Renee's picture was shown on the screen. When it was over, she took my hand.

"Katie, I gave you an impossible assignment. I apologize. I should never have called on you."

I repeated, "The evening isn't over yet." But my voice didn't carry much authority.

"I guess I'd better pack. How about you?"

"I think we should wait. We've come this far. Why leave until we are positive there is no chance?"

She turned away. "I'm going to do what he wants. It's his daughter."

I had my hand on the door when the telephone rang. This time Julie didn't run. She picked it up on the third ring and her voice sounded almost as tired and beaten as Eric's. Then suddenly she was crying and laughing at the same time. I heard her say, "Go, it doesn't matter about me. Katie and I will stay right here until we hear from you. Eric, I know it is going to be all right."

Then she said to me, "A cabdriver just telephoned the police station to say he picked up a girl answering Renee's description on Wednesday, late, at the bus station. He drove her to an area of rooming houses. He didn't watch television last night because he was working and he slept through the noon broadcast. But tonight he had stopped in a tavern to have his supper when Eric was talking. Wasn't it luck?"

I wanted to say it was more than luck. There was a beautiful planetary aspect culminating in the heavens that very night: Mars in Aquarius in a good fortune aspect to Jupiter in Sagittarius, meaning all is well. I had been waiting for it. Now all I could do was walk slowly over to the bed and sit down, collapse.

They found Renee at 9:40 P.M. She was in a run-down boardinghouse in a section where the less seen of the police, the better; an explanation of why nobody had reported her presence, even if she had been noticed. She hadn't gone out much, living on crackers and candy bars in her room. But at 3:40 that afternoon, she had come out of her confusion and gone to the pay telephone in the hall and tried to reach her father in Evanston. She'd continued to call him at intervals during the evening. In fact, she was in the telephone booth when Eric arrived at her boardinghouse. Recognizing his voice, she had slammed the door of the booth, screaming and kicking. Eric had to have help in getting her out to the car and back to the hotel, where he called a doctor. He sat up with her all night, trying to comfort her when she awakened from the sedation. But it wasn't until the next day that Renee was quiet enough to think coherently and agreed to extended therapy.

Julie and I, of course, didn't even see her. The cabdriver—a charming young student with his sun in Aquarius, in accordance with the aspect—drove us to the plane. The next day, Eric took Renee back to the hospital in Urbana.

I should have felt gratified. Eric and Julie were both warmly grateful. But by now I knew Renee's chart so thoroughly all I could think of was the inevitable trouble ahead. She had broken down and run away under a progressed full moon setting off her Mars-Pluto opposition. Two years hence, her progressed sun would form a 90-degree angle to Mars, triggering its destructive qualities. There were explosive times ahead for all of them.

To any outsider, however, things were going well. Instead of re-

turning to college, Renee took a part-time job in the hospital and
continued her therapy. The doctors felt she was making progress.
She visited her mother once a month for the weekend and Eric
went down to Urbana frequently to see her. Finally, the plans for
the long-awaited visit to Evanston became specific: she would arrive on June 24, 1962. I had to point out to Julie the date was as
badly aspected as possible.

Julie felt she couldn't ask her to change—"not when I'm meeting
Renee for the first time." I couldn't press my point, although
Eric's chart showed mixed aspects, both happiness and serious
trouble. I was convinced that the Uranus aspect in Julie's house
of marriage was still to have its full impact, that the stepdaughter
would threaten her marriage far more directly than she had before.
In addition, I suddenly saw that Julie's progressed Venus, the planet
of love and happiness, was in a trouble aspect to the eclipse point
in Libra which was in effect October 8, 1939—the day she'd first
met her married lover and one day after Renee was born.

But Renee was coming anyway, bringing trouble with her. She
arrived in such a rainstorm that her pink cotton dress, obviously
selected to impress a stepmother, was limp and wrinkled before
they got home to Evanston. Julie's more sober selection of dark
blue—chosen to make a sedate impression—weathered the storm
much better. It was a bad start, for Renee felt ill at ease, on the
defensive. Nor did the pink bedroom and little private bath ad-
joining, also in pink, have the desired effect of calming her, washing her in luxury. It was everything she had always wanted, yet she
felt it had been provided by a rival, that there was a trick, a hidden
catch somewhere.

Not until some weeks later did I hear the details of those awk-
ward early days. At first, on the surface, everything was placid,
Julie trying to do everything to please Renee—offering the use of
her car, her charge accounts in Evanston—and Renee outwardly
happy, girlish, charming. But beneath the surface, Renee was plot-
ting. Libra people are brilliant strategists; witness one of our great
ones, General Eisenhower. Ordinarily, they are fair, peace-loving,
they go far to back away from quarrels, they want harmony. Most
of them are influenced enough by Virgo to be instinctively tidy,
to enjoy harmonious surroundings, and Renee, with Virgo rising,
was naturally a careful, neat little girl.

But she was desperate. She had come planning to reclaim her
father, the sweetheart she had lost, expecting little or no com-

petition. She had been unprepared for someone as young-looking and as glamorous as Julie. In addition, having seen her father's attitude toward her own mother, she was utterly unprepared for his playful, sometimes fatherly way with Julie.

Julie's basic problem, the reason she'd been slow to find success in her career and even slower in finding the right man, had been emotional immaturity. Born on July 3, 1913, at 12:38 P.M. in what we call "the dark of the moon" and in the sign of Cancer, she had a double handicap. Just before we on earth see the new moon, there's a brief period when, according to folklore and fiction, witches come out to dance and work their spells on hapless mortals. That's why it's been said that it's unlucky to be born in the "dark of the moon."

Nonsense—of course. But the moon and sun do have an effect on babies. Infants born at high noon, when the sun is on the midheaven, love to shine, to be in front of the public. But they often lack the drive, ambition, found in midnight children. My theory is that the night babies, born without the sun overhead but with the same ambitions, have to struggle harder. And, "dark of the moon" babies, lacking the illuminating glow of that body, mature later. This has nothing to do with basic intelligence. Some of the most brilliant people are late bloomers. It is simply an inability to relinquish the patterns of childhood. And two zodiac signs also tend to produce people who mature late—unless other aspects offset this. Men and women—men particularly—born between April 21 and May 21, are apt to be emotionally immature, held back and spoiled by adoring mothers simply because Taurus babies are so enchanting. And men and women—particularly women—born between June 22 and July 22, cling so ardently to home and parents they grow up slowly.

Julie really hadn't been looking for a husband in her hopeless love affair. She'd been seeking a father to replace the one she'd lost through death. With Eric, her Saturn in Gemini meant something special. Although he was only seven years older than Julie, to her he was not only a lover, a husband, but a father; Saturn often represents a parent in a chart, as well as karma, destiny. And he was able to accept this role because he has a cluster of planets in Cancer, making him protective, loving, responsive to devotion—in other words, instinctively a father.

So, instead of a stepmother, Renee found she had competition from a sibling, another daughter. It was enraging, humiliating.

And she fought back with all the malice and venom of a woman scorned.

Among these were youth and enchanting looks. She had the Libra sweetness, the exquisite skin, the softly curved little budding body, the piquant face and the tiny appealing Virgo chin. Not a smashing beauty, the kind men followed in the street. But a girl who deserved a second look, a third, a fourth—and then you were caught up, unable to escape.

She always wore brief shorts and tight little sweater tops. When Eric came home, she rushed to the door, blocking Julie's way, and threw herself into his arms. She kissed him on the lips, she sat in his lap while they watched television. Once in a while, Julie caught her glancing over her father's shoulder, past him, to get his wife's reaction.

At first, she tried to tell herself the girl didn't know what she was doing. Later, when it became obvious that Eric, at any rate, should recognize what was going on, Julie withdrew, in characteristic Cancer fashion. She found herself outside in the cold, unable to enter into their plans, unable even to talk to Eric. As I pointed out to her afterward, what Renee at that point wanted was a confrontation, a demand that Eric choose between his two women. Even if she didn't win, she could tell herself she was the victim of a cruel stepmother.

But it wasn't in Julie's Cancer nature to act directly. So Renee, frustrated, became deliberately hostile, vindictive. She gave up all pretense of being helpful around the house. Her bed was left unmade. Her pink bathroom was a welter of cosmetics and damp towels. If she as much as touched a pan in the kitchen, she burned it beyond repair. When Julie got home, she found the kitchen filled with dirty dishes, bits of food scattered around the living room, soft drinks spilled on her gray rug and pastel upholstery.

Like many Cancer women, Julie loved an attractive, warm home. She wasn't methodical, but she was Cancer-practical. In the early days of their marriage, Eric used to complain that, after she dried the lettuce on paper towels, she hung the towels up to dry so they could be reused. But he had been very grateful for her Cancerian thrift when they were not so prosperous and he had grown used to the sweet comforts Julie provided for him. Renee's sabotage campaign defied all Julie's attempts to pick up after her stepdaughter. She left cigarettes burning great grooves in window sills. Impressions of her dirty feet were on the wall above the sofa. She used Julie's charge accounts to buy herself expensive cosmetics and scarves and useless trinkets, which she tossed aside after a few uses. When Eric demurred, she dimpled at him, saying, "It costs money to be a girl."

The crisis weekend, when Julie admitted to herself that Renee was trying to break up her marriage to Eric, came on July 7. I saw the aspects were bad and called Julie to say casually, "Don't worry if things go wrong this weekend. The planets are acting up. Lie low, if you can."

But Julie had planned a picnic at Ravinia, our wonderful park where we Chicagoans go and listen to music under the stars. She and Eric loved Ravinia and they hoped Renee would share their pleasure. Julie, who usually wore dark clothes in the city, underplaying her natural vivid coloring on TV, had bought a pretty red and white cotton for the occasion, gay and girlish. To her shock, when she got home from work, she found Renee wearing it.

"I thought you wouldn't mind," she said to Julie's complete astonishment. "Anyway, it's much too young for you. It looks better on me, I'm sure."

Julie went upstairs and changed into a sweater and skirt. When Eric came home, he said, "It was nice of you to lend Renee your dress. It looks cute on her." That night, after the picnic—at which Renee nibbled on chicken and turned up her nose at everything else—Eric sat with his arms around Julie, listening to the music. At intermission, Renee wandered off and did not come back. Finally Eric went to hunt for her. When he came back he said, "Renee said the chicken disagreed with her. She isn't feeling good. I put her in the car. I think we'd better take her home, don't you?"

Julie packed up in silence. When she went to bed, she found her new red and white dress, smeared with catsup and mustard, on the floor. It was ruined. She showed it to Eric. He said, "The poor kid was sick. I guess she didn't notice what she did to your dress."

Julie wanted to point out that the dress had been deliberately smeared—and that she'd had neither catsup or mustard in her picnic basket. Renee must have made a trip to the refreshment stand in order to give Julie the message: This is the way I intend to ruin you, mess you up.

On Monday, Julie came in to see me. She was white and shaking. "I'm leaving Eric. I spent most of the weekend in bed, saying I was catching cold. Eric was hostile, withdrawn. But I could hear him

THE GIRL WHO RAN AWAY

laughing downstairs with Renee. I didn't do any shopping; when I went to get my car I found Renee had used all the gas, it wouldn't start. This morning, I didn't fix breakfast for Eric. I stayed in bed until he had left. I'm going to stay downtown for dinner. Let them worry about it. In fact, I'm thinking of moving out to-night, taking a hotel room. The only question in my mind is, shall I bother to tell Eric?"

I frowned at her. "That is just what she is waiting for. You must not withdraw from Eric. You are his wife. He loves you. Whether you realize it or not, you are in control. Your chart shows that in every way, you are stronger than Renee—your south node is right on her progressed ascendant. Unless you defeat yourself, she can't win."

"What can I do?"

"The first step is to communicate with Eric. He isn't a stupid man. But he loves his child dearly, he is paternal—you know that —and he must be worried about harming her, knowing how much she has suffered already. Being a Gemini, he also knows how to tack with the wind, shifting and adjusting to what is going on. He remembers the years of his first marriage when he and Renee lived for each other, when she was the light of his life. But Mars is squaring Uranus now, badly aspected to Renee's progressed moon, making her erratic and rebellious. Unless you upset everything now by walking out, he will soon reach his limit."

"It is easy for you to be calm."

"But you've lived through so many things, Julie, and grown so much. In my opinion, this is your final lesson. You've always wanted a daughter. Now you have one, and you see what it is like, what other parents go through."

"She isn't my daughter."

"She has her moon 20 degrees in Cancer on your mid-heaven, which means you are going to learn a lesson through her, she is going to be good for you eventually. Your chart shows you have control over her, materially and spiritually, if you are only wise enough to use it and not retreat into your shell and sulk."

"I'm not sulking."

"Then let's say you are withdrawing, in Cancer fashion, to brood. There are two basic problems when I compare your chart with Renee's. She is a prima donna who wants center stage. You're a prima donna, too, and you resent her trying to take over your stage and your leading man. You are competing—instead of hanging on to your role of leading lady and making her maintain hers, the ingenue. Another thing, you both are stubborn, fixed. Neither of you will give in to the other. But there are better ways of fighting than retreating in wounded silence. Eric is your secret weapon. Don't reject him. You need him on your side. Ask for his help."

I walked her to the elevator, thrusting tissues into her hands, and bits of last-minute advice into ears I wasn't sure heard me. Finally I said, "Julie, last year you called me in the middle of the night to ask me to find Renee after she had run away. By astrology, I was able to show you where she was and when she would be found. Do you remember?"

She nodded, tears spilling over her navy blue eyes. The elevator came, but I pulled her back.

"Will you believe me again if I tell you that by August 18 your problems will be over? Your progressed full moon in Aries, squaring your Neptune—meaning a deceptive influence in the home—is approaching a conjunction to Renee's Saturn. An end is coming. Renee's progressed moon in Taurus conjunct Uranus will put her at a pitch of rebellion, culminating probably in a separation. Things will come to a head, chickens will come home to roost. On the full moon everything will be over."

On Monday, August 20, I had kept time open for Julie. And, as I expected, she wanted to see me. Renee had left the house and was staying with some friends of her mother in Oak Park. It was all over. Eric had finally chosen between his wife and his daughter. It had been—as his chart indicated—the worst summer of his life. But their marriage had survived. And here I again give astrology—and the clients who have the wisdom to accept what it can tell them and use it—credit.

After Julie left my office, her first step had been to re-establish communication with Eric. Her silence, her cold rejection, had left him mystified. To a Gemini, talk is of paramount importance; he must be able to read you, silence confuses and hurts. That night, as they were going to bed after a stormy dinner during which Renee said she couldn't eat the "lousy meal" Julie had cooked and had gone out for pizza, which she deliberately spilled on the carpet, Julie had crept into Eric's arms and asked for his help.

His answer was, "Yes, my darling, I know how difficult she has been. But you must be patient."

Her instinct was to withdraw again. She felt she had been patient beyond all reason. But then my final bit of advice came back to

her: "As one Cancer person to another, I can only remind you of
our built-in characteristics which some people think of as faults.
We love so deeply we sometimes smother those close to us because we want to be protective. We hold on, cling. You were so
eager to please Renee in the beginning that she must have sensed
your vulnerability, thought you would be easy game. Now you
must let Eric make the decisions, let go and make no demands. A
Gemini resents restrictions, fencing him in only makes him
nervous, irritable. The instant a Gemini feels he is being held on a
tight leash, he will slip his collar and run away."

So she waited, trusting Eric. And finally, under the influence
of the oncoming new moon, everything came to fruition. The night
of August 18, a Friday, there had been a television special she
wanted to see because the star was going to be her guest the next
week. As usual Renee had the set tuned to the station she wanted
and was wandering around the house. When it came eight o'clock,
Julie switched to the proper channel and turned down the blaring
volume.

In a flash, claws out, Renee was back in the room. "What in hell
do you think you're doing?"

Julie said nothing; she'd had practice schooling herself to
silence, ignoring Renee in the past weeks. But Eric caught Renee's
wrist as she reached out to the set. He ordered her to leave the
room. She reached up and drew her long, sharp nails down his
cheek, drawing blood. He didn't fight back. He simply said,
"Renee, get out. You are trying to break up my marriage, which
has given me the greatest happiness of my life. You can't, because Julie is more important to me than you are."

Stunned, she asked, "Where can I go?"

"I don't care. To your mother, I suppose."

"She's driving up to get me, next week."

Eric and Julie looked at each other; Renee had kept that information, among other things, to herself. He said, "If you want to
stay here next week, you can. But you must act like an adult, behave yourself."

"I won't stay here another minute! I'm going to people who
love me!"

In the end, in a wild fury, she packed her bags and Eric drove
her out to Oak Park, where she stayed with friends of her
mother's until Paula drove up for her. Julie didn't say good-bye.
She simply went up to her bedroom and sat, staring at the ceiling,
until she heard Eric's car leave. Then she burst into tears.

"I've never behaved that way to another human being," she told me. "The horror of being so hated that I couldn't even bring myself to say a word to the child before she left."

"She isn't a child," I said, "and you and Eric have learned from the experience. Your marriage is more solid because it has been able to weather a severe strain."

Suddenly, Julie was able to smile, her eyes still wet. "And I've finally had the daughter I've always wanted, only to learn that children can bring heartbreak and tragedy, as well as joy, to parents."

That was eight years ago. Renee never went on with her projected nursing career, never graduated from college. She married, had a child and now lives in California. Only rarely does Eric hear from her. Once, after a quarrel with her husband, she telephoned her father and announced she was coming "home" to him with her little girl. He said, "No, Renee, you must work out your own problems. You are a grown woman with a child."

Julie said to me not long ago, "You were so right to have insisted I wait, let Renee show her hand. Eric has told me so many times how much he admired my self-restraint that summer. And I understand him better, too, now. When he seems to withdraw, to turn cool and pull away, it's because he is going through torment and wants to work out his problems alone, not burden others. As you've so often pointed out to me, Geminis have a deeper side they so often hide from the world and this is territory which is posted, 'Keep out.'"

And one evening just last week when the four of us, Eric and Julie, Ralph and I, sat with long glasses in our hands looking out over the lake, Eric said to me, "Katie, would astrology help Renee?"

My answer: Astrology can help anyone, because it enables us to know ourselves as we really are, so that we don't waste time and energy fighting against the pattern. Life is not easy. It never was. It never will be. But if you know the woof and warp of your life pattern, the designs set by the planets as you drew your first breath and became part of the universe, you are never really confused again. For day by day, hour by hour, even minute by minute, as the planets come together and separate, exerting their pull on the electromagnetic field of your body, you are brought into periods of trial you can recognize, as well as those times of serendipity when, if you just put out your hand, you cannot be denied.